FACILIT
MANAGEMENT
BRINGS ECONOMY
BENEFITS

TO ORGANIZATIONS EDITION 2

JOHN LOK

Copyright © John Lok
All Rights Reserved.

Contents

Preface   *v*

Prologue   *ix*

● **Human Resource Training Raises ● Productive Efficient Research**

  1. ● Reward Management Strategy   3

  2. ● Organizational Development   24

  3. ● Human Resource Role In Business   32

  4. ● Training And Learning   60

  5. ● Performance Management   71

  6. ● Sourcing And Staffing   88

  7. ● Employee Engagement   95

  8. ● What Is The Relationship Between Human Resource ●   103
     Strategy And Corporate Strategy

  9. ● Solving Human Resource ● International Organization ●   117
     Strategic Challenges

 10. ● Human Resource Assists ● Organizational Development   143

 11. ● How Human Resource Development ● Assists Organizations   165
     To ● Raise Productive Efficiency

● **Facility Management Raises ● Productive Efficient Research**

 12. ● Facility Management Can Reduce ● Maintenance Service   187
     Expenditure

 13. ● How (fm) Space Moving Management ● Can Bring Valued   195
     Add To Organizations

 14. ● The Relationship Between Facility ● Management And   202
     Productive ● Efficiency

● **Psychological Methods Raise ● Productive Efficiency**

 15. ● How To Impact Of Workplace ● Management On Well-being   231
     And ● Productivity

 16. ● Organizational Environment Factor ● Influences The New   238

Contents

Employees ● Production Efficiencies

Employee Efficiency Psychological Research

17. Employee Satisfaction Measurement ●   267

18. ● How To Learn Qualificative Research ● Interviewing In   299
    Order To Raise ● Efficiency And Effectiveness

19. Human Resource Department And Organizational Performance   316
    Relationship

Factors Influence Organizational Overall Performance Effectiveness

20. What Is Efficient Achievement Of Technological Inputs Factor In 327
    Construction Industry

21. Can Effective Departmental Communication Factor Influence   331
    Successful Organizational Effective Change

22. Can Human Resource Development Training Factor Influence   335
    Organizational Productive Performance

23. Factors Influence Employee Motivation To Achieve   340
    Organizational Effective Performance

24. Performance Measurement Influences Effectiveness   344

25. Facility Management Brings Economic Benefits To Organizations 350

Preface

Summary

This book concerns how to apply how behavioral economic and psychological methods to attempt to explain whether your organization can be influenced to raise your employee individual productive efficiency as well as improve service performance to achieve to let your clients feel more satisfaction by effective human resource training or/and facility management methods. My research questions include: Can effective human resource training or/and facility management influences your organization's employee individual productive efficiency raising and/or service performance improving? Can effective workplace working environment facility management influence your organization's employee individual emotion and working attitude to be changed more positive to raise productive efficiency and/or service performance?mCan effective human resource training program improve your organization's employee individual skill level in order to raise productive efficiency and/or service performance?nHas it relationship between effective human resource training and facility management to influence organization's employee individual productive efficient level and service performance in long term?

I shall apply psychological method to attempt to recommend whether it is the right time to your organization ought need to find methods to raise your organization's human resource trai8ning course(s) quality and/or improve your organization's facility management in-house service quality to let your employees feel more comfortable to work in your organization's any working environment in order to achieve the raising productive efficiency and/or improving service performance consequence in possible.

This book divides five parts. The first part indicates how organizations can attempt to apply different psychological methods to research how and why employee individual selects to do the behavioral performance in organizations in order to let any organization leaders can judge whether it is right time that whose organization ought need to attempt to change human resource training courses quality in order to let employees' skills can be improved more effectively and/or applying facility management to be implemented more comfortable to let employees to feel in order to achieve the productive efficient raising and/or the service performance improving possible consequence in long term.

The second part indicates to explain whether effective human resource training courses can help to raise employee productive efficiency and/or improve service performance. I shall indicate the whole HRM successful elements to explain whether it can still help the organization to raise employee efficiency and/or improve service performance, if the organization neglects to implement an effective human resource training course program to let whose employees to attempt to learn any work-related skills.

The second part concerns challenge of HR management it is as a HR specialist, what are the challenges you may face and what HR intervention mechanisms would you consider using in an attempt to drive individual and organization performance in a multinational company? Critically evaluate this question by utilizing the appropriate academic literatures.

The challenges of the HR specialist when there engage in attempt of increasing the individual and organization performances in Multinational companies through developing a set of HRM best practices, especially relating to employee recruitment and selection, performance management and staff retention. Since the organizations are multinational number of concerns are arises such as dealing cultural issues with the organizational goals as well as individual goals.

Furthermore organizational behaviors and tools such as engagement, motivation and empowerment are basically highlighted; without those it is merely a dream to achieving the business goals. Basically Multinational companies are aiming profits and there for individual and organization performance are very vital for their existence.HR has been organized in a different ways over the years. Some functions have emphasized delivery by location or by business structure.

In these models an integrated HR team has serviced managers and employees at specific location or with in specific businesses units, with some more strategic or complex tasks reserved for the corporate center. The degree to which these different arms of HR were centralized or co-located and the question of whether they were managed by the business unit varied. Within the HR teams, depending up on their size their might have been specialization by work area (especially for industrial relations in the 1960s and 1970s) or by employee grade or group (responsibility, say, divided between those looking after clerical staff from those covering production) The advancement of personal management starts around end of the 19th century, when welfare officers came in to being. There are some organizations where HR is seen as a central, corporate function with little advancement to business units. Some other organizations position themselves in the opposite direction, with a very small corporate center and all the activity distributed to business units. The question of best structure is how the function best organizes itself between the pulls of centralization and the pushes of decentralization.(The changing HR functions)

This part explains why human resource strategy can bring organizational benefits. It will explain how reward strategy can bring what kinds of benefits to organizations. Reward management is nowadays considered as an important topic in order to achieve the goals of a company. Employees are considered as the main factor which plays an important role in the organization. The success of each and every organization is its dedicated employee's .Current world is filled with changes and competition. In order to survive in the current situation companies should be having employees who are loyal and expert in their own field. New technologies are developed constantly and the companies are eagerly trying to catch up those talented employees with right expertise in their own areas. So, fair award management can attract talented employees to choose the organization to work.

When the organization has good reward management, then it will bring good organizational development, good learning and training , good performance management, good sourcing and staff, good employee engagement. In my this book, I shall explain how and why good reward management will bring all above these any one of human resource related issues to let readers to make accurate and reasonable analysis.

The final part indicates whether organization's facility management in-house department or outsourced department can achieve to improve its office or warehouse working environment to be more comfortable to let employees to feel in order to influence their productive efficiencies to be raised or improving their service performance to bring customers' more satisfactory feeling.

I write this book aims to hope any organization leaders can attempt to apply psychological methods to predict whether their in-house facility management service is enough or/and human resource management strategy and training course program strategies which both have relationship to influence their employees' productive efficiency and service performance in order to achieve aim to raise more satisfactory feeling to their customers. I believe that effective facility management can improve better workplace environment to influence employee individual productive efficiency raising as well as effective human resource training course program can improve employee individual service performance in order to achieve customers to feel more satisfactory service performance in consequence for the organization's service.

Whether do any organizations need facility management department? What function of benefits will bring when the organization sets up one facility management department? If the organization lacked one facility management department, what the disadvantage it will bring to influence the organization's operation? Does it has relationship between raising efficiency or improving performance and facility management department? I shall indicate some evidences and causations to explain what will be occurred when the organization owns one facility management department or it lacks one facility management department in its organization. Any readers can make judgement whether in what situations , the organization needs to set up one facility management department in order to bring advantages or waste essential human resource or raise service cost from the facility management department.

In the final part, I will explain how any why effective department communication, excellent technological input, effective human resource developement training, good employee motivation strategy and effective performance measurement strategy can influence any organization's overall performance to be more effective. I shall indicate the reasons to explain why above any one of these factors have indirect relationship to influence the organization's overall performance effectiveness. Readers can earn fresh opinions to acknowledge that these any one factors can be possible to influence organization's overall performance effectiveness.

Prologue

Table of contents

Part One
Human resource training raises
productive efficient research
    Chapter 1
Reward management strategy p.4-25
    Chapter 2
Organizational development p.26-39
    Chapter 3
Human resource role in business p.40-55
    Chapter 4
Training and Learning p.56-73
    Chapter 5
Performance management p.74-91
    Chapter 6
Sourcing and staffing p.92-120
    Chapter 7
Employee engagement p.121-139
    Chapter 8 p.140-159
What is the relationship
between human resource
strategy and corporate strategy
    reference

● How human resource brings
benefits to organizations p.160-174
    reference
    Chapter 9
Solving human resource
international organization
strategic challenges p.175-190
    reference

● Developing countries Human resource development whether need to be improved p.191-215

● The relationship between human resource department and raising employee individual productive performance efficiency p.216-229

Reference

Chapter 10
Human resource assists organizational development p.230-248

Chapter 11
Effective human resource department characteristics p.249-260

reference

Chapter 12
How human resource development assists organizations to raise productive efficiency

● Human resource raising productive efficient factors p.261-290

Reference

Part Two
Facility management raises productive efficient research
Chapter 13
Facility management can reduce maintenance service expenditure
● Facility management role in organization p.291-318

Chapter 14
How (FM) space moving management can bring valued add to organizations

Reference

● Predictive the choosing right
data asset and (FM) analytics
solutions to boost public
transportation service quality p.319-337

Chapter 15
The relationship between facility
management and productive
efficiency

● The relationship between facility
management and consumer
behavior p.338-350

Chapter 16
Facility management influences
consumer satisfactory service
feeling p.351-370

Part Three
Psychological methods raise
productive efficiency

Chapter 17
How to impact of workplace
management on well-being and
productivity
● Health and safe work environment
influences productivity p.371-380

● Employee personal
empowerment factor influences
performance p.381-390

Chapter 18
Organizational environment factor
influences the new employees
production efficiencies

● Raising efficient and effective
interview psychological methods p.391-415

Chapter 19
Interview psychology methods

What are common psychology methods of
recruitment choice?
Why does need to test the applicant's
psychological behavior in the
interview process?
● Occupation psychological
test methods p.416-439
How to apply psychological recruitment
strategies effect/manage in the
recruitment process?
How to apply occupational psychological
test method to test applicant's ability?
● Selecting and evaluating
assessment methods p.440-458
How selection assessment methods are applied
to choose the best applicants ?
How to criteria for selecting and evaluating
assessment methods in interview?
Reference

Part Four
Employee efficiency psychological research
Chapter 20
Employee satisfaction measurement
● How to measure employee satisfaction ? p.459-470

● How can leaders satisfy employee needs?

● How does one company raise
employee efficiency

Chapter 21
Organizational behavior theory
● What is system approach? p.471-488

Employee satisfaction methods
● How can satisfy to employees' needs?

● How to achieve work motivation strategy ?
● How can influence organizational
positive behaviors ? p.489-500
    Reference
    Chapter 22
How to learn qualified research
interviewing in order to raise
efficiency and effectiveness
reference

● Psychological methods predict
employee individual productive
efficiency and service performance p.501-518
    Chapter 23
How to apply psychological
methods to predict employee
individual productive efficiency
and service performance
        ● Aims and hypotheses in employee
performance psychological research p.519-528

● What are variables, concepts and
measures meaning to any employee
performance psychological research p.529-538
    reference
    Chapter 24
Human resource department and
organizational performance
relationship p.539-550
    Part Five
Factors influence organicational
overall performance effectiveness
    Chapter 25
What is efficient achievement of
technological inputs factor in
construction industry p.551-568
    Chapter 26
Can effective departmental

communication effective change p.569-580
    Chapter 27
Can human resource development
training factor influence organizational
productive performance p.581-600
    Chapter 28
Factors influence employee motivation
to achieve organizational effective
performance p.601-620
    Chapter 29
Performance measurement influences
effectiveness p.621-640
Chapter 30
Facility management brings economic
benefits to organizations p.641-660

● Human resource training raises ●

productive efficient research

CHAPTER ONE

● Reward management strategy

●

● 1.0 What is reward management strategy?

1. Can effective human resource training or/and facility management influences your organization's employee individual productive efficiency raising and/or service performance improving?

2. Can effective workplace working environment facility management influence your organization's employee individual emotion and working attitude to be changed more positive to raise productive efficiency and/or service performance?

3. Can effective human resource training program improve your organization's employee individual skill level in order to raise productive efficiency and/or service performance?

4. Has it relationship between effective human resource training and facility management to influence organization's employee individual productive efficient level and service performance in long term?

I shall apply psychological method to attempt to recommend whether it is the right time to your organization ought need to find methods to raise your organization's human resource trai8ning course(s) quality and/or improve your organization's facility management in-house service quality to let your employees feel more comfortable to work in your organization's any working environment in order to achieve the raising productive efficiency and/or improving service performance consequence in possible.

●

● Why does organizations need reward management strategy that is concerned with the formulation and implementation of strategies and policies that aim to reward people fairly, equitably and consistently in accordance with their value to the organization. Reward management consists of analyzing and controlling employee remuneration, compensation and all of the other benefits for the employees. Reward management aims to create and efficiently operate a reward structure for an organization. Reward structure usually consists of pay policy and practices, salary and payroll administration, total reward, minimum wage, executive pay and team reward.

● Reward is the generic term for the totality of financial and non-financial compensation or total remuneration paid to an employee in return for work or service rendered at work. Reward, which is sometimes been refer to as compensation or remuneration, is perhaps the most important contract term in every paid-employment. Its impact on workers (or employee's) performance is in most instance greatly misinterpreted. The understanding of this term is very important; this is because the incentive scheme given to an employee will influence the behavior and level of engagement to the organization. However, basic pay, it is a straightforward payment scheme which may not provide incentives to individual workers because they are not based on output or performance. This pay is often in relation to a given period like an hourly rate, weekly wage or annual salary. It's also an established rate for all workers in one category. Incentive for group, Plant/enterprise-based it is refer to as grain sharing within large group or the whole organization. This pay scheme is use in organizations where the workforce can clearly see the results of their efforts.

● Award can include two kinds. Intrinsic reward include- Achievement, feeling of accomplishment, recognition, job satisfaction, personal growth and status, job enlargement, job enrichment, team working, empowerment. Otherwise, extrinsic rewards also include formal-recognition; base wage or salary, incentive payments, fringe benefits, promotion, social relationship and work environment. This study will explain and define different type of pay and non-financial scheme use in today's organizations.

● Reward Management is concerned with the formulation and implementation of strategies and policies that aim to reward people fairly, equitably and consistently in accordance with their value to the organization. Reward management forms the organization relationship. This if an HR manager is to succeed in successfully managing the employment relationship, he/she will have to do well in reward management, otherwise these will be an in balance in the employment relationship, such as strikes, lockouts. Objectives of Reward Management may include: Support the organization's strategy, recruit & retain, motivate employees, internal & external equity, strengthen psychological contract, financially sustainable, comply with legislation and efficiently administered.

- Basic Types of Reward include
- Extrinsic rewards
- – satisfy basic needs: survival, security
- – Pay, conditions, treatment
- Intrinsic rewards
- – satisfy higher needs: esteem, development
- Rewards by Individual, Team, Organization
- Individual: base pay, incentives, benefits
- – rewards attendance, performance, competence
- Team
- – team bonus, rewards group cooperation
- Organization
- – profit-sharing, shares, gain-sharing
-
- In general , a profitable reward management system should have these characteristics: Simplicity must be easily understood by everyone in the organization. People must understand why they are getting, what they are getting from the employment relationship . Fairness and equitability, every component of the system must be justifiable and consistently applied. But reward management has related problems, such as strike, staff turnover, dissatisfaction etc. An effective participatory reward management system should be negotiated and agreed better management and employees.
-
- What is the role of Compensation and Reward in Organization? Compensation and Reward system plays vital role in a business organization. Since, among four Ms, i.e. Men, Material, Machine and Money, Men has been most important factor, it is impossible to imagine a business process without Men. Land, Labor, Capital and Organization are four major factors of production.
- Every factor contributes to the process of production/business. It expects return from the business process such as rent is the return expected by the Landlord. Similarly Capitalist expects interest and organizers i.e. Entrepreneur expects profits. The labor expects wages from the process. It is evident that other factors are in-human factors and as such labor plays

vital role in bringing about the process of production/business in motion. The other factors being human, has expectations, emotions, ambitions and egos. Labor therefore expects to have fair share in the business/production process.

●

● What are the advantages of Fair Compensation System?

● Therefore a fair compensation system is a must for every business organization. The fair compensation system will help in the following:

● If an ideal compensation system is designed, it will have positive impact on the efficiency and results produced by workmen.

● Such system will encourage the normal worker to perform better and achieve the standards fixed.

● This system will encourage the process of job evaluation. It will also help in setting up an ideal job evaluation, which will have transparency, and the standards fixing would be more realistic and achievable.

● Such a system would be well defined and uniform. It will be apply to all the levels of the organization as a general system.

● The system would be simple and flexible so that every worker/recipient would be able to compute his own compensation receivable.

● Such system would be easy to implement, so that it would not penalize the workers for the reasons beyond their control and would not result in exploitation of workers.

● It will raise the morale, efficiency and cooperation among the workers. It, being just and fair would provide satisfaction to the workers.

● Such system would help management in complying with the various labor acts.

● Such system would also bring about amicable settlement of disputes between the workmen union and management.

● The system would embody itself the principle of equal work equal wages. Encouragement for those who perform better and opportunities for those who wish to excel.

●

● Factors affect an organization's reward policy and strategy which include: affordability, it means what an organization can afford to pay the argument is that an organization can't borrow to reward employees, but should reward from the value created by the employees themselves. However, an organization has to afford to pay above legal minimums, legislation sets the minimum base pay (minimum fixed pay rates), which becomes the starting point in calculating for all of an organization's policies. Workers committees/trade unions depend on the power of a union, pay levels are determined through collective bargaining. The most powerful ones will strike higher levels, external job value means the market value of the job, e.g. what is the market value or HR manager or clerical assistant? Internal job value means the value or perceived value of a job compared to other jobs which the organization will determine the reward that job, e.g. HR manager compared to finance manager. Value of the person means employees holding similar jobs can be paid differently depending on the value of the organization performance and the economy environment influence means (labor supply/demand). Some authors explained a depressed economy increased the supply of labor, which reduced its price and have effect reward policy strategy.

●

● Thus, reward system strategy means a benefit plan management procedure and it needs to implement these steps in order to achieve its fair reward as below:

●

● Step one, deciding objective to assess what the company wants to achieve through its benefit strategy and policy, and its ability to pay for the changes;

●

● Step two, obtaining view points and input from employees to collect employees' view points through employee surveys, focus groups and individual interviews;

●

● Step third, analyzing competitiveness to establish or determine the company's competitive position, though conducting a customized survey or collecting available market data from external providers;

●

● Step fourth, designing the benefit package to determine the mix and scale of the benefit package, the allocation of benefit, the scope for flexibility and the cost of benefit provision;

●

● Step fifth, consulting the senior management team and employees on the proposal to get input and buy in from senior management team to make amendments if necessary, collecting comments and effort the non-financial rewards as benefits; step sixth, planning the communication to inform everyone concerned what is happening, why it is happening and how it affects them,

●

● The final step , evaluation to review the plan on a regular basis and obtain input from employees and management for evaluation purposes.

●

● Strategy reward system pay for perform two elements: Financial reward includes base salary, pay incentives, employee benefits. Non-financial reward includes intrinsic rewards, centers in the work itself, praise, recognition , time off. Reward system is a key driver of-HR strategy, business strategy organization culture strategic reward system related to HR system. Such as skill-based pay to training, overtime pay rules to labor relations, sign-on bonus to employment, merit pay to performance management and merit pay to performance culture.

● Thus one successful reward strategy system will have these characteristics. Performance and reward strategy, identify requirement and develop strategy, analyze data and performance and reward information on individuals or group and achieve colleges to aid decision making, work with managers to certain and develop reward requirements for key individuals within their area, review and analyze the organization strategy demographic profile and market activity against current reward activity to identify current reward activity to identify current and long term reward requirement to assess internal and external factors driving reward requirements against plan. Explain to employees how pay and reward fits and supports overall people processes and activities, such as performance management.

● In conclusion, what is award's aim ? For the organisation, reward should aim at; recruiting the quantity and quality required, encourage suitable staff to be loyal and remain in the organisation, provide rewards for good performance and incentives for further improvement in performance, maintain appropriate differentials relative to values of different levels of job, the reward adopted by organisation should be flexible enough to accommodate changes in the market rate for different skills and should be cost effective. For individual employees the reward system should be fair and equitable in valuation of the worth in comparison with others. The third which is the union of employees, the system should ensure maximum benefits for members without undue prejudices to their future security by making their reward to pace with the cost of living and the prosperity of the organisation.

● What kinds of benefits of reward strategy which can bring to organizations? Good employee benefits and services can help the organization by reducing potential employee discontent, satisfying their needs and discouraging labor unrest or raising labor turnover. Thus, with competitive benefit programs , an organization can be more effective in recruitment and employee retention, thus reducing labor turnover.

● Employee benefits may include legally required payments, such as workers compensation, long service pay or retirement payment, sickness allowance and end of year payment, bonus as well as optional welfare plans, such as life insurance, medical/hospital /dental coverage to self and family' education allowance, housing allowance, quarters, subsidized loans, retirement, pension plan, meal allowance, travelling allowance, paid time off, pay sick leave, other special paid leave, five day week, paid annual leave and maternity leave.

● Employee service mean the organizations can choose to provide various services ranging from work related to those satisfying personal or family needs, in order to encourage employees to work happily and stay with a particular organization. The service may include social functions or recreational activities, e.g. New Year dinner, annual ball, company picnics, free transportation service, food service or canteen ,purchase of used equipment no longer required by the company, credit unions, low-interest loans, legal services, child care and elder care services, free holiday apartment, air ticket allowance etc. employees' welfares.

●

●

●

● 1.1 Why does organization need reward management system?

●

● Some HR professionals feel reward management can earn these benefits to organizations. In compensation and benefits reward management aspect, it is not possible to imagine an offer of employment that does not indicate a salary or wage and possibly other terms of compensation as well as description of the various benefits available with the employment. So, a candidate accepts or rejects the job offer, he/she will regard how a compensation package with a monetary of non-monetary value, such as a fair exchange for whose labor. So, the award management plan will include monetary reward and non-monetary reward both is better than monetary reward only. For example, piece rate pay is good for factory workers, commissions have long been a major part of the compensation of salespeople and merit pay and bonuses are well established methods of rewarding good performance for car salespeople. So, the variable or incentive pay is a good reward implementation plan for salespeople, insurance agents.

● How to evaluate the base pay level is the more accurate? Leon, M. (2002) indicated that when a company needs to determine levels of base pay, the best companies have several objectives. The most important , in a global business environment characterized by strong demand for talented experienced employees is to be competitive. The determination of base pay level does not depend on only in one's own industry, but also in other industries competing for the same talent. In fact, a firm's closes competition for human resources often is not its closet industrial competitor. In addition, the best companies are attractive to the levels of compensation appropriate to the different regions and countries where facilities are located or where workers originate. At the same time, some are developing truly global talent managers, whose pay scales are most pay level to similar manager in other companies than they are with typical rate of pay in either the firm's headquarter country or its overseas locations.

● Is one company achieves higher profits, it needs to raise higher wage to its all employees? I feel that it depends on whether situations to make decisions to raise all employees' wages , due to it has higher profit reason in the year.

● Robert, P.V. (2006) summarized these rules in dealing with subordinates, their performance should be enhanced. These rules includes using fair differential rewarding, it means that many managers try to treat all subordinates alike. When all employees receive equal rewards, superior performers begin to feel that their efforts are unappreciated, when poorer recognize that they won't be penalized for minimal effort. In response, over time, most above-average performers will drop their performance to the minimal level.

● A few superior performers may persist absolutely , but most will lower their efforts to the level that they feel equals their rewards. So, when rewards are commensurate with performance, however, subordinates receive a quite different message. Superior performers get the signal that their efforts are valued, and potentially high performers are encouraged to try harder, identifying valued rewards for individual , it means that if a manager hopes to influence an employee's behavior through the use of rewards, the rewards must have value to the employee. One of the best ways to obtain such information is simply to ask employees what rewards they could like to receive. Younger workers may prefer more paid vacation days, (non-monetary value reward) or greater participation in decision making (high position management role) . The older workers may choose better medical insurance or a longer contribution to their pension plan, instructing subordinated on how rewards are tied to performance. It means that in order for maximizing organization's effectiveness, employees must clearly understand how rewards and performance are connected. When specific information is lacking, subordinates may try to second-guess their manager's intentions by constructing their own imagined system of rewards. Thus, much under productivity can be avoid of a manager clearly states goals for performance and explains how rewards will be related to performance, providing information feedback on performance means that in order to meet their manager's standards of performance, employees must have instructive feedback. Their manager must evaluate their information for them, indicating how well or how poorly they are doing and suggesting specific ways to improve. In addition to providing guidance, feedback can also serve as an additional form of suggestion.

● Thus, when an organization earns higher profit, it seems that it ought not raise all employees salaries to be higher, because some hard working employees will feel unfair if the lazy employees can raise the same salary level to same to the hard working employees in the year. On the consequence, the hard working employees will be possible to under productivity or productivity in below level efficiency or inefficiency to perform their unsatisfactory or disagreed feeling to complain whose employers. Then, the organization will encounter low productivity in possible. Hence, fair reward management plan to all employees which is needed in any organization.

●

●

● 1.1.1 Why do IT and bank and property management and school organizations need reward management system?

●

● In IT and bank and property industries which need reward strategic reasons: Reward management systems have major impact on organization capability to catch, retain and motivate high potential employees and as a result getting the high level of performance. I also believe reward of employee performance can lead to differentiation between the productivity of the bank employees. In fact, bank employee performance is originally what on employee does or does not do. Performance of employees could include quantity of output, quality of output, timeliness of output, presence at work, cooperativeness.

● Reward management in bank service industry, bank organization needs have effective and attractive reward management system to attract talent human resource applications. But banks are facing global saving bank competition. Reward management system is a core function of human resource discipline and is a strategic partner with company management. An good reward management can raise bank service employees performance in loan, saving mortgage etc. different departments. An effective reward management system can shorten service timeliness to raise talent employee individual bank service performance, raise the talent employee team cooperative effort in loan, mortgage, counter etc. different service departments.

● However, reward management system tool includes both financial and non-financial rewards which are also called as extrinsic and intrinsic rewards. In bank industry financial rewards include salary increase, bonus, commission, housing loan allowance, education loan allowance. The non-financial rewards include promotion and title, authority and responsibility, appreciation and praise, participation to decisions, vacation time, comfort of working place, social authority, customer and management positive oral and written feedback, flexible working hours, design of work recognition , social rights, etc.

● Property management industry reward management practitioners include property managers, caretakers, attendants, security guards, facility maintenance workers and cleaners. It is essential for employers to formulate strategic plans and coordinate labor relations of human resource with the development. In responds to the people-related challenge and opportunities to property management industry. It includes six aspects: communicating and improving staff benefits, promoting work-life balance and health and enhancing work arrangements, enhancing staff's career development and promotion prospect, improving the professional image of the industry, friendly employment practices for mature persons. Through these practices enterprises can make their job vacancies about attractive and answer misunderstandings about the property management industry.

● Thus, the manpower shortage challenge will be avoid , when the people have interest to join the industry and they feel the reward is attractive to them to develop career. How to improve staff benefit? It includes new recruit entry bonus schemes, giving out little gifts and bonuses, during celebrations and festive occasions, and granting gratuities to critically ill employees or on the death of the employee's immediate family members, offers employees insurance plans, offering award schemes for employee's children by granting scholarships to outstanding students in recognition of their excellent exchange scholarships are available to subsidize their children's study abroad, promoting working-life balance to staff, such as organizing interest classes, setting up sports teams, organizing gatherings, participating in charitable activities, encouraging employees to organize social gatherings, promoting happiness at work, strengthening occupational safety and health arrangements to employees, e.g. setting up occupational safety and health committee / departments, formulating occupational safety and health policies, entertainment of work arrangement: compressed working days, five-day work week, flexible working days, flexible rostering, job sharing, part time work pattern, most rest time for frontline employee, job nature or workflow modification / re-engineering, improvement of employee's workplace environment, intra-district redeployment.

● Reward is an important element in information technology industry. The IT industry had been needing a leader in changing traditional compensation strategy. Pay for performance needs to be designed effective reward system to encourage IT employee to work hardly in order to reward and contribute the most to an IT organization's technological productivity and profits.

● The compensation mix depends on deliverable and the impact it has on the IT business. Consequently higher the responsibility greater the variable content in the pay package. IT industry has many IT professionals , such as programmers, software or hardware engineers, e-commerce website designer etc. different IT professionals. Hence, different IT professionals need have different skills to evaluate pay performance level fairly. However, performance related pay plans, it is a motivator the improves productivity. It helps in improving IT product productivity and performance levels when making every IT professional individual equally to encourage or motivate them to work to hardly in their IT unique professional aspects. It is a greater motivator for top performances and teams as they can get fair and reasonable reward and pay according to their contributions.

● In fact, there is no standard formula for a performance -related incentive plan, it is unique for each IT professional. However, the incentive plan should need to be design to each IT professional with an organization's objectives. They include, communication and understanding of objectives, consideration of different IT professional performance against objectives, translating evaluation into the kid of IT professional performance rating, a link between ratings and pay to the kind of IT unique professional skill.

● University HR strategic reward management system(review promote monitor scheme) aims to improve systems and skills for teaching employee communication, support teaching management to play a move active role in communication key messages, ensure school reward policies and procedures are fair to teaching staffs and administrative non-teaching staffs in salary rank increasing level, establish improved consultation procedures at academic and teaching service level, demonstrate the values and ethics by the university through management practices and communication with teaching staffs and non-teaching staffs, improve the profile and performance of the university by recruiting and developing talent teaching employees with appropriate external recognition , certain academic disciplines present more different recruitment challenges and profile of the university as an employer could be improved in the academic labour market, recruiting sample of selection decisions through early stages of employment to assess quality of appointment and identify learning points, support and encourage recruitment messages to improve selection practice including skills and high quality appointment decisions, raise the profile of the university as an employer regionally, nationally and internationally, establish succession planning for all key roles and positions linked with clear career progression with job families, to face in a difficult economic climate the university needs to continue to attract and keep high quality staff to work in an efficient and cost effective manner. The extension of workload allocation models to all academic units is an important tool to assist in managing workload fairly and more effectively, well targeted and designed training and development is very effective in motivating and enabling staff and support productivity.

●

● 1.1.2 Why do small organizations need reward strategy?

● Reward strategy can be applied to large organization, it can be also applied to small organization, e.g. family business, family business also needs compensation policies, the result encourages professional growth among family members and other employees as well as strategic business goal accomplishment. In general, compensation can be divided into the categories of base pay (equity as a basic for fairness , benefit, e.g. health care insurance, salary , wages, incentive compensation (e.g. bonuses, deferred compensation, stock or share options) and perks e.g. club membership, use of the company's private mountain, beach for holiday entertainment or sport activities e.g. free golf sport and company 's automobiles to provide to employees to drive in their private time.

● Craig, E. A (2011) indicated that although small business has less employees , but it also needs compensation adjustments. The reasons include: (1) performance-based increases i.e. a rise, (2) annual wage adjustments e.g. cost of living increases to remain with what comparable businesses are paying and corrective adjustments to more pay for a position into with other position in the business increases are considered to be a key component of compensation by managers and non-management employers alike. The difference between one small organization's and one large organization's performance based increase is possible that one large organization has more a rise amount of performance -based increases in every time performance review. Otherwise, one small organization has less a rise amount of performance -based increases in every time performance review.

● A good reward strategy can develop a philosophy of compensation that builds a framework for base pay and incentive tailored to the special values, goals, and needs of the particular family firm. Hence, one family or small firm's compensation -reward strategy can be explained to be needed, due to these factors : the firm can compare pay and performance levels with those of businesses with whom which compete for employees, the firm's goal is to provide total compensation between median and the percentage of comparable groups, base salary will be made more accurate decision at or high or below the median level for the comparable groups, individual salaries will be made more accurate decision within how much percent of the midpoint for the firm's comparison group's salary range, the firm can make more accurate decision on emphasizing whether performance -based incentives ought be spent at the expense of the salary, whether annual incentives ought be exceed those of comparably sized competitors, whether long-term incentives ought be based on results that add shareholder value.

● However, culture can influence some business owners how to make compensation issues, culture means beliefs, values, assumption, habits and behavior patterns of the organization. The reasons staffs are paid the way, they are may be partly unconscious and may arise from the personal and family history and the deeply felt personal needs of the business leader or leaders. So, any family or small business will ought try to develop a philosophy of compensation (reward) strategy , which may learn a great deal about itself in the process. For example, a entrepreneur has confidence in her or his ability to manage compensation on a case-by-case basis and maintain tight personal tight personal control over each individual pay, perks, incentives, dividends, and gifts in order to encourage its employees can raise more effort to increase the sale number to its different kinds of product in its shop. Otherwise, if a family member working in this kind of culture asks for a raise, the business owner will not talk to about how to raise compensation to his/her salespeople in Christmas period. Hence , culture seems to influence the large organization and small organization how to make itself compensation to salespeople in Christmas period.

● However, a basis for fairness to base pay which can let the large organization or small organization's staffs to feel, it is very important , when the large or small organization needs to focus on filling a vacancy and getting new skills into key areas quickly to meet customer needs with quality and efficiency. Because if the large organization or small organization expects it sale turnover may increase or staff turnover may decrease, but hiring needed talent may become more difficult, indicating that the company's pay structure may have lost internal logic if it's basic pay is unfair to attract talent staffs choose to join to its organization to work, when they feel that the organization's base pay is not reasonable to compare its competitors (pay for one job compared to another), and comparable jobs outside the company, the process is logical , objective and fair to be needed to judge the base pay structure to any organizations. Having a consistent, explainable ration for how compensation or reward is critical for employee and shareholders judgements about fairness. Hence, individual employee will usually compare his/her job in the company's salary and his/her similar job in another company's salary whether whose salary is same or more or less between whose company salary and similar company salary. Hence, a company needs to establish equitable base pay in a market value and merit system, with any adjustments , pay raises being a function of performance merit in order to make more reasonable compensation or reward to let its staffs to feel to avoid staff turnover number raises.

● A rational compensation system steps can include: creating job description for all jobs, conducting a job evaluation to rank order jobs and determining which jobs that are similar in their importance to the business, obtaining external wage and salary survey information for representation jobs, utilizing other sources for comparable external data when needed, determining the company's reward strategy for compensation and deciding whether it wants pay to be set at the market average , whether it wants compensation at levels above or below the market average, or whether it wants to make a culture statement with pay levels, creating a wage and salary structure of starting pay levels, (minimums) and levels of pay for the most experienced workers (maximums). Analyzing current pay levels against the new structure pay levels against the new structure to determine which jobs are paid appropriately and which ones are not, considering individual, unique jobs that may have qualitative more or less important than external market comparable might suggest, making pay adjustments for those that are not of the range, accelerating regular increases for positions below the target range and decelerating or not making increased that are above the range. Finally , it needs to periodical check or review the wage and salary structure against outside bench market (external similar competitors positions to maintain external equity).

● The point factor job evaluation tool can help the organization to make decision whether the staff ought pay how much salary level is the most reasonable. The point method include the elements such as : The experience element means the factor appraises the length of time normally required for an individual to acquire the necessary knowledge and ability to affectively perform the duties of the job. The experience level element means that whether the worker individual working experience in the firm, e.g. up to three months, he/she can earn the lowest points, till to comprehensive over right years, he/she can earn the highest points. The direction of others element means this factor appraises the responsibility to the job , it includes for organization, selection , assignment , guidance and review of personnel and the performance of other supervisory tasks. The direction of others level can indicate the employee earns none points when whose jobs involves no responsibility or authority for the direction of others, till to the highest points when the employee can confirm to own administrative ability,whose job is responsible for general administrative or executive supervision of all or broad segment of company operations as well as he/she can establish general policies and procedures and formulates and applies broad plans of operations.

● Compensation specialists can help the company to select representative jobs from a company and find good external comparisons. They will need to make adjustment. Some criteria for determining a jobs' market value can include position title and job description, industry, size of company, sales or revenue volume, cost of living, based on location etc. data to determine whether their company's salary level is acceptable or reasonable to a job's market value. They need to gather the data concerns the job's market value. This is helpful because the latest supply and demand factors can affect certain positions may not show up in surveys. They must need to gather similar industry's organization size, sale or revenue volume data, daily cost of living and transportation cost how to influence their employees' income and similar competitors' employees income in order to make more reasonable and accurate salary structure adjustment.

●

● 1.2 Reward management aims to bring positive influence to work performance, how to achieve high work performance?

●

● How can reward management strategy raise job performance? In organization, work performing is affected by job characteristics and physical work environment, ability and skills and the willingness to performance to the individual employee. The major strategic rewards decisions to reward employees which include: What to pay employees, how to pay individual employees, cognition programs? Concerning about what to pay? The employer needs to establish a pay structure balance between internal equity, (the value of the job for the organization) and external equity , the external competitiveness of an organization's pay relative to pay in its industry.

● What does reward management mean? The management discipline is concerned with the formulation and implementation of strategies and policies, the purpose of which are to reward employees fairly, equitably and consistently in accordance with their value to the organization. It deals with design, implementation and maintenance reward systems (processes, practices, procedures) that aim to meet the needs of both the organization and its stakeholder. Thus, total reward can include non-financial as well as financial element is developed, implemented and treated. Usually , the components of total reward include two aspects: tangible rewards (base pay, contingent pay and employee benefits) as well as relational intangible rewards (learning and development), the work experience and achievement, growth , non-financial rewards . Then, it is the total reward. However, reward can include these tangible and intangible elements:

payment, such as salary, bonus, shares etc. Praise, such as positive feedback, commendation, staff-of -the year award etc. Promotion, such as status, career development. Punishment, such as disciplinary action, criticism, withholding pay. Thus, if one employee can not achieve the satisfactory performance, he/she ought need to get disciplinary action to be punished in order to let he/she learns how to revise his/her performance to raise working efficiency.

● How to implement strategic reward management? Where do we want our reward practices to be in a few years time (vision)? How do we intend to get these (mean)? So, a declaration of intent that defines what the organization wants to do in the longer term to develop and implement reward policies, practices and processes, that will further the achievement of its business goals, and need the needs of the stakeholders, it can give a framework to other elements of rewards. So, the structure and content of a reward strategy may include: Environment analysis, macro-level, social, economical, demographic, industrial level, and micro-level competitors, analysis of job evaluation, financial conditions, gap analysis.

● When the organization expected to apply reward strategy to raise employee individual performance successfully? It needs to know what job evaluation means. It is a systematic process for defining the relative worth/ size of the jobs roles within a organization, for establishing internal relatives, for designing an equitable grade structure and grading jobs in the reward structure. For example, reward strategy can attempt to reduce wage gaps, when the wage gap can occur in the company, it can use international benchmarking in job evaluation. However, the cause is simple. The market of top managers is usually international, they earn international wage, or they leave the firm. The market of workers with little or no qualification is local in nearly every case. They can earn local wages. In less developed countries , this can lead to raise wage gaps between the top and bottom employee. Hence, if the firm discovered it has large distance of wage gaps between its top and bottom level positions. It ought need to find methods to adjust these positions' salaries to be reduce large distance of wage gaps fairly in order to let these large distance of wage gaps of position employees , they can feel their company is more fair to treat every employee.

● Moreover, firm also need to consider that whether it ought choose which type of individual payment to excite its employee individual performance to be improved. They may include: performance -related increases basic pay or bonus -related to assessment of performance, contribution-related pay is related both to inputs and outputs, skilled-base pay is related to high or low skilled to the individual effort performance, service -related pay is related to whether the employee needs to spend how long service-time to satisfy customer's need in order to measure every service employee's performance, team-based pay is related to team performance, it can encourage teamwork, loyalty and cooperation and it can be demotivating on individual level.

● All of these any types of reward method will improve or encourage the low performance employee individual working efficiency or raise productivity more easily as well as fair reward strategy can upgrade the high performance employee individual efficiency or encourage them to exceed their productive level or raise their productivity to achieve the maximum number. Hence, reward management has direct relatively to influence every employee's performance in order to bring either long term positive or negative influence to their organizations.

●

● 1.3 What factors can influence organization's reward strategy?

● What is reward management strategic principle to employment relationship? employees needs to pay tangibles (salary, wage, cars, educational , holiday allowance etc.) or/and intangible (recognition, career development growth etc.) rewards to employees aim. Individual balance to achieve tangible output, sales and/or intangibles loyalty , service performance, commitment. Hence, reward management forms the employment relationship, if an HR manager is to succeed in successfully managing the employment relationship, he/she will have to do well in reward management.

● The reward management principle includes simplicity, it must be easily understood by everyone in the organization, fairness and equitability , every component of the system must be justifiable applied. This element is arguably the most challenging to implement and is the cause of most reward management related problems , such as strike, turnover, dissatisfaction etc. Hence, an attractive communication and training to the low skillful labour to have chance to upgrade high skillful which is needed, a participatory chance is effective one should ideally be negotiated and agreed between management and employees.

● In fact, traditionally companies have always adopted the base pay strategy. It pays the legal minimum wages and salaries. However, it does not adequate in new work cultures and in terms of attracting , retaining and motivating top performers for strategic purposes, but still very commonly for lower level employees. The new reward strategic options include as below:

● 1. Knowledge and skills based strategy, because of the proven relation job performance, organizations have sought to encourage continuous skills development by trying it to rewards. A organization simply varies its pay structure according to one's level of knowledge and skill (job evaluation systems. It can define which skills, it values and will pay for and must have a supportive training and development strategy. It is based pay with an equal base pay and a variation based on skills and knowledge. It may be costly in the short-term , but it is beneficial from a knowledge HR base through increased productivity and quality of product.

● 2. Performance based (varied pay based structure strategy), employees should be rewarded only for the value they create. A company will reward employee in the same grade variably depending on each employee's performance.

● 3. Incentive based pay structure strategy, it measures but being different in that it focuses on group performance rather than individual performance. The starting point in strategy is to define group performance targets , such as productivity sale volumes or profitability.

● What factors can influence organization's reward strategy? They include: Affordability, the argument is that an organization can't borrow to reward employees, but it should reward from the value created by the employees themselves; legislation sets the minimum base pay minimum fixed pay rate; union/workers committees' pay level are determined through collecting bargaining. For example, strike issue will bring higher salary level in possible; external job value, the market value of the job, e.g. what is the market value of an HR manager or clerical assistant; internal job value, perceived value of job compared to the other jobs which the organization will determine the reward for the jobs , e.g. HR manage compared to finance manager; value of the person, employees holding similar jobs can be paid differently depending on the value to the organization performance; the economy changing factor (labor supply/demand) in labor market, e.g. it is a depressed economy increases the supply of labour, it will reduce the labour wage/salary market prices, due to the economy is bad , employers won't need to raise to any employees number and it has excess labour supply number to affect reward policy strategy.

●

● 1.4 What is reward system of McDonald ?

- For McDonald's Corporation U.S. employees at corporate, division and region offices, McDonald benefits are organized into four Performance management includes processes that effectively communicate , company aligned goals, evaluate employee performance and reward them fairly.
- Your Pay and Rewards (ref from McDonald's reward system)
- Attractive program follows a "pay for appearance" beliefs: The better your results, the greater your pay opportunities.
- Base Pay
- Since employees' bottom pay is the most important portion of their recompense, McDonald's maintain the competitiveness of our base pay through an annual review of both external market data and interior peer data. In our business, division and region offices, McDonald's has a broad banding compensation system. Broad banding allows for suppleness in terms of pay, movement and growth.
- Incentive Pay
- Inducement pay gives our workers with the possibility to earn spirited total compensation when performance meets and exceed goals. For our corporate, parting and region office, the Target Incentive Plan (TIP) links employee presentation with the presentation of the business they hold up. TIP pays a gratuity on top of employees' base salaries base on business presentation and their person appearance.
- Long Term Incentives
- Long term incentives are granted to entitled workers to both prize and retain key employees who have shown continued presentation and can crash long-term value creation at McDonald's. for the befits of employees the long term incentives are very helpful because when the organization has a policies of incentives or long term incentives then the employees of the organization feel secured and work hardly for the organization. Similar like this any company or any Originations rewarding system always brought positive crash.
- Recognition Programs
- Mc Donald's recognition programs are intended to reward and recognize physically powerful performers. For our corporate, separation and region offices, these take in the president Award (given to the top 1% of individual performers worldwide) and the Circle of fineness Award (given to top teams worldwide to be familiar with their aid for advancing our vision). Once start to hesitation your honesty, and then no one is leaving to alter their activities Appraisal system is also very helpful and makes a positive

competition and encouragement in between the employees of the organization. Promotions will be appraisal based which encourage employees for hard work.

● Company Car Program
● Mc Donald's company car program provides entitled employees with a company car for both business and individual / personal use. If entitled, employees can decide from. This is also very encouraging and motivating incentive for employees. It creates competition between employees and they work hard to get this incentive.

● In conclusion, the assumptions the company is creation about their prospect service and its intention to support their progress. Practical processes for deploy people and delivering enlargement which are consistent with these intention. The reserve and promise for taking these types of program used. If we see in past we can get that simple ways in which the company could use the out test for the planed strategies and special and important clues for the good results.

●
●

● Reference
● Craig, E.A. & Stephen, L.M. & John, L.W. (2011) family business compensation: New York, US, Palgrave Macmillan, p.35
● Leon, M. (2002). High performers, how the best companies find and keep them: US, Jossey - Bass, John Wiley & Sons, Inc, US pp.133-134
● Robert P. V, (6 edition, 2006). organizational behavior: core concepts: US, Thomson, pp.58

●
●
●
●
●
●
●
●
●
●
●
●
●

CHAPTER TWO

● Organizational development

●

● Why do organizations need develop?

●

● Organizational development (OD) is defined by theorists and practitioners in different ways. Essentially, it is a planned, organization-wide effort to increase an organization's effectiveness and/or to enable an organization to achieve its strategic goals. Before working on organizational development activities, an essential first step is to map the organizational context in which the changes , you are hoping what will occur. It means to understand function what affect your work, which approach you may be bringing to the activities and being able to determine an organization's readiness to work with you and develop for themselves the required innovations.

● Many OD projects focus on providing the more visible material resources, building skills, improving organizational structures and systems. Moreover, culture values have an impact on several elements of as including: the way change occurs, perception about whether change is needed, perception about leadership and ownership , perception about risk and uncertainty, perception about relationship and partnership and perception of what success looks like. It is described internal changes as relating to organizational structures, processes and human resource requirement, whereas external changes involves government legislation, competitor movements and customer demand.

● In general, organizational development aims to expect to raise awareness, e.g. improved understanding, attitude, confidence or motivation , enhanced knowledge and skills, e.g. increasing ability to act through teamwork, e.g. strengthened ability to act through improved with a group a people tied by a common task. This may involve for example, among them members, a stronger agreement or improved, communication, coordination, contribution by the team members to the common task, enhanced networks, e.g. improved processes for stronger incentives for participation in the network or increased traffic or communication among network members; increased implementation know -how , e.g. discovery and innovation with learning by doing formulation or implementation of policies, strategies, plans for UD aims in possible.

● Why do organizations need to changed? Our business would is fasting to increase technology new methods of production and new taste of customers and new market trends as well as new strategies for best control of the organizations and motivation of employees like to accept to use new products in popular nowadays. Hence, managers need to concern how to decide about the change management in the organizations, because business activities now are globalize, and every organization needs to attract loyal customers , trained the employees, introduce and adapt new methods of production and best control the activities of the organization.

● How will change organization in the good condition? The question arises in present scenario. Organizational change or change management aims to raise ability of the management benefits and support from change with reduced inefficiencies and ineffectiveness from the side of employees and encourage appreciate acceptance and support. The process of changing the activities of the organization as well as the implementation of the procedures and technologies to achieve the design objective. If the organization usually needs to change management includes different aspects, such as control change, adaptation change and effecting change.

● Consequently, organizational change simply means to change the activities of the organization, it concerns change the culture of the organization, technology, business process, change of employees, rules and procedures, recruitment and selection, design of jobs, methods of appraisal , human resource , technology, physical environment of the organization, methods of training and development, job skill, and knowledge etc.

● However, when the organization decides to implement change. Some employees should feel not adapt the change easily. They will quickly respond by complaints, engaging in work slowdown, threating to go on strike etc. How to overcome change management implementation successfully. The organizations need to implement change fairly , selection people who accept change, education and communication.

● However, organization development also plays an important role in the change management. It can be defined as a collection planned change, built a humanistic values and benefits and welfare needs, that need to improve the organizational effectiveness and employees work performance and well-being.

●

● Why does General Motor organization need change management?

● For General Motor (GM) change management case example, GM taking swift cost cutting action (2008) showed GM established in 1908s, till 1920s it was becoming the world largest motor manufacturing company, it could produce new style and design car every year. These were different brand cars which were producing by the company that time, and this every there were no other competitors to compete in the company different cars. But, the Japan automakers the company, GM felt threatened, specially Toyota Japan. Hence, GM needed to again get his position in market by restructuring and making change in the company. Now the GM company is again operating business in core brands in America, such as GMC.

● GM taking swift cost cutting action (2008) also indicated that however, the change to GM was the high wages cost to employees as the company was paying US$74 per hour as compared to Toyota US$44 per hour, because GM was an agreement with trade union and GM run the plant with minimum 80% capacity whether it was needed or not.

● Hence, what types of changes are decided to bring or make change to GM. In fact GM decided to bring changes on some areas of the motor business. These were included, structural change, cost change, process change and cultural change. The steps which as taken to change by the GM is about cost cutting, it has reduced cost of some brands to maintain the profit level. Similarly , GM also cut pay of employees which was the major problem. The GM also changed the culture of the company. GM removed it automate producing board and automate strategy up to 8 men board. It can changed the culture to improve the efficiency of the employees and such change is to speed up the day to day decision making.

● But, GM also encounters problems to change process. Such as problems in cultural change, the cultural plan was based top down approach, which ignored totally the involvement of the employees as compared to other companies, some suggested that it has not down up approach in which employees feel satisfaction. So this regard , it empowered the employees by introducing in tailoring the down top approach. Rather then telling to employees what they do, due to its employees hope have change to discuss with top management to express their opinions. Moreover, the other problem with cost cutting from the agreement of trade union, as it was an agreement with not lowering the pay of the employees and maintain the capacity level.

● Driving change at GM (2005) indicated that better result of cost cutting of GM seems from its employment figure of 98 to 2009. It was reduced from 226,000 to 101,000 workers and now the GM is concentrating on sale rather than to further cut off and also GM is deciding to reduce the worker force of the factory from 60,000 to 40,000. It certainly leads to cost saving to GM. Another better result of cultural change to GM, employees now becoming aware about the responsibility, as well as GM as empowered the employed to give better productivity. Hence, GM can success to solve change management problems to bring profit and win its competitors in motor sale market in global successfully.

●

● Culture can influence organization development

● Culture is not the way we do things around here. Culture is which we cooperate and the through we view the organization. If we view an organization as a system of interacting and interrelated part, culture defines , creates and supports that system.

●

● IBM computer organizational culture influences whether it's computers will be out dated feeling to computer consumers

●

● For IBM computer example, IBM had brought to change a culture means changing our fundamental view of how the world works. However, IBM ran into serious financial difficulties in the late 1980 and early 1990s in large part because it was unwilling to change the ways in which it was approaching the computer market, even though the market was rapidly changing around it to break with tradition.

● How is culture created to IBM? Stephen, R.B(2011) indicated IBM founder , or the influential leader, had reinforced the values of culture. When he worked for IBM many years ago, he discovered the IBM leader was one considerable person to his employees. Such as one case, how when an IBM employee was badly injured and his family killed in a car accident, the leader Tom Watson was there at the hospital when the man woke up, promising to cover the medical bills and do whatever he could. Hence, he can let IBM employees feel that IBM was seem to their home family.

● Hence, what makes a successful culture to IBM ? Stephen, R.B(2011) also showed that a culture is successful if it is in harmony with its environment and unsuccessful if it it unable to function in its environment. The environment is the world in which the culture operates. So, when environment changes faster than cultures. When the environment changes, the mechanisms of the culture may no longer be valid. Such as the advent of the PC changed the business environment for IBM, and the company found it difficult indeed to adjust. Today, with the accelerating shift from desktop computers to mobile devices and the Internet, Microsoft is still. In 1992, IBM had a loss for the first time, closed down numerous divisions. However, IBM's culture contained a very strong ethic of " analyze the problem, determine the solution, and execute the solution even, if it 's unpleasant." IBM realized that it needed a fresh perspective, so it brought in Lou Gerstner, the first non-IBM to become CEO. As Ed Schein points out, Gerstner came from a very similar marketing background to IBM's founder, Tom Watson, Sr. Gerstner didn't so much change IBM's culture as revitalize an aspect of it that had become dormant. Over the year, IBM's engineering culture had become dominant, and the marketing culture had benefit to become into the background.

●

●

● IKEA organizational culture influences whether it's China furniture market in success?

● Why does IKEA management cultural diversity needs to regard its staffs in China challenge? Multinational company, such as IKEA furniture company aims to increase profitability and it also needs to seek to for solutions to problems related with the saturation of existing markets, it needs to make an effort to expand operations to overseas market, such as China. However, it will face cultural difference challenge to be needed to deal if it want to enter China furniture sale market successfully.

● Kumar, S. (2005) indicated IKEA is the world's largest furniture retailer since the early 1990s. It offers a wide range of well- designed, functional home furniture products at low prices as many people as possible will be able to afford them. However, IKEA planned to enter China market, but it will face the cultural difference challenge between China and itself Swedish regional cultural of their staff communication and co-operational relationship.

● In deed, the "IKEA" facilities its successfully international expansions

, it needs to combination vision, characteristic leadership and business principle between China and Swedish culture effectively. IKEA opened its first store in China in 1998. Although, the company has succeeded with their global strategy in the past in most of the markets, it has entered , it quickly learnt the success in the Chinese market required a different strategy in the areas of marketing and HR (Kumar, 2005, p.2).

● What are the cultural difference to influence IKEA's success to develop furniture sale in China market? The standardized strategy which is adopted by IKEA could lead to some disadvantages because Swedish managers are needed to send to other branches in other countries in other to ensure the IKEA way is implemented in the local areas. Thus, it brings the conflict between the Swedish management and local employees could occur due to the cultural differences. Especially, in the country like China where the traditional cultures and value are different to such as Swedish culture. So, Chinese employees will have their mind for long a working culture differs from the Swedish way that IKEA wants to influence to their employees, problems were unavailable.

● When IKEA were keen to increase revenue in Asian markets like China, they faced the challenge to mange their staffs from the conflicts and the diversity of Chinese cultures, such as how to train people within IKEA perform in a standardized format to keep its essential value, and how to avoid the misunderstanding when improve employee performance and understanding the importance of cross cultural management between Sweden and China. So, IKEA managers definitely have responsibilities to spend time, energy and effort to understand the differences of national corporate and functional cultures before starting an arranging the strategic plans in China furniture sale market.

● The another cultural difference challenge concerns China and Sweden both countries have problems on law, price competition, information, language, delivery, foreign currency, time differences and cultural differences etc. different aspects. Thus, such as this IKEA Sweden furniture international company plans to enter China furniture sale market. It will have great barriers are caused by cultural differences, such as difficulty of communication, higher potential transaction costs, different objectives and means of cooperation and operating methods.

● These problems have led to the failure to IKEA furniture to enter China furniture sale market in possible. Therefore, IKEA needs to concern questions how to do business in China and understand China's culture and how to do business with Chinese people. It is possible that Chinese labors dissatisfy IKEA's provided cheap labor as well as the strong serious organizational bureaucracy system, high job duty demand is needed to satisfy customer's behavior in China. Hence, IKEA's culture difference challenge to China furniture sale market , it has relationship to human resource management and reward challenge.

● HR development aims

● Human Resource Development is the framework for helping employees develops their personal and organizational skills, knowledge, and abilities. Organizations have many opportunities for human resources or employee development, both within and outside of the workplace. By the end of this paper i will be able to devise a human resource plan for a work area, to meet organizational objectives, identify and plan for individual development to meet organizational objectives and also initiate a personal development plan for an individual and evaluate progress. Healthy organizations believe in Human Resource Development and cover all of these bases.

● The focus of all aspects of Human Resource Development is on developing the most superior workforce so that the organization and individual employees can accomplish their work goals in service to customers. We need to learn new skills and develop new abilities, to respond to these changes in our lives, our careers, and our organizations. We can deal with these constructively, using change for our competitive advantage and as opportunities for personal and organizational growth, or we can be overwhelmed by them. With all the downsizing, outsourcing and team building, responsibility and accountability are being downloaded to individuals. So everyone is now a manager. Everyone will need to acquire and/or increase their skills, knowledge and abilities to perform their jobs. By developing our knowledge and skills, our actions and standards, our motivation, incentives, attitudes and work environment we will be able to cope up with the ever changing work environment.

●

●

●

●

● Reference

● Driving change at general motor, 2005, online retrieved 15 Dec. 2009,

● ● www.cioleadershipnotes.com/p/gm/htm

● General motor talking swift cost cutting action, 2008, online retrieved

15 Dec. 2009 from dailymarkets.com/stock/2008/11/24/General- motor-takingswift-cost-action-cutting

● Kumar, S. (2005) "IKEA's globalization strategies and its foray in China", IBS center for management research

● Stephen, R.B. Organizational development, U.S., The McGraw- Hill , 2011, pp.5-8

●

●

●

●

●

●

●

CHAPTER THREE

● Human resource role in business

●

● HR function in organization

●

● HR role in business functions: HR ethics and code of industry includes that HR people should act legally, ethically and professionally as these aspects: Act legally, it represent the most core of obligations. HR is responsible for keeping current with changes in employment law and keeping management informed of risk or possible library. Act ethically, HR represents all employees at all levels of the organization, regardless of sex, age , race , color, material status, religion, disability or other protected class. At the same time, HR promotes the ethical culture of an organization. They must model the highest level of ethical behavior, administer all company policies and procedures fairly in handling disciplinary.

● HR must conduct thorough investigations and make recommendations or decisions based on facts. Act professionally, HR must keep employees' and companies' information in the strictest confidence and protect company information when dealing with employees or individuals outside of company. HR must follow changes in employment law, company policies and employment issues. They are also responsible for continuing education to remain expects in the field to be a successful strategic business partner. HR staffs need own business knowledge and understand the cost of people-related activities and responsible for measurement to all HR programs and processes, subject matter expert, in this role, the HR person should passes HR knowledge in relation to the most up-to-date employment law at the best HR practices for sourcing and staffing, remuneration strategy and systems, performance management, employee relations, and people development and advice business as appropriate.

● At all time, a professional HR will keep his/her management informed of any potential risk and liability to the business , due to the change of employment law. Creating good working environment, HR needs to motivate , engage, contribute good and happy working environment to le staffs to work in the organization. HR needs to help to establish and promote the organizational culture in which people are willing to do the best performance to the jobs, and commit customer's needs and concerns.

● In this role, the HR person identifies and facilitates overall talent management strategies, employee development opportunities, employee assistance programs, long term incentive and effective communication opportunities and channels between management and employees. HR is such as one change agent. The HR person needs to know how to link changes to the strategic needs of the organization and being able to show empathy and concern employee needs to minimize employee dissatisfaction change. So, HR person needs have the ability to execute successful change strategies.

● HR functions in organization include: workforce planning, sourcing staffing, organizational development, skills training , learning , talent development, reward management, compensation and benefits, employee relations, communication, engagement, HR policy and legal recommendation, change management, employee welfare, workplace health and safety.

● Staffing sourcing means the success plan or buy recruit from external. It is a process , a company ensures that employees are recruited and developed to fill the key roles. Through high-performing employees, develop their knowledge, skills and capability and prepare them for advancement or promotion into even more challenging roles in 3 to 5 years' time. So, it asks to develop the employees to special projects, team leadership roles, internal and external movement to training and development opportunities.

● The success plan should identify key position, its key roles and contributions, key success factors of key positions, skill, knowledge, capabilities, reasons cause of turnover, potential success identification, development plans for potential successor to reach the required success factors.

● Recruit from external or buying recruiting resource from the labour market is suitable to meet company short-term staffing needs for the junior to middle level positions. It can help new skills and new experience. Sources of supply can be from a combination of full time/part time employees, recruitment agencies' temporary workers and contract workers.

● The contracting applicants arrangement stage means the HR needs to contract the job applicants and invite for an interview, conducts the job interview, prepares the resume in advance and highlight areas to require further during the interview, knowledgeable about the company, the role in discussion and the job application process the applicants able to answer questions they might have, enthusiastic , friendly and courteous , so the applicant will be viewed the opportunity move positively, resourceful and helpful to hire managers , such as sharing tips ar interviewer, how to manage interviewees' expectation etc.

● Arranging interview stage providing the shortlisted candidates with helpful information about the interview includes: when and where the interview, who will be in the interview, how the interview will be conducted. Facilitating effective interview, the interviewer needs to ensure the interviewing environment is comfortable one free no noise, not leave the candidate waiting for too long. When closing the interview, the interviewer should advise the candidate of the possible must steps, online screening of application forms, using online to search and compare job applicant's information, job skills, years of experience, education level to identify suitable candidates for further selection processes.

● Reward management is concerned with the formulation and implementation of strategies and policies that aim to reward people fairly, equitably a fact, employers nowadays can hardly rely solely on base salary to attract and motivate their employees. More emphasis has other benefits , such as retirement benefits and learning opportunities. Performance and reward system should be market-based, equitable and cost-effective. Rewards do not only depend on skills, capabilities and experience of individuals, but also performance. In order to encourage top rate performers, employers must not only offer rewards for good work, but they must also have consequences for substandard work. Although, employers usually do not want to follow through with negative consequences, it is sometimes a necessary process. Otherwise, employees have no incentive to correct unacceptable behavior.

● Employers also needs to clearly know about what is recognized by the company and how these will be measured. So that they understand the relationship of performance and reward. Total reward may include anything value resulting of employment relationship to the employee with a goal to attract, motivate and attract talent. It can include financial and non-financial rewards and that these can change over time depending on their personal circumstances. Employers need to find out what attracts, engages individuals and explore how best they can meet these needs. It is important that the company how design's the elements of the reward package to support.

● What factors can determine rewarding for performance, qualification, experience, potential, behavior, effort, achieving goals, meeting targets. How the employees will be rewarded, the awards whether are company's work culture/characteristics are whether driven the right behavior/performance/efforts the awards are be valued by the employees, the awards are how often to be given, how often the rewards are reviewed, the award is long or short term.

● Legal framework for reward system , such as payment of wage, restriction on wages deduction, minimum wage, benefit, such as share options or housing benefits. Major benefit plans may include: retirement benefit schemes, personal security, e.g. healthcare, dental , hospitalization, accident or life insurance, financial assistance, e.g. mortgage interest subsidies, rental subsidies, staff discount, education subsidies, personal needs, e.g. holidays and leave with pay child care, fitness and facilities, use of holiday house, employee shares purchase plan, company car etc. welfares.

●

● 3.1 What is HR's role in corporate social responsibility?

● The HR function should help formulate and achieve environmental and social goals when also balancing these objectives with traditional financial performance metrics. The HR function can serve as a partner in determining what is needed or what is possible in formulating corporate values.

● At the same time, HR should play a key role in ensuring that employees implement the strategy consistently. For example, encouraging employees, through training and compensation to find ways to reduce the use of environmentally damaging chemicals in the products, assisting employees in identifying ways to recycle products that can be used for play grounds for children who do not have access to healthy places to play designing a company's HRM system to reflect equity development avoid well-being , thus contributing to the long-tem health.

● How HR policies shape the workplace and how HR can improve employee well-being through better working conditions and more positive workplace a cultures. Top-management can encourage particularly supervisory support, also has been identified as key to employee environment actions. In addition, adopting HRM and communicating a pro-environmental image can have a positive reputational effect. This helps to staff , the company leading to lower recruitment and training costs and a better financial bottom line. In fact, in some cases, a pro-environmental stance may be more important to potential employees. It can help a company address wider social problems that are affecting not only its external community, but also the company's financial bottom line. For example, The US postal service employees participate in more than 80 cross-functional teams across the US do drive energy reduction and resource conservation. These teams helped the postal service reduce energy, water, solid waste to landfills and petroleum fuel use as well as recycles more than 222000 tons of material. Thus, HR-related activities that can support , such as responsible workplaces, human rights, safety practices, labor standards, performance developments, diversity, employee compensation and more.

●

● Human resource role in Hong Kong business environment

●

● Andy, W.C. el.(2002) indicated that economic

● downturn which began in early 1998 had dramatic effects on Hong Kong's prosperity and increasing rates of Gross Domestic Product, especially during the 1990s and the early years of the 21st century. In late 2002s, Hong Kong's unemployment rate stood at 7 per cent and showed no immediate prospect of diminishing. This has huge implication for human resource professionals and especially for their training, as managers of the organization's most precious resource, its people. Moreover, downsizing and consequent increases in the rate of unemployment were logical consequences of this process.

●

● However, Hong Kong's strengths in finance, trade, services and tourism provided benefits from the effects of these recessionary forces. But, Hong Kong was faced with the poor of dealing with the human resource implications and other aspect of workforce reduction. Hence, it explains why HK organizations need to consider HRM functions as part of the acquisition, development , motivation and maintenance of human resources in order to bring direct relevance of the strategic decision-making on which profits and productivity depend.

●

● Human resource management is focused on the development and application of policies in relation to human resource planning, recruitment, selection, placement, and termination, management education , training and career development, terms of employment and methods and standards of remuneration, working conditions and employee services, formal and informal communication and consultation through employer and employee representative at all levels, negotiation and implementation of agreements on wages and working conditions , as well as procedures for the avoidance and settlement of disputes and the creation of a fairer and more equitable workforce in which discrimination in any form is viewed as unethical behaviors.

●

● HRM responsibilities include to conduct research into local wage levels to ensure the firm's reward system is competitive with those in other companies, devising remuneration systems to excite or encourage or persuade workers into enhanced effort and efficiency, administering superannuation schemes, e.g. retirement welfare plan, and advising employees about their pensions, maintaining personnel records and statistics, preparing accurate job descriptions and other retirement documentation, implementing health and safety regulations, accident prevention and the provision of first-aid facilities, e.g. safe construction site environment, designing and evaluating management training and development schemes linked with succession planning and developing and implementation systems with facilities organizational communication.

●

● Role of HR manager includes the control function, such as analysis of key operational data in human resource areas of labor turnover, wage cost, absenteeism, monitoring of staff performance (staff appraisal) and recommending appropriate remedial action to managers; the advisory function offers expect advice on human resource policies and procedures, e.g. which employees are ready for promotion, who should attend a certain training course, arrangement contracts of employment, health and safety regulations etc. related human resource related issues.

●

● The future role of HR manager needs to concern to adopt an international insight in their work, growing concern for the application of ethical approaches to human resource management, implementation of equal opportunity , data privacy, and arranging flexible working models, such as job sharing, job rotation, permanent part –time work, increased awareness to encourage or persuade for effective employee participation in company production systems in order to achieve raising efficiencies and effectiveness, concerning the consequences for HR management of the ageing workforce discussed issues, such as prolonging / shortening working age or shortening /prolonging retirement age policy, participating legal system in human resource issues, including laws on hiring , dismissing, equal opportunities, age, country discrimination conduct of industrial relations.

● HR planning can help management in making decision in the following areas: recruitment. , avoidance of redundancies (increasing labor turnover, training, management and development, estimates of labor cost, productivity bargaining, raising effectiveness or efficiency , accommodation requirements. In order to achieve company's maximum benefits purpose, HR planning needs continuous readjustment (annual review) , because the goals of an organization are subject to change and its internal and external environment is uncertain. It is also complex because it involves to many independent variables, e.g. increasing skillful immigration job seeker number to compete in the country's local labor market or decreasing skillful labor, e.g. computer programmers, doctors, accountant, lawyers etc. occupation professionals sudden emigrate to other countries to seek jobs, consumer demand increases or decreases to the product. Hence , it must include feedback because if the plan can not be achieved, the objectives of the company will have to be modified so that they are feasible in human resource terms.

● The human resource plan process to one company
● is a cycle process. The first step may include that it
● needs to follow issues from corporate plan's
● strategies and objectives. The main points to be
● considered such as capital equipment plans,
● reorganization, e.g. centralization or
● decentralization, how to change in product or in
● output, marketing plans and financial limitations.
●
● After it gathers the company's corporate
● strategic plan data. Then, it will implement its

● second step. This step may include three aspects:
● How to achieve the reasonable present utilization of human resources in particular: numbers of employees in various categories, estimation of labor turnover for each grade of employee and the analysis of labor effects of high or low turnover rates on the organization's performance, amount of overtime worked, amount of short time, appraisal of performance and the potential of present employees and general level of payment compared with that in other comparable firms. All these HR related data is essential to be recorded in accurate attitude.
● The external environment of the company analysis, such as recruitment position, population trends, local housing and transportation plans, government policies in education and retirement.
● The potential supply of labor analysis, such as effects of local emigration and immigration, effects of recruitment or redundancy in local firms, possibility of employing categories not now employed, for example outsource employees number, part time and semi-retired workers number and changes in productivity , working hours.
●
● The final step is that HR planning needs to be
● achieved. It includes recruitment/redundancy program, training and development program, industrial relations policy and accommodation plan. The issues will appear in this plan, such as jobs which will appear, disappear or change, to what extent redeployment or retraining is possible, necessary changes at supervisory and management is possible, necessary changes and supervisory and management levels, training needs, arrangements for necessary and details of arrangements for handling any human problems arising from labor deficits or surpluses , e.g. early retirement or other natural wastage procedures. Following , it needs to give feedback , what will be possible modification to company objectives to company's corporate level to review its HR plan whether it can achieve company's objectives and strategic aims.
●
● Human resource manager can be one human resource relation consultant to give recommendation how the organization should be better equipped to cope with the HR consequences of changed circumstances, careful consideration of likely future human resource requirements could lead the firm to discover new and improved ways surpluses might be avoided, it helps the firm to create and develop employee training and management

succession program, some of the problems of managing change may be foreseen or consultations with affected groups and individuals can occur at an early stage in the change process and decision can be taken and by considering all the relevant , options, rather than being taken in crisis situations, management can assess critically the strengths and weaknesses of its labor force and HR policies, wasting or excess of effort among employees can be avoided and coordination to worker's efforts is improved to raise efficiencies and productive effectiveness.

●

●

● HR role in bank industry development

●

● What is human resource (HR) role in organization? What factors can change to influence HR? They include workforce changes, globalization, ethics, organizational growth, increased accountability. These factors can influence HR's role change in the organization. So , when you assume be one HR manager, you need to concern : How have you used you awareness of internal and external changes to guide the decision making of your stakeholders ,e.g. discussing the impact of trends in workforce skills with function leaders? Which of your knowledge , skill, abilities or other characteristics have been useful in consulting with stakeholders?

● Hence, HR role needs to understand the organizational goals and the role each function plays, serves of a cross-functional bridge. Locates talent throughout the global organization, identifies and supports need for resources or training, advices core functions on how with adapts to organizational strategy. Moreover, HR leaders need own knowledge of other business functions and whose organizations' business influences specific actions by HR , e.g. understanding the type of experts needed by R&D and future trends for that need. Also, the HR leader needs to know which of whose knowledge, skills, abilities or other characteristics have been useful in responding to this challenge?

● HR also needs to consider how its organizational functions. They have disadvantages and advantages in order to achieve HR staff skill, talent to satisfy different departments' needs effectively and efficiently. Organizational structure has three types: Firstly, functional type advantages of easy to understand, specialization develop economies of scale, communication within function, career paths, fewer people and disadvantages of weak customer or product focus , potentially weak communication among function, hierarchical structure. Secondly, product type advantages of economies of scale, product team culture, product expertise and disadvantages of regional or local focus, more people, weak customer focus. Finally, geographic type advantages localization, quicker response time and disadvantages of fewer economic of scale, more people potential quality control.

● HR also needs to concern when it's company needs to implement outsourcing employment need rea third party contractors' successful outsourcing depends on choosing the right activities to outsource, cooperation of contractor's performance objectives with strategic requirements.

● Confirmation of contractors' reliability, capacity, expertise and ethical behavior. So , when the organization feel it needs to employ outsource contractors. The HR has responsibility to lead and know how to apply whose ethical practices competency in contracting for HR services or performing , due diligence or organizational sourcing, e.g. taking steps to protect employee data. The HR leader or manager also needs to know which of his/her knowledge skills, ability or other characteristics has been useful in responding to this challenge.

● Standard chartered had have good talent management strategies to train its staffs. The talent management at standard chartered bank (SCB) features include: Standard chartered bank has good performance appraisal or measurement strategy. By making it a global standard to conduct face-to-face performance appraisals every six months. SCB is reviewing its own performance management objectives to make sure that those objectives stay relevant and achievable. Being sensitive to different cultures by employing different appraisal methods, also show that SCB understands the importance of managers and staff identifying and dealing with real, actual problems in a way that is most familiar and effective to them. Through appraisal, SCB also classifies their employees into 5 categories ranging from high potentials to critical resources, then to core contributors, followed by underachievers and finally underperformers. By identifying areas in which they are lacking and act.

● What are the relevance HR problem to bring bank crisis to SCB. SCB view of employees as human capital in the organization, it could have at least minimized the less to a certain extent. For one, discussions between employers and still could have been more open and problem issues could have been identified at an earlier stage inefficiencies in the organization would have been uncovered , influence their performance against regional offices. In a way, having a certain amount of centralized control through talent management would also enable the monitoring of its offices globally.

● What are performance appraisal aims? Performance appraisal is the measurement of the effectiveness of an employee's job performance. The process is described as the collection and use of judgements, ratings, perceptions or more objectives sources of information to understand better the performance of a person, team, unit, business, process program in order to guide subsequent actions and decisions. The result or performance outcomes represent the contributions that an individual's job performance makers to an organization and its goals.

● Performance appraisal focus on measuring or appraising the job performance of a individual, e.g. use of surveys or rating focus to assess and evaluate employee behavior. It brings the either positive or negative feedback to the employee in the performance view and the new goals for the next performance period may be discussed.

● 3.4 HR role in India automobile industry

● Human resource development (HRD) is the part of human resource management in any organizations. It deals with training employees in the organization when the industry feels it have need to upgrade skills to its staffs. It aims to let them to learn new skills distributing resources that are beneficial for the employee's task. For automobile industry in India example, India automobile sale companies will need effective HRD in their organizations if they expect to sell automobiles to global customers attractively.

● Authors (May, June 2014) from internet essay indicated the India automobile sector is divided in four different sector which are as follow: two wheeler, which comprise of mopeds, scooters, motorcycles and electric two-wheelers passenger vehicles which include passenger cars, utility vehicles and multi-purpose vehicles, commercial vehicles that are light and material heavy vehicles and three wheelers that are passenger carriers and product carriers.

● Why do India automobile sale companies need to concern HRD? Authors (May, June 2014) indicated the automobile industry is one of the key drivers that boost the economic growth to India. However, the year 2013-2014 has seen a decline in the industry's growth . High inflation , high interest rates, low consumer sentiment and rising fuel prices with economic slowdown and rising fuel reason for the downturn of the industry.

● Except for the two wheelers, all other segments in the industry have been weakening. These is a negative impact on the automakers and dealers who offer high discounts in order to push sales. To match the decline in demand, automakers need good skillful of automakers to manufacturers attractive automobiles in order to attract foreign automobile buyers to choose to buy themselves any kinds of automobiles.

● Despite the comprehensive market being under extreme burden, the luxury car market has observed a robust double digit like during the year 2013-2014, as a result of rewarding new launches at lower price points. Hence, foreign robust luxury cars competitors influence India automobiles sale number to be reduced. Hence, India automobile manufacturers felt automobile manufacturing workers' skills need to be train or improve in order to manufacture more comfortable and good design vehicles to satisfy future global automobile consumers' driving enjoyable needs.

● In fact, India automobile industry employment opportunities will trend increase in the future with the number of vehicles available on the road today, the need and requirement for people who can fix these machines is fast increasing. The automobile jobs like automobile technician, car or bike mechanics are a great option. Becoming a diesel mechanic is also a significant alternative in India, auto labor market. Diesel mechanics are responsible for repairing and servicing diesel engines. As they are also required to repair engines of trucks and buses, other than cars. Even if communication with people instead of repairing cars in what interest to Indian, then Indian have opportunity of becoming a salesperson or sales manager in an automobile company. Career opportunities in automobile design, paint specialists, job on the assembly line and insurance of vehicles is also available.

● Future India automobile industry employment trend is as the destination choice for design and manufacture of automobiles employers who need to automobile production skillful worker number will rise, because India manufacturing heavy vehicles, passenger vehicles, commercial vehicles automobile production skillful workers need number will rise.

● Hence, India automobile sale employers will need have good human resource development model for the automobile companies, if they expect to raise automobile sale competitive effort in global automobile sale market. At the implementation level, India executives of the automobile companies need to strengthen their training, net working and more towards providing a satisfactory human resource development climate for its automobile industry car production, design, repair, salespeople employees and suggest suitable changes and corrections in the policy decisions for management of automobile companies and policy makers. Hence, future HRD practices in automobile industrial organizations for India automobile companies aim to identify the HRD mechanisms implemented in the selected automobile companies to achieve the training function to be effectively managed in the automobile companies in order to raise automobile sale competition effort in global automobile market.

●

● 3.5 Challenge of HR management

●

● As a HR specialist, what are the challenges you may face and what HR intervention mechanisms would you consider using in an attempt to drive individual and organizational performance in a multinational company? Critically evaluate this question by utilizing the appropriate academic literatures.

● The challenges of the HR specialist when there engage in attempt of increasing the individual and organizational performances in Multinational Companies through developing a set of HRM best practices, especially relating to employee recruitment and selection, performance management and staff retention. Since the organizations are multinational number of concerns are arises such as dealing cultural issues with the organizational goals as well as individual goals. Furthermore organizational behaviors and tools such as engagement, motivation and empowerment are basically highlighted; without those it is merely a dream to achieving the business goals. Basically Multinational companies are aiming profits and there for individual and organisational performance are very vital for their existence.

● HR has been organized in a different ways over the years. Some functions have emphasized delivery by location or by business structure. In these models an integrated HR team has serviced managers and employees at specific location or with in specific businesses units, with some more strategic or complex tasks reserved for the corporate center. The degree to which these different arms of HR were centralized or co-located and the question of whether they were managed by the business unit varied. Within the HR teams, depending up on their size their might have been specialization by work area (especially for industrial relations in the 1960s and 1970s) or by employee grade or group (responsibility, say, divided between those looking after clerical staff from those covering production)

The advancement of personal management starts around end of the 19th century, when welfare officers came in to being.

●

● There are some organizations where HR is seen as a central, corporate function with little advancement to business units. Some other organizations position themselves in the opposite direction, with a very small corporate center and all the activity distributed to business units. The question of best structure is how the function best organizes itself between the pulls of centralization and the pushes of decentralization.(The changing HR functions)

● The HR assumptions and HR practices observed in high performing firms are the key elements to the formation of the Best Practice theory. Employment security, selective hiring, self managed teams, high pay contingent on company performance, extensive training, reduction of status difference, and sharing information are the key element of the theory. However less concern about the organisational goals and culture are given as draw backs for the theory.

● According to the "best fit theory" a firms that follows a cost leadership strategy designs narrow jobs and provides little job security, whereas a company pursuing a differentiation strategy emphasizes training and development. In other words this argues that all SHRM activities must be consistent with each other and linked to the strategic objectives of the business. HRM uses various technologies to direct employees behavior towards objectives and tasks that deliver approved organisational performance. Many organizations try to frame these 'levers' with an overall performance management system, and attach incentives and rewards to achievements of objectives and targets within this. HR will need to reduce employment expenses to help organizations to save income. Direct costs include: Recruitment costs (advertising, admin, etc.),Induction/training costs, other admin costs associated with new hires, Overtime/ cost of temporary workers, reduced productivity cost etc. which are related to HR expenses.

●

● In conclusion there is evidence to suggest that including the practice out line within this organisational behaviours and tools can used to drive organisational and individual performance in Multinational companies. It is essential to have suitable recruitment and selection process, performance Appraisal System and staff Retention plan to ensure the right people, In the right place, at the right time with right attitude. Training and development is also vital to improve HR performance. In addition HR Specialists role will be more specific when these techniques applying in to multi cultural environments where people perceptions and behavioral patterns are different from each other.

●

● 3.6 The nature of the employment relationship

●

● John, B. & Jeff, G. (6 edition, 2017) indicated Human resource management defines a distinctive approach to employment management, which seeks to achieve competitive advantage through the strategic deployment of a highly committed and capable workplace using an array of cultural, structural and personnel techniques. Also, human resource management is a strategic approach to managing employment relations which emphasizes that leveraging people's capabilities and commitment is critical to achieving sustainable competitive advantage or superior public services. This is accomplished through a distinctive set of integrated employment policies, program and practices in an organizational and societal context. Moreover, human resource management underscores the importance of people, only the " human factor" or labor can provide talent to generate value. It should draw attention to the notion of indetermination or uncertainty, which devices from the employment relationship: Employees have a potential capacity to provide the added value desired by the employer. It also follows from this that human knowledge and skills are a strategic resource that needs investment and skillful management. Moreover, in the environmental change factor influences to any organizations need to provide a role for HRM in improving an organization's performance in terms of overall sustainability.

● What is the nature of the employment relationship ?

● The nature of the social relationship between employers and the social relationship between employees and employer is an issues of central analytical importance to HRM. The employment relationship describes a relation between employees (non-managers and managers) and their employer. Through the employment contract, inequalities of power structure both economic exchange (wage or salary) and the nature and quality of the work performed whether it is routine or creative. They can be short-term, primarily but not economic exchange for a relatively well-defined set of duties and low commitment or they can be complex long-term relationships defined by a range of economic inducements and relative security of employment, given in return for a set of duties and a high commitment from the employee.

● Airline services: the demands of emotional labor of employment relationship between airline and airline staffs.

● Positive emotion at work offers an apparent win to win situaton for airline organizations and individuals as it suggests that if a job or work is correctly designed, individuals will feel better and perform better. What was once a private act of emotion management is sold now as labor in the public contract jobs? What was once a privately negotiated rule of feeling or displaying is now set by th airline company's standard practices division. However, such as airline service waiter job, a private emotional system has been subordinated to commercial logic and it has been changed by whose airline employers.

●

● HR role in business maximizing efficiency method

●

● John , H. (2013) described the work of police officers, we might discuss the functions of preventing come and catching criminals, the practices of patrolling, filling in report forms, breaking up disturbances, making arrests, and the qualities of commitment service. He also indicated police work is much more complicated than the brief suggestions and management work (including the management of police work) is much more complex still. It is hard to describe the functions without detailing the practices or to make sense of the practices without involving the functions.

● John, H. (2013) defined characteristics of management is responsibility for an organization or organization unit and for the work of its members. The unit might be anything from a small retail outlet with one or two shop assistants to large corporation with tens or even hundreds of thousands of employees, but most managers are directly responsible for managing the organization of a manage number of people, typically between two and twenty and of the various processes in which they are engaged. So, we have sales managers and production managers and marketing managers and IT managers etc. organizing the work of specialists. The at the level, of the business unit or agency or regional subsidiary, we have general managers whose jobs is to organize and coordinate the work of different specialist groups.

● Maximizing efficiency method

● Maximizing efficiency was a work study or time-and-motion to be exercise designed to calculate how the work could be most efficiently carried out. This involved the analysis of different possible divisions of different possible tasks of labour into specialized tasks. The optimization of the tools and machines, and the optimization of the physical movements, required to operate them, assuming workers well suited to the specified tasks concern. The optimized system would then be so as to become a standard requirement to be implemented with absolute regularity, so that the whole workplace operated as a machine. Workers would be selected with the skills and strengths to perform each specialised task, and trained to follow the standard procedures. They would be fairly paid for what was scientifically established to be a reasonable level of performance (assuming they were well pay introduced, to encourage over- performance and punish (underperformance). Both owners or employee would benefits.

● It indicated conclusion was that output was determined less by working conditions or incentive systems than by the informed social pattern of the work group. Feeling mattered and wherever managers took a personal interest in the workers, made them feel important and generated mutually supportive and cooperative environment, output are enhanced management. It seems was not about mechanical optimization processes, but about leadership and team dynamics. The management characteristics were however critical and with some rearrangement they can be summarized as follows: A strong people orientation, every body is treated s part of the team and just as an replaceable resource, flexibility and teamwork value driven value system is through the company.

●

● six situation factors can influence management's choice of HR strategy

●

● Beer , M., et al. (1984) explained that HRM and the issue of management goals and specific HR outcomes. The Harvard framework consists of six basic components as below:

● Beer, M., et al. (1984) indicated these six situation factors can influence management's choice of HR strategy. Firstly, situation factors include workforce characteristics, business strategy and conditions, management philosophy, labor market, unions , task technology , laws and societal values. Any one of situation factor can influence management's choice of HR strategy. The situation factor can bring influences to other two components. Stakeholder interests component means shareholders, management, employee groups, government, community, union as well as human resource management policy choices component, it means employee influence, human resource flow, reward system and works systems. It emphasizes that management' decisions and actions in HR management can be fully appreciated only if it is recognized that they result from an interaction between constraints and choices will be influenced by situational factor component and share holder interests components and long-term consequences component influences.

● The human resource management policy choices component will influence the human resource outcomes component, it includes commitment, competence, cost -effectiveness. It means that it needs to understand the importance of management's goals, the HR outcomes of high employee commitment and competence are linked to longer term effects on organizational effectiveness and societal well-being.

● The assumptions are built into the framework are that employees have talents that are rarely fully utilized in the workplace and that they show a desire to experience growth through work. The, the human resource outcomes component will influence the long-term consequences component. It includes individual well-being, organizational effectiveness and societal well-being . The long-term consequences distinguish between three goals: individual , organizational and societal. At the level of the individual employee, the long-term HR outputs comprise the psychological rewards that workers receive in exchange for their effort. At the organizational level, increased effectiveness ensures the survival of the firm. The societal level, as a result of fully utilizing people at work, some of society's goals (for example, employment and growth are attained.

● Finally, the sixth component is a feedback loop component, it is through which the outputs flow directly into the organization and to the stakeholders. However, long-term outputs can influence situational factors, stakeholder interests and HR management policy choices in cycle two way relationship.

●

● Knowledge management at hotel industry

● Hotels' realization led to the design and implementation of a computerized knowledge library that was accessible to every site manager in every hotel across the Australia/South pacific/ South East Asia region. The system was designed to initiate a long-term knowledge-sharing culture by making it easier to share value-added practices and processes, thus reducing wastage of time and resources through replication.

● The problem- The knowledge library operated as a two way system whereby managers could both add ideas or effective innovative practices and find solutions to some of their own operational problems that demanded new ideas or innovation. To simplify its use, the system was designed to store ideas by hotel function (that is food and beverage, housekeeping etc.) with both functional and key word search tools available , knowledge transfer was considered to have occurred once an idea had been implemented at another site.

● Hotel management realized that they would need to create support systems to motivate sharing between the sites and geographical regions. This opened up an opportunity to achieve the desired knowledge, sharing actions and behaviors. Throughout the performance management system, as a result, for each site manager to pass their annual performance review, they had to retrieve a minimum of two ideas from the system and implement these in their hotel, as well as add two ideas to the system for others to be able to access and use.

● The idea that the hotel different site managers' knowledge and expertise can play a strategic role in achieving competitive goals to expect to achieve a strategy results in superior performance, or a competitive advantage. Achieving high performance, improving employment skills, pay-for -performance, profit sharing, performance appraisal, team working, job evaluation, information-sharing, employment security, selective hiring, self-managed teams or team working, high pay contingent on company performance, extensive training, reduction in status differences, information sharing(knowledge management) benefits.

● Manpower planning role in business

● Manpower planning (workforce planning) means personnel and HR managers need to ensure that necessary supply of people was forthcoming to allow targets to be met. In theory at least, a manpower plan could show how the demand for people and their skills within an organization could be balanced by supply. The idea of a balance between demand and supply reflects the influence of the language of classical labor economics, in which movement towards an " equilibrium" serves as an ideal.

● The utilization, improvement and preservation of an organization's human resources. The four stages of the planning process may include: the first stage is an evaluation or appreciation of the existing manpower resources. The second stage is an estimation of the proportion of currently employed manpower resources that were likely to be within the firm by the forecast data. the third stage is an essential or forecast of labor requirements needed if the organization's overall objectives were to be achieved by the forecast date and the fourth stage, it needs to measure to ensure that the necessary resources were available as and when required that is the manpower plan.

● There were two main reasons for companies to use manpower planning. To develop their business objectives and manning levels and to reduce the " unknown" factor. Firstly organization implements strategy and targets, it brings organization practices and methods, it brings manpower review and analysis (internal and external factors) , it brings forecast (demand and supply), it brings adjust to balance (recruit, retain and reduce).

● Way of working includes: annualized hours, working time organized on the basis of the number of hours to be worked over a year rather than a week; it is usually used to fit in with peaks. Compresses hours, which allows individuals to work their total number of agreed hours over a shorter period. Flexi-time, employees have a choice about their actual working hours, usually outside certain agreed core times. Home working, either on a fully time basis or an a part time basis where employees divide their time between home and office. Job-sharing , which involves two people employed on a part time basis but, working together to cover a full time post. Shift-working , giving employers the scope to have their business open for longer periods than an 8 hour day. Staggered hours, employees can start and finish their day at different times. Term-time working, employees can take unpaid leave of absence during the school holidays.

●

● Recruitment, selection and talent management stages include:

● Internal factors and external factors bring to workforce planning staffing needs options: internal via external brings to recruitment attraction via sources brings to applicant pool brings to selection assessment brings to job performance measurement brings to job analysis brings to workforce planning staffing needs opinions in cycle processing again.

● Capable people who will apply for jobs within a organization. First, there is a need to attract people's interest in applying for employment. It implies that people have a choice about which organizations they wish to work for, even though during times of recession such choices might be limited. People may be capable of fulfilling a role in employment, but the extent to which this will be realized is not totally predictable. How capability is understood is increasingly determined by an organization's approach to talent management and development.

● Under different labour market conditions, power in recruitment process will change between buyers and sellers of labour, the employers and employees respectively. Thus, in conditions of recession, employers are likely to reduce recruitment budgets and costs, paying more attention to developing the talent that has already been employed.

● Online recruitment

● Budgetary factors will also affect how recruitment channels are used, with more use of online recruitment. For example, the ageing profile of the workforce around the world requires an adjustment of recruitment policies, the use of the internet and agencies for recruitment reflected to younger applicants, whereas older workers were more dependent on formal channels of recruitment, such as newspapers and journals. In addition, there have been many more graduates leaving university, and graduate employment is becoming very competitive. Many graduates will take longer to find employment that matches their skills. This might affect perceptions of the value to be gained from studying for a degree compared with the price of a degree.

● There is a difference, however, in what recruiters think is important to this generation and what the generation itself thinks . Although HR policies will be designed to achieve particular organizational targets and goals, those policies will also provide an opportunity for individual needs and be satisfied . This view assumes that a fit between a person and the environment can be found so that their commitment and performance will be enhanced.

● This an indication that the person to environment fit includes a person to organization fit, person to group fit and person to environment fit. If there is a match between the values within each of those areas expressed by the organization at the recruitment stage. The organization and the new recruits have a clear employees and can therefore manage those expectations.

● HRM could help to shape the direction of change, influence culture and help bring about the mindset that would decide which strategic issues more considered. HR considerations, including the results of a review of the quantity and quality of people, the goals , objectives and targets whether they can achieve performance in an organization and for how work is organized into roles and jobs.

● There has been a rapid growth in online recruitment , e-recruitment. As a result, organizations are advised to consider the design of websites and the terms that applicants might use to carry out job and vacancy searches. The usability of a company's website affects an applicant's perception of a job, with a focus on hyperlinks and text rather than graphic images and navigation links. However, issues with e-recruitment , including the one-way communication system, the fact that it is impersonal and passive, and the fact that it creates an artificial distance between the individual and the company.

● recruitment agent

● However, once a recruitment strategy has been formed, an organization might outcomes its implementation to reduce costs and take advantage recruitment expertise, especial a large number of staff are recruitment. Recruitment agents act as "labor market inter-mediaties" between individual recruits and recruiting organizations. Financial service organization assessment and measurement of creating customer service performance indicators include as below:

● Anticipating customer needs and planning accordingly, identifying the customers who will be of value to the company, recommending change to current ways of working that will improve customer service, arranging the collection of customer satisfaction data and acting on them. The analysis and definition of competencies should allow the identification and isolation of behavior that are distinct and are associated with competent or effective performance. On this assumption, the assessment of competencies is one means selecting employees.

● Recruitment channels may include walk in, employee referrals, advertising, particularly online job boards, websites, labour market intermediaries, such as social media , social professional networks, recruitment agencies, educational associations, professional associations.

● job description

● Job description includes job title, department, reponsible to , relationships, purpose of job/overall objectives, specific duties and responsibilities, physical and economic conditions as well as personnel specification includes physical characteristics, general intelligence, specific attitudes, interests, impact on other people, qualification and experience, abilities, motivation. Both job description and personnel specifications have been key elements, it replies too much on the analyst's subjective judgement in identifying the key aspects of a job and the qualities that related to successful performance.

● Selection

● An organization wishes to recruit new employees to define criteria against which it can measure and assess applicants. Increasingly , such criteria are set in the form of competencies composed of behavioral characteristics and attitudes. Organizations have become increasingly aware of making good selection decisions, as selection involves a number of costs include: the cost of the selection process itself, including the use of various selection instruments, the future cost of training new staff , the cost of labor turnover if the selected staff are not retained.

● There are good reasons why organizations need to consider the reaction of applicants to selection methods. If the selection is viewed as the attraction of the organization may be diminished, candidates who have a negative experience can dissuade others, a negative selection experience can impact on job acceptance , selection methods are covered by legislation and regulations relating to discrimination, mistreatment during selection will put off future applicants and may also stop applicants from buying the organization's products or using their services.

●

● role of HR technology

●

● What is the role of technology in Human Resource Development? Identify some key forms of e-learning and critically evaluate their advantages and disadvantages, providing appropriate examples from organisations. It will define what Human Resource Development is and why it needs technology. Also it will discuss what electronic learning (e-learning) is, and will explain some key forms of e-learning and why we need to use e-learning. It will give a brief indication as to what technology actually is, and also the progression of technology. The essay will critically evaluate the advantages and disadvantages of using e-learning in Human Resource Development. There will be appropriate examples used to show how different organisations use e-learning within their company/ organisation. Finally it will offer conclusions as to why I think technology should or should not be a part of Human Resource Development.

● Why does HR development need technology?

● Technology is always progressing and this is very good for companies who need or even sell technology. If we look at how a few years back within companies the secretary would need to file documents manually and this could take a long time, also apart from the time issue there were more serious problems like documents going missing or being damaged. This is where technology began to progress because there was a new technology progressing and this was the database and this could hold all the documents you needed safely onto the computer and that way it would be a lot faster and more secure for the secretary to file the documents. This is just one example there are many more ways in which technology has helped to progress companies. The example given here is just to show that technology is progressing and it will keep progressing much further in the future years to come.

● Human Resource Development is all about learning, training, developing and education the employees in the workplace. There is a difference between these four concepts but there all correlated. If for example we looked at learning; this can be learnt anywhere and you can be learning yourself the new skills, but on the other hand if you looked at education you are being taught something but in a formal way but the two are linked because from both of these you are learning new skills and then you can go on to training and developing them skills.

● HRD was not always known as this, there was a shift from welfare officers to HRD. HRD was initially set up for training and development and this was to help the employers in crafts such as electricians, or engineers as an example and from this they would be learning from their masters and will be developing their skills to be able to perform in the workplace. HRD created an integration of people management and development and this could become CIPD which stands for the chartered institute of personnel and development.

● HRD likes to be strategic and is more for the organisation than the employees; it is also a long term method to help to build the company. HRD does like to implement change into their methods and this is why e-learning will be very convenient to help within organisations because it is constantly changing and this change would help employees improve on their learning and training and will be able to implement new skills within the workplace.

● Why does HR needs e-learning in organization? Firstly before I go into detail about how e-learning helps HRD perform you will need to know what e-learning actually is. E-learning used to be known as computer-based learning, this is basically what it still is, it is a way of learning but on a computer or even these days there is even m-learning which is through the mobile. We need e-learning in everyday life to be able to adapt the required skills in education, employment, even at home. It can be defined as any learning activity supported by information and communication technologies which is known as ICTs. There are arguments out there concerning the labels, an example of this is whether ICT-based learning is the same as e-learning, we can gather information from the world wide web channel and this would be our online materials, but we can also get materials from this intranet would could be confused as being from the world wide web but instead this material is delivered through an internal network of personal computers. E-learning is in fact taken to mean any form of electronic technology which can support learning this can be opposed to the chalk and blackboard technology which used to be the main form of learning.

●

● Why is HR strategy important to influence organizational success?

● In organizational level, humans do formalize strategies as a function to direct and focus their efforts. However, in a business organizational (a firm), such efforts will focus on creating value for profit. In fact, the environment is a market with limited resources and therefore it causes competition exists. This environment mght be more or less stable, but it is in constant change.

● HR Strategy will become a systemic and rational act, a process that can be managed in order to successfully attain in the golas of the firm. HR Strategy can divide these three kinds. Firstly, a HR plan is intended to achieve a particular purpose and to develop a HR strategy for dealing with unemployment. It is overall HR strategy to gain promotion. For government (public organization's economic HR strategy example. Secondly, it is the process of HR planning or putting a HR plan into operation in a skillful way. Finally, for war strategy, it is the skill of HR planning to be trained to the movements of armies in s battle or war. An example, of military HR training strategy, defend, strategies compare tactic.

● However, nowadays, business organizations need " office of general", " command" , " generalship" skillful actions, leadership and leading welfare from one leader, such as CEO who have any effective HR strategy to manage staffs and tasks as well as leading them to serve their organizations successfully. So, an effective HR strategy can give good HR planning direction to let the organization to know whether it ought need how to do in order to achieve its HR development goals successfully.

● An effective HR planning direction can achieve the organizaton's HR allocation goals more easily. For example, knowing how it can use of common resources (e.g. available human and technological resources). A basic HR strategic advantage tool win and prevail over rivals in the market comes from the differentiated used of such resources.

● In beverage competitive industry example, Coca-Cola soft drink organization example, it was still keeping its predominance in the beverage market product " Coke", Pepsi Co was advancing fast on the base of a successful "image" HR strategy targeting the youngest segment of the beverage market under the taste of the new generation. So, it can select to employ more young workers to work in its organization in order to persuade many youngest soft drink customers to believe it is one young soft drink health drinking company. By 1983, Pepsi had begun to outsell coke in supermarkets when coke maintained its edge only through soda vending machines and fast food restaurants. Although, different marketing strategic breakthrough by far unexpected. It follows all time successful formula of coke. In 1985, the " New Coke" was introduced after an extensive study of market trended, surveys, focus group and taste tests strategies. In these survey investigation process, it must need to employ many part time or full time questionnaires staffs, they can include students, housewives, freelance workers, unemployed workers. So, HR department needs have enough time to select the right applicants to finish the whole questionnaire investigation project efficiently and effectively. The HR arrangement need to gather information to conclude this goals, such as how to design the new formula (or taste) was based on a different (lower cost) source of sugar, high fructose corn syrup to replace cane sugar. All of Coca (the plant from which comes the allealoid cocain) derivates were also removed from the old formula. So, how to design the taste is the main survey information gathering aim. Also, how HR arrangement which can have enough questionnaire staffs to carry on gathering information from the taste tests in the limited time to achieve to finish the taste test questionnaire project efficiently and effectively.

● What are HR strategic benefits? They include: It can assist an organization to protect its HR capital base. It is a well accepted business principle, it can also help the organization to extend this notion to the world' natural and human resources, it can help leaders to plan and measure HR employment and reward and welfare and performance management systems of business enterprises more accurately, it can help business leaders to do the best balance between narrow self-interest and actions takes for the good of unemployment or creating more opportunity solution benefit in society as well as they can do actions in pursuit of financial survival more easily.

● Why can HR strategy help organizational change in success? Knowing the importance and implication of organizational change and admitting the fact that organizational change success and leader / leadership can play a key role in bringing and implementing these changes by deciding the desired form of an organization and taking the potential steps which are needed for the process. So, when one organization has one good HR strategy, it can assist its organization to change more people and non-people resources effectively and efficiently.

● Why do organizations need to change HR strategy? Nowadays, dynamic business environments influence organizations that respond quickly and effectively to constant change. A dynamic enterprise has two important tasks. It must adapt the current business environment, e.g. people skillful shortage in the industry into a shared HR strategy and then quickly and effectively to employ talent people or potential people to do the skillful job for its organization.

●
●
●
●
●
●
●
●
●
●
●
●

● Reference
●
● Andy, W.C. and Barry, J. B. and Wai, M.M. (2002) , Managing human resource in Hong Kong, Hong Kong: Thomson, p.6
●
● Source: The harvard model of HRM
● Beer , M., specter, B., Lawrence, PR. and Mills, D. Q. (1984). managing human assets. New York: Free press.
● John, B. & Jeff, G. (6 edition, 2017). Human resource management

theory and practice, Palgrave, Macmillan publishers ltd. UK , London,pp.4-5

●

● John, H. (2013) managment a very short introduction, Oxford university press, UK, pp.11-13

●

●

●

● Sources

●

●   http://info.shine.com/industry/automobiles-auto-ancillaries/2.html retrieved on 14 th May 2014

● https://www.kpmg.de/docs/auto-survey.pdf retrieved on 17 the June 2014

CHAPTER FOUR

●

●

●

●

● Training and Learning

●
● What are the technique sector to solve above aspect of problems to HR?
●
●
● John, A (2018) identified the major problems relate to HR personnel management, they include that selection of personal problem aspect, he explained that even if one knows precisely what qualities are required of man to do a given job well, it is still difficult to determine whether any given candidate has these qualities. On training problem aspect , he indicated that the cost of training staff is rapidly increasing, due largely to the increasing level of skill needed to operate modern equipment in the factory and office. Poor training will bring low earnings, high proportion of scrap production, mistakes, accidents results. Finally on salary and wage structure aspect, paid problems concern complaints of unfairness in the wage and salary differentials between levels of age, or skill, or between sections of the company.

● What are the technique sector to solve above aspect of problems to HR? John, A (2018) explained that productivity bargaining, job evaluation, consultation and management by objectives techniques can be attempted to solve human relation problem; aptitude tests, intelligence tests, manpower planning, personality tests techniques can be attempted to solve selection of personal problem; needs analysis, programmed learning, business games techniques can be attempted to solve training problem; productive bargaining, job evaluation, merit rating, incentive schemes, salary progression curves, time span of discretion techniques can be attempted to solve salary and wage structure problem.

● John, A(2018) , he explained that how to apply the aptitude test to solve selecting personal problem. He assumed that increasing technology needs an ever larger number of skilled and semi-skilled employees in almost every field of industry , e.g. machines and processes are more complex to operate and maintain, computers must be programmed. However , training employces to the new higher standards is expensive and it is becoming increasingly important to select any those who will be able to reach the necessary standard. One way to determine whether a candidate will satisfactorily complete his training to be test his aptitude for the proposed task before his/her training starts these kinds of aptitude tests as below:

● The technique consists of analyzing the physical and mental skills required to perform the task successfully and then estimating each candidate's aptitude in these by means of special tests. Typical examples of the testable skills are: manual desterity, ability to understand complex progress for chemical plant operators, mental aptitude for system analysis. Also standard training tests are now available for estimating certain aptitudes and where exist little training is required to give a test to a candidate. The training test is often a highly specialized job. Usually it will be able of someone in the personnel department to use this training test technique, but executives should be aware of its existence. Aptitude test advantage concerns buying a standard test is low, but the cost of having are specially prepared by an expert can be high. The training required to use them and interpret the results is slight. For some of the standard tests the correlation between those failing the test and failing a achieve the necessary standard of skill after training is good, i.e. substantial savings in training costs can be made by unsuitable candidates before spending money on their training.

● John, A(2018) explained that how to apply brainstorming technique to generate new ideas. He assumes that new products have appeared on the market an ever-increasing rate, that is to say many product life-cycles are declining. So, new ideas in advertising in display in production technique to HR development is needed . Many companies are finding that their employees think creatively. They begin to the problem is that most employees not only fail to think creativity, but tend to use the old product, old market , outlets, old methods and old equipment for as long as possible habitually. He indicated that brainstorming strategy is a way of promoting new ideas. The usual method is for six to fifteen people need to meet for half an hour and propose answer to a question from the session leader. The questions may be that how many ways, we could increase sales of product (x), how many new market , we can think for product (y), in what ways we can redesign product(z). Hence, each member needs to present and they can be drawn from all levels and from any departments in the company. The leader speaks his/her idea to let the every member to listen and no one is permitted to criticize this idea, his/her idea provokes member to think of another.

● Eventually, several ideas may be developed into one that is entirely new. Only when the session has ended do they start the rational process of determining whether the ideas can be practices or not. Then, any promising ideas can be subjected to " reverse brainstorming" in which the question in how many ways might this idea fail? is asked. Hence, brainstorming technique is good training to let staffs to create new idea method.

● John ,A (2018) explained that intelligence test can be applied to select the right man for the job. he assumed that this problem of one of the requisites for any job is a minimum level of intelligence. How can this be measured? He explained that intelligence tests intelligence tests consist usually of a long list of questions to be answers and problems to solved within a set time. The number of questions answered correctly within this time is an indication of IQ of the candidate. Some training is required to apply an intelligence test to a candidate and to interpret the results, even when the test used is one of the well known standard ones.

● How to design a test of this sort is a highly specialised job. All personnel officers should know about this technique and in large companies it may be desirable to train one officer in their use. Its advantages include cost is low, it only takes an hour or to test one candidate or a group of them. The effort is hotly debated. Without doubt these tests accurately measure IQ is a large proportion of cases.. In particular they can indicate whether a candidate has a very high or very high or very low IQ , although some doubt exists as to their accuracy in the middle ranges. However, the real debate concerns the accuracy of the results so much as their value. For IQ is said to be a measure only of a certain type of intelligence and not a guide to other types which may be more relevant to industry. Psychologists would certainly agree that an IQ test must be supported by an impression formed of the candidates ability in other ways, such as at an interview.

● John , A(2018) indicated that a clear job description is needed to define what each employee is to do. In some companies , the employees have not been told exactly what their job is, with the result that sometimes two people attend to the same task neither knowing whose responsibility it is, or some task is not carried out at all, each man believing that someone else is attending to it.

● In large organizations this can lead to cause the company has intense frustration and annoyance to individual employees. The job description technique is simple, the supervisor writes a description of each job, specifying each major activity as accurately as possible and limitations. Very little training is requires, but obviously it is necessary for someone with a fairly detailed knowledge of the company to draw up such descriptions. This is usually done by the supervisor of the job cooperation with the present job. It needs seldom take more than half an hour of two people's time to write out a fairly comprehensive description of any job. It's content may include job title , tasks , authority, superior, committees, limitations.

● John, A (2018) explained that job evaluation is one effective method to select the right rate of pay for each job. He assumes that the all levels of wage or salary earners is the differential in rate of pay or between one job and another. How much more should the driver of a bus get than the conductor, how much most should a crane driver get than a fork life driver, how much more should a manager get than a foreman?

● The first step in job evaluation is to carry out a job description for on can not evaluate a job unless each of several headings according to the requirements of the job. Headings according to the requirements of the job. Headings used often include such aspect as: skill needed to carry out the job, possible effects of careless number of months experience required to each proficiency, working conditions, including any unpleasant circumstances, such as excessive, temperatures or dustiness. Each job is evaluated in this way and then arranged in order of ascending total points into financial terms. For example, the dockside crane driver, process plant operator, canteen cleaner job's maximum points possible may include headings of skill (10), effect of carelessness (20), experience required (10) and working conditions (10) , maximum points possible.

● John , A (2018) explained joint consultation is the effective method to improve human relations. He assumes that a large company feels junior employees who feel that nothing they can do will have any effect, and the top management is indifference to them or their happiness. The result is sometimes indiscipline and always indifference towards the company, its products, its reputation, its managers. Joint consultation is one effective employee engagement method , which is one way of drawing junior employees into the company and making them feel part of it is to allow them or encourage them to participate in management decision making or at least to discuss with them the consequences of management decisions. Many of decisions that managers take are highly technical and need great skill, long experiences and the use of time very advanced management techniques, e.g. capital expenditure appraisal is on such area. However, many decisions are more of a moral nature or affect employees more than they affect the company. Thus, joint consultation advantage can make a systematic attempt to consult with the employees to seek their opinions, ideas, reactions.

●

● What are on-job training advantages?

● On -the-job training means that having a person learn a job by actually performing it. Virtually every employee, from mailroom clerk to company president, gets some on-the job training when he/she joins a firm. It usually involves assigning new employees to experiences workers or supervisors who then do the actual training.

● Coaching or understudy method means that the employee is trained by an experienced worker or the trainee's supervisor. At lower levels, trainees may acquire skills for, e.g. running a machine is observed by the supervisor. Top management level, to the position of assistant is often used to train and develop the company's future top managers.

● Job rotation, in which an employee usually a management trainee, moves from job to job at planned schedule. Special assignments similarly, give lower-level executives firsthand, experience in working on actual problems. Its advantages include relatively inexpensive trainees learn when producing and there is no need for expensive off-job facilities like classrooms or programmed learning devices. The method also facilities learning , since trainees are learned by actually doing the job and get quick feedback about the correctness of their performances.

● Stages in training needs analysis includes as below: Preparation , deciding the objectives and scope of the training needs analysis; data collection is from employees in the real world; data analysis is needed to analyze the training needs in a systematic way; recommendation to propose the training budget, training design and evaluation methods; action is needed to identify the responsible person and time frame, and implement the plan,

● Training principle means the effective motivation of the trainee is needed by the design of the training program and the methods which are used, the designing a training course is needed to consider the training requirements: attitudes, skills, knowledge. For example, a shop assistant in a convenience store, would require a certain friendly service attitude towards customers, skill in selling, displaying arrangement and knowledge of stock, sale procedures and the company's general policy.

● On -the -job-training is given in the normal work situation, the trainee needs to use the actual tools, equipment, document, or materials, that he/ she will use when fully trained. The trainee is regarded as a partly productive worker from the time training begins. Off-the-job training is taken away from the normal work situation, usually employing specially simplified tools and equipment. The trainee is not regarded as a productive worker from the beginning, it is exercise practice. Off-the-job training is needed to implement on the company's premises at a training center or at an educational institution.

● On-the -job training advantages include that it is less costly because it uses normal equipment, the trainee is proficient, there is no transfer of learning problems, the trainee is in the production environment, he/ she does not need to adjust to it after the less realistic conditions. Its disadvantages include the trainee may be a poor teacher and may not have enough time to give proper training, if there is a payment-by-results scheme, if may discourage the trainer from training, the training may be implemented in an inefficient way, a large amount of spoiled work and scrap material may be produced, valuable equipment may be damaged, the production conditions, which are stressful, i.e. noisy, busy, confusing, stress of this type usually inhibits learning. Otherwise, off-job-training advantages include the training is given by a specialist trainer and it should be of higher quality, special equipment, simplified of necessary can be used, the trainee can learn the job from easy to difficulty in planned stage, it is fee pressure of payment-by-work scheme, noise, danger, publicity, the trainee will learn correct methods from the beginning, the trainee does not damage valuable equipment or produce spoiled work or scrap, it is easier to calculate the cost of off-the -job training because it is more self contained. It's disadvantages include the higher costs of separate premises, equipment and trainers, learning difficulties to the trainee, when he/she needs to change training equipment to production equipment and a classroom environment to a production environment.

●

● The four steps of learning requirement

● Any learning requirement include four steps: identifying the problem, seeking a solution, selecting an applying training and setting objectives. In seeking solutions steps, common performance problems and solutions include: lacks of skill problem can be solved to provide suitable skill training, insufficient knowledge problem can be solved by training to broaden understanding, lack of motivation problem can be solved by training might-enthuse, attitude problems can be solved by training of management commitment.

● The important concern is that the training's topics and contents need to achieve this aim to improve employee (trainee) individual behavior, such as improvement of efficiency is concerned primary with doing things right, when effectiveness is about doing the right things well. Because highly efficient training courses do not mean that the training courses and contents are effective relevant to the company or individuals concerned needs.

● Why does training need to set objectives? Because it can let the trainer gins a better understanding of the desired behaviors when it is seeking to encourage to achieve the training efficiently and effectively, let participants to know what the course details will help to overcome any uncertainty, and assist in motivating the individual and training objectives can indicate what the needs and requirements of the company. It can reduce the waste a quantifiable return on the time and capital invested before it has clear objectives for the training achievement.

● Why does know what the main objective for training is more important? It has difference between aims and objectives. Aims mean to provide a direction or statement of intent. So, aim is at target, but the objective could be more clear. Whether this objective is realistic one would depend on the people involved and the circumstances under which they operate. This means that when an aim might express a desired outcome, it is the objective which will seek how and when this is attained or desired more easily. So, when the trainer can predict what (are) is the more accurate objective(s) , when this objective(s) is (are) confirmed the real need to the organization's benefit. The training will be more effective or avoids ineffective training consequence (irrelevant training courses and contents) to let trainees (participants) to learn, it means that time and money wasting of the training course.

● David, L. (2016) explained that why a lesson plan is necessary. He indicated that " the existence of lesson plan can have positive effects. It depends on whether the methodology of knowledge (the how we do it) , but at this stage we are simply examining the knowledge itself (what knowledge are we trying to communicate). However, there are three principle classifications of information. Firstly information that the group must know, it means that there are items of information which are essential to the understanding of the topic in question. In most cases, they will have already been identified in any training need analysis and as they are fundamental to the success of any training course on the subject they must be given the highest priority. Secondly, information which trainers should know would include anything which related directly to the information in the must show category. For example, this might include other practices and procedures which interlink with those requires for safety reasons. Finally, the could know matters are those which can be described as useful to the group , but largely incident to the subject. These are items of information which , if time permits, could provide a useful background to the topic , but won't directly assist in its effective execution. This category would include historical details, boarder aspects, of the task, further areas of interest and general information."

● The classification of information into these three categories allows each aspect of the subject to be examined and assigned to the appropriate category. In this way, it is possible to provide a degree of prioritization , enabling all the essential elements to be concerned in time available and any secondary information to be incorporated as and when circumstances permit.

● However, these are number of other factors which will have an impact upon the structure topic and content of any training course . These include: level of understanding, course size, availability of equipment and material, financial constraints and timing. For example, a person's existing knowledge or cognitive inventory will influence whose level of understanding whether it is more or less easily when the trainee is learning the training course, the number of people participation will affect how much can be accomplished and what facilities and trainers are necessary for the course size arrangement, the availability of equipment and materials, e.g. what materials are needed and are available to avoid the kinds of equipment limited supply shortage, the financial constraints' aim to satisfy the course objectives at the lowest cost feasible, and achieve the highest standard of training possible at a cost that is acceptable to the organization. If the objectives of the course can't be achieved within the limits of available budget, then it is better not to run the course at all then to run unsuccessfully. Finally, the training course whether it has enough time to prepare all teaching arrangement to avoid bad or ineffective training consequence and not to cover-estimate what can accomplished during this period.

●

● Training and development steps

● Gary, D. (2000) indicated that employee orientation provides new employees with basic background information, who need to perform their jobs satisfactorily , such as information about company rules. Orientation is actually part of the employer's new employee socialization process. Socialization is the ongoing process of researching in all employee the attitudes, standards, values, and patterns of behavior that are expected by the organization and its departments.

● Training refers to the methods used to give new or present employees the skills, they need to perform their jobs. Training might mean showing how to operate its new methods, a new supervisor how to interview and appraise employees. Training is used to focus mostly on teaching technical skills, such as teachers devises lesson plans. However, technical training likes that is no longer sufficient. Employers have had to adapt to rapid technological changes, improve product and service quality and boost productivity to stay competitive. Improving quality (quality improvement programs) require employee who can produce charts and graphs and analyze data. Similarly, employees need skills (training) in team building, decision making, and communication, as well as technological and computer skills (such as desktop publishing, computer aided design and manufacturing) . And as competition demands better service, employees require customer service training for the tools and abilities require to serve customers.

● Gary, D. (2000) also explains the five step training and development process, such as below:

● First step is needs analysis, which identifies specific job performance skills needed to improve performance and productivity, analysing the audience to ensure that the program will be suited to their specific levels of education , experience and skills as well as their attitudes and personal motivations, using research to develop specific measurable knowledge and performance objectives.

● Second step is instructional design, which gathers instructional objectives, methods, media description of and sequence of content examples, exercises and activities. Organizing them into a curriculum that supports adult learning theory and provides a blueprint for program development. Making sure all materials, such as video scripts, leaders' guides, and participants' work tools, complement each other are written clearly into the started learning objectives, carefully and professional handle all program elements, whether reproduced on paper, film or tape to ensure quality and effectiveness.

● Third step is validation, which introduces and validates the training before a representative audience. Base final revisions on pilot results to ensure program effectiveness.

● Fourth step is implementation, when applicable , boost success with a train-the-trainer workshop that focuses on presentation knowledge and skills in addition to training content.

● Fifth step is evaluation and follow up, assess program success according to: reaction to document that learners' immediate reactions to the training, learning to use feedback devices or pre to measure what learners have actually learned, behavior to note supervisors' reactions to learners' performance following completion of the training. This is one way to measure the degree to which learners apply new skills and knowledge to their jobs, result to determine the level of improvement in job performance and assess needed maintenance.

● How to choose learning or training method

● Methods of learning, training and development plans, training sources can be internal to the company or employees are trained from an external organization. Training can range from short term to long term, from online to in-person and from low cost to high cost development program for senior or specialist staff could learn techniques , such as coaching and mentoring or second, formal or off-the-job learning or educational arrangement.

● The choice of learning methods depend on several factors include: the nature and degree of priority of the learning needs, type of occupation, level of seniority and qualifications/educational background of learners, organizational culture, evaluation of the effectiveness of previous learning and training results, experience, time required to complete training, learner preference, each individual may prefer learning in different ways, some prefer classroom learning over real-life practicing , learner preference's over learning ways and styles and their individual characteristics need to be taken into account when selecting , developing and delivering learning methods. For example, in-house courses provide an opportunity to focus on company specific issues. External courses involves interaction with people from other companies. For example, in-house, on the job training aims to deliver on a one-to-one basis at the trainee's place of work, allocated time to a specified , planned and structured activity.

-
-
-
-
-
-
-
- Reference
-
- David , L. (3 edition, 2016). The Group Trainer's
- Handbook, Designing And Delivering Training For groups , Kogan Page , US pp. 18-19
- Gary, D. (8 edition, 2000), Human resource management , Prentice hall, New Jersey.pp. 248-251
- John, A. (2018) Management techniques, a practical guide, London, UK and New York , US: Routledge, pp. 27, 34-37, 67, 70-71,133, 140-144.
-
-
-
-
-
-
-
-
-
-
-
-

CHAPTER FIVE

● Performance management

●

● Pay structure steps

●

● Human professionals might create the pay structure for their organization, or they might work with an external compensation consultant. There are several steps to design a pay structure: job analysis, job evaluation, pay survey analysis, pay policy and development and pay structure information (Milkovish, G., & Newman, J. 2008).

● Milkovich, G. & Newman, J. (2008) explains that the pay structure steps include as below:

● Step one : Job analysis is the process of studying jobs in an organization. The outcome of this process is a job description that includes the job title, a summary of the job tasks, adjust of the essential tasks and responsibilities and a description that includes the knowledge, skills and abilities needed to perform the job.

● Step two: Job evaluation is the process of judging the relative worth of jobs in an organization. The outcome of job evaluation is the development of an internal structure or hierarchal ranking of jobs. Job-based evaluation is used more often than person-based evaluation and so the former will be the focus in this case. There are three methods of job-based evaluation: The point method, ranking and classification. The job evaluation helps to ensure that pay is internally worth perceived to be fair by employees.

● Step three : Pay policy identification is the process of determining whether the organization wants to lead or meet the market in compensation. The pay policy or strategy will likely influence employee attraction. Pay policies can vary across families , i.e. groups of similar jobs, and job level of the top management feels that different areas of the organization.

● Step four: Pay survey analysis is the process of analysising compensation data gathered from other employers in a survey of the relevant labor market. Gathering external data , e.g. base pay, bonuses , stock or share options and benefits is the essential to keep the organization's compensation externally competitive within the industry. Employee attraction can be improved by maintaining externally pay structures.

● Step five: Pay structure creation is the final step, in which the internal structure (step two of job evaluation) is combined with the external market pay rates . Step four: Pay survey analysis in a simple regression to develop a market pay line. Depending on whether the organization wants to lead or meet the market, the market pay line can be adjusted top or down. To complete the pay structure , pay grades and pay ranges are developed.

● In this organization's job analysis, it can influence these positions or job titles. For example, office support department has the lower level, front line receptionist, middle level, admin. assistant and top level, assistant to the director of operations. Operations department has the lower level, operations trainee, operations trainee, middle level , operations analyst, top level, director of regional operations, top level, director of regional operations. Human resource department has the lower level, payroll assistant, the middle level, benefits counselor and benefits manager, the top level, HR director.

● In this organization, the administrative assistants, perform similar administrative tasks across departments and do not handle function-specific tasks , e.g. HR. Thus, this organization's administrative assistant ought be suggested grouping the front-line administrative jobs in a separate job family called office support. However, in some organizations, administrative assistant has possible to need to handle function-specific tasks, e.g. HR. Hence, in these organizations administrative assistant can be the low level group to HR department.

● In the job evaluation step, this organization chooses to apply point method to evaluate the pay worth to every job title. The evaluation points method can be weights for example the four degrees for education level are identified as below:

● 1=high school, 2=assocaites, 3= bacholors, 4=master/graduate points are then calculated by multiplying the degree by the weights.

● The compensable factor for the evaluation for front desk reception as below:

● skill (50%) degree(1,2,3,4) weight points

- education level 1 25% 25
- degree of
- technical skills 1 25% 25
- responsibility(30%)
- scope of control 1 10% 10
- impact of job 2 20% 40
- degree of
- problem solving 1 10% 10
- task complexity 1 10% 10
- 120
- The ensure that the pay structure is extremely competitive, a pay survey will be conducted. The market pay data must be from the relevant labor market. Surveys can include i.e. six organizations who recruit and hire similar jobs in the regions. Base pay salary data from the responding organizations are reflected to ensure the summary job descriptions , sample data are appropriately similar to those in this organization in order to compare and analyze the pay data between other similar organizations and this organization.
- Finally , it need to implement how to design the pay structure. it can be settled the pay ranges for each pay grade, pay ranges create upper and lower pay rates for each job in the pay scale. Each pay grade will have a minimum and maximum pay rate. It is important to remember that all jobs in a paygrade will have the same minimum and maximum pay rates. Percent guidelines below the midpoint the pay range will reach . For example, the maximum might be 10% percent above the midpoint and the minimum might be 10% below the midpoint. The percent guidelines can be based on input from the organization's job evaluation committee, e.g. clerical and office positions: 10% above and below the midpoint. Enter to mid-level professional and management positions: 30 % above and below the midpoint.
-
- What is key performance indicator (KPI) components?
- Performance management strategy of performance metrics are a powerful tool of organizational change. It can measure organizational performance really. Companies define objectives , establish goals, measure progress, reward achievement, and display the results for all productivity. Executives can use performance metrics to define and communicate strategic objectives tailor to every individual and role in the organization.

Managers can use them to identify forming individuals or teams and guide them and employees can use performance metrics to focus on what is important and help them achieve goal defined in their personal performance plans.

● But wrong metrics can have unintended consequences: They can threaten to prolong on organizational processes, demoralize employees and undermine productivity and service levels. If the metrics do not accurately translate the company's strategy and goals into real useful actions that employees can take on a daily basis. Employees will work hard but have nothing to show for their efforts, everyone will feel tired and frustrated, also the company will be efficient but ineffective.

● Performance metrics are a critical ingredient of performance management, performance management has a four steps cycle involves strategize misson, value, goals, objectives, incentives, strategy maps. Then, it needs to plan budgets, forecasts, models, targets. Next , it needs to monitor / analyze performance report, analytical tools. Finally, it needs to adjust or make action to assess, decide and track in execution step.

● A performance metrics measurement tool can fasten the business, distill an organization's strategy to serve its stakeholders, linking strategy to processes. A performance metrics can give visual information delivery system that lets users measure, monitor, and manage the effectiveness of their tactics and their progress toward achieving strategic objectives . Collecting , a performance metrics measurement tool enable users to identify problems and opportunities, taken action and adjust plans and goals as needed.

● What is key performance indicator (KPI) components? The only difference between a metric and KPA is that a KPI is a strategic objective and measures performance against a goal. KPI is a strategic objective , KPI measure performance against specific targets. Targets are defined in strategic planning, or budget sessions and can take different forms , e.g. achievement, reduction, absolute zero, targets have ranges of performance, e.g. above on, or below target. Targets are assigned time frame by which they must be accomplished. Time frame is often divided into smaller intervals, targets are measured against a baseline or benchmark. The previous year's results often serve as a benchmark.

● The goals associated with KPIs are known as targets because they specify a measuerble outcome rather then a conceptual destination. Ideally, executives, managers and workers collectively set targets during strategic planning or budget discussions.

● In performance management view point, target can be defined five types: Achievement means performance should reach or exceed the target. Anything over the target is valuable but not required, e.g. revenue and satisfaction. Reduction means performance should reach or be lower than the target. Anything less than the target is value, but not required, e.g. absolute means performance should equal the target. Anything above or below is not good, e.g. in-stock percentage and on time delivery. Minimum/maximum means performance should be within a range of value. Anything above or below the range is not good , e.g. mean time between repairs, zero means performance should equal zero, which is the minimum value possible, e.g. employee injuries and product defects. All above these target will be key performance indicator performance tool.

● For time frames example, performance targets have time frames, which affects hoe KPIs are calculated and displayed. Many organizations establish annul targets for key processes. To keep employees on track to achieve those long -term targets, many organizations divide time frames into intervals, that are measured on a more frequent basis. For example, a group may divide the annual target to improve customer satisfaction from 60% to 68% into four quarterly inter with 2% target improvement each quarter. However, in some cases, such as a retail environment is affected by seasonal shopping, groups many back weighs. The targets toward the end of the year, since most holiday season, during the Dec. holiday season.

● Finally, KPI targets could be measured against a benchmark that becomes the starting point for improving performance . Typically, the benchmark is last year's output. So, for example, a sales team may need to increase sales by 20% compared to last year. Or the benchmark could be an external standard , such as the performance level of an industry leader. So, a company might want to set a goals of closing the gap in market share with its closet competitor by 50% next year.

● Users can read KPIs to look at a visual display that has been properly encoded and know whether a process of project is on track. To assist users can understand KPI (key performance indicator) performance measurement more easily. It has seven attributes for each. They include: status measures performance against the target and is usually shown with a stoplight. Trend measures performance against the prior interval or another time period and is often displayed using arrows or trend lines. The actual and target values are self-explanatory and usually displayed with text.

Variance measures the gap between actual and target and is displayed using text or a micro bar chart in performance report variance percentage divides the variance against the target. These seven attributes can combine to provide valuable insight into the state of performance.

●

● How to Implement a Performance Management System

● Depending on what kind of changes have been made we will have to prepare a communication and change management plan in order to transfer the organization smoothly from one to another PMS. While the small changes can be covered by simple communication informing about the changes in the system, major changes may even require change of mindset and old habits, which will need a more serious change management plan.

● It is a system that is linked to and feeds many other HR tolls and systems meaning that the final results of those tools are highly dependent on the inputs that they get from the PMS. Having that kind of importance and influence this system, though complex in its nature, from one side has to be as simple as possible so that all managers can willingly and easily use it, while on the other side it has to offer quality results that can be used as inputs for the other HR tools and systems.

● The quality of the system and the results it offers depend on the process of setting up the system itself. Doing a good job in planning, defining and introducing the system will do half of the job in securing quality results from the system. So how do we set up a Performance Management System?

● Implementation of a Performance Management System is a project of its own... as every other project it needs serious approach towards all project elements and phases.

● The implementation of a Performance Management System is a project of its own so it should be treated as one. So, as every other project of this character it needs serious approach towards all project elements and phases such as defining, planning, people, resource and stakeholder management, implementation, monitoring, measuring etc..

● The performance management system may contain all of these components, but it is the overall system that matters, not the individual components. Many organizations have been able to develop effective performance management systems without all of the following practices.

●

● A performance management system includes the following actions:

●

● •Develop clear job descriptions using an employee recruitment plan that identifies the selection team.

● •Recruit potential employees and select the most qualified to participate in interviews onsite.

● •Conduct interviews to narrow down your pool of candidates.

● •Hold multiple additional meetings, as needed, to get to know your candidates' strengths, weaknesses, and abilities to contribute what you nced. Use potential employee testing and assignments where they make sense for the position that you are filling.

● •Select appropriate people using a comprehensive employee selection process to identify the most qualified candidate who has the best cultural fit and job fit that you need.

● •Offer your selected candidate the job and negotiate the terms and conditions of employment including salary, benefits, paid time off, and other organizational perks.

● •Welcome the new employee to your organization.

● •Provide effective new employee orientation, assign a mentor, and integrate your new employee into the organization and its culture.

● •Negotiate requirements and accomplishment-based performance standards, outcomes, and measures between the employee and his or her new manager.

● •Provide ongoing education and training as needed.

● •Provide on-going coaching and feedback.

● •Conduct quarterly performance development planning discussions.

● •Design effective compensation and recognition systems that reward people for their ongoing contributions.

● •Provide promotional/career development opportunities including lateral moves, transfers, and job shadowing for staff.

● •Assist with exit interviews to understand WHY valued employees leave the organization.

● •Performance Appraisals Don't Work tells you why you want to move away from the traditional appraisal system.

● •Performance Management Glossary Entry provides a basic definition of performance management.

● •Performance Management Is Not an Annual Appraisal provides the components of a performance management system.

● •Performance Management Process Checklist gives you the components of the performance management process.

● •Performance Development Planning provides the steps for preparing and implementing performance development planning.

● •Performance Development Planning Form is used to write out specific goals and measurements, to be updated quarterly.

● •Goal Setting: Beyond Traditional SMART Goals discusses goal setting.

● •Tips to Help Managers Improve Performance Appraisals provides concrete suggestions about how those of you who have to manage in a traditional performance appraisal culture can make them better—for both you and the employee.

● •Common Problems With Performance Appraisals identifies the most common reasons why appraisals are not effective.

● •Phrases for Approaching Performance Reviews and Difficult Conversations shares tips about successfully holding a comfortable appraisal meeting.

● Finally, performance appraisal is one part of performance management system. The process by which a manager or consultant (1) examines and evaluates an employee's work behavior by comparing it with preset standards, (2) documents the results of the comparison, and (3) uses the results to provide feedback to the employee to show where improvements are needed and why. Performance appraisals are employed to determine who needs what training, and who will be promoted, demoted, retained, or fired.

● Performance management aim

● Performance management means the goal of reward programs are to attract, motivate people and it is essential for the company to clearly identify the performance and competency levels required of their employees in different roles at different levels. The company will then evaluate , differentiate and reward the employees in a fair and consistent way.

● Performance management is one of the most important functions in human resource management. It is also an important tool to link individual objectives with departmental targets. It is a part of a comprehensive human resource management strategy. It needs to let objectives into practical and realistic performance goals at each level of the company. It provides employees clear aims and forms on job expectation motivates employees to perform better, helps focus on the desired results, improves communication, helps develop employees, capabilities and helps achieve organizational objectives.

● It's elements include : planning means agreement on performance goals and targets, based on job descriptions and business objectives, goals and targets have to be specific to clear, measurable, specify quantity, quality, time, money etc., achievable to solve challenges, but within each of competent and committed person, relevant to the company's objectives. So, that the individual's goals can contribute towards the company's objective, monitoring and coaching means on ongoing and continuous process, monitor performance against agreed goals and targets, provide direction/ support and feedback on how well people are doing, recognize and reinforce desirable behaviours, coach and help solve difficulties in achieving desirable performance, identify problem at early stage, take corrective action in a timely manner.

● Then, performance review or appraisal meeting means that it is a formal review on the individual's performance, it is usually done once or twice a year to review, monitor and employees for promotion, help identify the training and development needs of employees, achieve a better two way communication between the line manager and the employee with regards to performance.

● Next, preparation for the appraisal meeting, it is necessary to keep a record of the individual's performance and achievement with gives support to rating, allow sufficient time for preparation on, what performance problems are to be mentioned, views on the possible reasons for success or failure, any suggestions to solve the problem, give sufficient notice to employee regarding the meeting and respect employee to have a self-appraisal before the meeting they can identify their own achievements and problems. Finally preparation of the appraisal form, it should be as simple and brief as possible and allow sufficient time for comments, terms should be easily understood, with some notes for guidance, information to collect on the form includes: Key result areas, agreed objectives/targets , assessment of performance against the key result area details of the development plan to improve performance.

● What are the development activities participated for current appraisal period mean? Review the development activities are participated by the employee for the past appraisal period and to agree on a development plan for the coming appraisal period. Management coaching for performance means that managers and supervisors have an important role to play in performance management, which is to provide feedback and coaching on employee's performance when necessary, coaching is a process that helps the employee gain how to win overcome barriers to improve job performance on a as need basis, when training uses a structured design to provide the employees with the knowledge and skills to perform a task.

● The other difference between coaching and training is that the former is normally done in real time. That is , it is performed on the job, at the workplace. The coach uses real-life tasks and problems to help the learners increase their performance. Otherwise, training and learning is taught to a group students to learn in a coaching is effective when it is specific to the individual and it is positive and it is positive and occurs as soon as performance problems are identifies.

● Coaching for individual benefit performance includes to identify performance problem by pointing out the facts/describing the behaviours observed in a professional manner, support with evidence if possible, clarify the expectations/standards of the job, explain the consequence of inappropriate actions/behaviours, ask for the employee's view point and how they assess their own actions/behaviours , discuss the causes of the problem/analyze reasons for sub-standard performance, develop and agree on solutions, decide on specific action(s) to be taken.

● Why is reward communication important? for this case, a company could be wasting the money spent on salaries and benefits by leaving employees when they listen the true value of the total package. Without employee understanding, reward programs won't motivate employee effort reward achieving business objectives. So, effective reward communication can let candidates existing staff appreciate or understand the value of the retirement scheme or other benefits, such as subsidized meals, life insurance and critical illness insurance. However, if rewards are used to motivate employees, or to encourage higher performance aims, it is essential to have an effective communicating information about pay scales, the provision of benefits and allowances, grading systems, job evaluation , performance-related pay schemes and how pay decisions and made for different individuals or groups of employees.

● In conclusion, performance management is not an annual appraisal meeting. It is not preparing for that appraisal meeting nor is it a self-evaluation. It's not a form nor is it a measuring tool although many organizations may use tools and forms to track goals and improvements, they are not the process of performance management.

● Note: Performance management is the process of creating a work environment or setting in which people are enabled to perform to the best of their abilities.

● Performance management is a whole work system that begins when a job is defined as needed. It ends when an employee leaves your organization. Performance management defines your interaction with an employee at every step of the way in between these major life cycle occurrences. Performance management makes every interaction opportunity with an employee into a learning occasion.

● Performance management aims at building a high performance culture for both the individuals and the teams so that they jointly take the responsibility of improving the business processes on a continuous basis and at the same time raise the competence bar by upgrading their own skills within a leadership framework. Its focus is on enabling goal clarity for making people do the right things in the right time. It may be said that the main objective of a performance management system is to achieve the capacity of the employees to the full potential in favor of both the employee and the organization, by defining the expectations in terms of roles, responsibilities and accountabilities, required competencies and the expected behaviors.

● The main goal of performance management is to ensure that the organization as a system and its subsystems work together in an integrated fashion for accomplishing optimum results or outcomes.

● The major objectives of performance management are discussed below:

● ?To enable the employees towards achievement of superior standards of work performance.

● ?To help the employees in identifying the knowledge and skills required for performing the job efficiently as this would drive their focus towards performing the right task in the right way.

● ?Boosting the performance of the employees by encouraging employee empowerment, motivation and implementation of an effective reward mechanism.

● ?Promoting a two way system of communication between the supervisors and the employees for clarifying expectations about the roles and accountabilities, communicating the functional and organizational goals, providing a regular and a transparent feedback for improving employee performance and continuous coaching.

● ?Identifying the barriers to effective performance and resolving those barriers through constant monitoring, coaching and development interventions.

● ?Creating a basis for several administrative decisions strategic planning, succession planning, promotions and performance based payment.
● ?Promoting personal growth and advancement in the career of the employees by helping them in acquiring the desired knowledge and skills.
●
● Some of the key concerns of a performance management system in an organization are:
● ?Concerned with the output (the results achieved), outcomes, processes required for reaching the results and also the inputs (knowledge, skills and attitudes).
● ?Concerned with measurement of results and review of progress in the achievement of set targets.
● ?Concerned with defining business plans in advance for shaping a successful future.
● ?Striving for continuous improvement and continuous development by creating a learning culture and an open system.
● ?Concerned with establishing a culture of trust and mutual understanding that fosters free flow of communication at all levels in matters such as clarification of expectations and sharing of information on the core values of an organization which binds the team together.
● ?Concerned with the provision of procedural fairness and transparency in the process of decision making.
● The performance management approach has become an indispensable tool in the hands of the corporates as it ensures that the people uphold the corporate values and tread in the path of accomplishment of the ultimate corporate vision and mission. It is a forward looking process as it involves both the supervisor and also the employee in a process of joint planning and goal setting in the beginning of the year.
●
● 5.4 What is the difference between performance management and performance appraisal?
● Performance appraisals are one of the crucial aspects of professionally managed organizations across the world. Each organization has set an appraisal system in place in order to raise its employees' performance over a period of time. They are based on a review of the performance of an employee on the tasks assigned to it. They are used for many aspects such as salary revision, bonus provisions, promotions etc. These reviews are mostly conducted annually, but may be considered quarterly or half-yearly as well

depending upon the HR policies of the organizations. Mostly, Human Resource department takes the lead in conducting formal performance appraisals.

● Otherwise, performance management systems are set in place to guide the employees to achieve a desired level of performance. It is basically a definition of what organization expects from employee over the next appraisal period. Specific objectives are set for short term (say next quarter), and employee is prepared to achieve the desired outcomes by meeting these short term targets. These targets are defined by the job description along with the desired outcome of the jobs. This helps employees to determine the gaps in their performance and thus helps them to improve before the final performance appraisal happens after a year or six months. However, performance management aims at overall personal development of the employees. It is a form of constructive feedback which encourages continuous improvement. It is helpful to both employee as well as appraiser. There is frequent communication between them which helps in setting right goals for the employee and possible guidelines from appraiser to achieve those goals in an effective manner. It therefore saves employees from the bitter feeling that comes at year end when they feel that they have wasted one whole year without any substantial value addition.

●

● What are performance management system

●

● The common goals of performance management system consider our daily work routine about our purpose in an organization. It is important to let organizational members understand what their organizations' visions and goals are, how their work fits into the organization, and how they contribute to their mission accomplishment. Hence one effective performance management system can encourage and improve the organization's members to raise their effort to contribute to their organizations. So, it brings this question: How to design one effective performance management system?

●

● A clear understanding of job expectations is needed. When employees and supervisors have a clear understanding of their specific job duties in the workforce are eliminated. Each employee will be expect to contribute their own duties and responsibilities efficiently. All effective performance management system can empower employees to think about and clarify every employee's role in the organization. Organizations need to set clear goals and expectations to help with them. Employee performance plans must provide for balanced, credible measuring expected results, the performance plans include results, the performance plans include appropriate resources, such as quality, quantity, timeliness, and/or cost-effectiveness. Moreover, performance expectations must be based on job analysis and understandable, reasonable and attainable and clear specific.

●

● Regular feedback facilitates better communication in the workplace factor is important. Performance strengths and weaknesses. How can employee individual performance can get improvement? In fact, performance management can be a motivational tool, when this tool can let employees to feel more satisfactory. Then, the supervisors can have a performance feedback process that facilitates between the supervisors and their employees. Hence, performance feedback ought need to be regular feedback facilitated better communication in the workplace. It can reduce from normal pressures of work.

●

● How to design effective performance management system ? AN effective management system can measure organizational and employee performance. Performance management involves multiple levels of analysis, and is clearly linked to the topics studied in strategy HRM as well as performance appraisal. The objectives of performance management system often include motivating performance, helping individuals, developing their skills, building a performance culture, determining who should be promoted, eliminating individuals who are poor performers, and helping implement strategies.

●

● Hence, the main purposes of a performance include: The work is performed the best by employees, employees have a clear understanding of the quality of work expected from them, employees effectively these are performing relative to expectation, awards and salary increases based on employee performance are distributed, opportunity for employee development and finding reasons and solutions why the employee performance that does not need expectation. These issues will be performance management usually main purposes.

●

● However, performance management system usually have these phases:

Phase 1 (developing and planning performance) , It includes outline development plans, setting objectives and getting commitment for the organization. Phase 2 (managing and review performance), it includes assess against objectives, feedback, coaching , document reviews, . Phase 3 (reward performance) , it includes personal development, link to pay , results performance. What is the performance management aim? On setting objectives stage, the management needs to know how to achieve and help to encourage commitment and understanding by linking. The employees' work with the organization's goals and objectives. It needs to let employees to know how to achieve its missions clearly. So, targets need to be settled for each performance and goals setting is the fundamental aspect for an organization. They further indicated that productivity gains will be supported for and employees' participation in the process of setting objectives. It is a motivational process which also gives the individual the feeling of being involved and creates a sense of ownership for employees.
●

● In management and review stage, this involves maintaining a positive approach to work, updating and revising initial objectives, performance standard and job competency areas as conditions change, requesting feedback from a supervisor, providing feedback to supervisors, suggesting career development experiences, employees and supervisors working together, managing the performance management process.
●

● Hence, performance needs to be compared. It is between desired performance and actual performance. When they are measured , then they will give feedback and development. Then, feedback will five opinions to desired performance in order to make performance revision again, even again. Finally, when the desired performance can be achieved the best actual performance measurement result and it will bring actual performance development to achieve actual vision, mission, strategy, value drivers consequently.
●

● IN the rewarding performance, it has three activities: personnel development, linking to pay and identifying the results or performance. In fact, all personnel development is basically self-development. Opportunity for development is valuable only if the individual capitalizes on himself/ herself. Development should be designed to improve performance on the current job and then prepare the employee for promotion. In fact, it is only the employees who get promoted , who are currently doing outstanding work and this have been able to demonstrate their capacity to assume greater responsibilities. Furthermore, training activities should ideally to based on performance gaps that are identified during the performance review phase.

●

● So, regular performance feedbacks are important factors to influence skills development. In addition organizations need a growing interest in pay-for -performance plans focused on small groups or teams. Small group pays provide monetary rewards based on the measured performance of the group or team. However, high performing, effective organizations have a culture that encourages employee involvement. Therefore, employees are more willing to get involved in decision-making, goal setting or problem solving activities, which subsequently result in higher employee performance.

●

● Thus, one effective performance management system needs to follow these steps to implement, such as developing and planning performance step: it includes to set what the main objectives , the organization needs. Then it is managing and review performance step, the organizations need to review whether what differences are between its desired performance and actual performance to prepare review their performance difference. Next, it is reward management implementation, the organization needs to give better record to the talent employees in order to encourage they develop their skills in the maximum effort as well as it also needs to punish the poor performance employees in order to expect they can review their error. In consequence, all these steps must be followed step by step to implement the performance management system effectively.

●
●
●
●
●
●
●
●
● Reference
● Milkovich, G., & Newman, J. (2008). Compensation, MC Graw-Hill Irwin.

0*NET. Available at http:// online.onetcenter.org

-
-
-

CHAPTER SIX

● Sourcing and staffing

●

● How to build talent staffing source

● Marion, D. & Michel, S. (2014) explained talent is the sum of a person's abilities, his or her intrinsic grifts, skills, knowledge, experience, intelligence, judgement, attitude, character and drive. It also includes his or her ability to learn. At the international level, talent shortages are more severe. During the past decade, an internationally mobile group of employees, who can pick and choose where they work. As firms in employing markets also begin competing in the global economy, these people are in ever-greater demand. For example, Singapore has had on an intensive recruitment program for skilled foreign workers, with more liberal criteria for eligibility to work in the country. Some 90,000 now work in the city-state, the majority from the US, UK, France, Australia, Japan and South Korea.

● Marion, D. & Michel, S. (2014) indicated several factors need to be taken into account to understand the market for skilled labour. Hays and Oxford Economics pooled their data to identify seven components that together give a better picture of skill shortages as below:

● Labour-market participation means the degree to which a country's talent pool is fully utilized, for example, whether women and older workers have access to jobs; labour -market flexibility means the legal and regulatory environment is faced by business, especially how easily immigrants can fill talent gaps; wage pressure overall means whether real wages are keeping pace with inflation; wage pressure in high-skill industries means which wages in high-skill industries outpace those in low-skill industries; wage pressure in high-skill occupations means rises in wages for highly skilled workers are a short -term indicaton of skills shortages, talent mismatches means the mismatch between the skills are needed by businesses and those available, are indicated by the number of long-term unemployed and job vacancies; educational flexibility means whether the educational system can adapt to meet the future needs of organizations for talent, especially in the fields of mathematics and science.

● Firms operating in knowledge-intensive industries depend on their most capable staff to help create value through intangible assets, such as patents, licence and technical know-how. In fact, globalisation and technological competition brings to much complexity of many jobs and occupations. Firms are now looking for individuals with an range of abilities that might include specialized skills, broader functional skills, industry expertise and knowledge of specific geographical markets. The skills include: digital skill means the fast growing digital economy is increasing the demand for highly skilled technical workers. Companies are looking for staff with social-media based skills, especially in " digital expression". Agile thinking means the regulatory and environment uncertainty, such as life sciences and energy and mining industry's talent knowledge, ability skill is needed for employee's personal effort and characteristic needs; interpersonal and communication skill, H R managers predict that co-creativity and brainstorming skills be greatly in demand, it will bring relationship building and teamwork skills; global operating skill means that ability to manage diverse employee is seen as the most important global operating skill,, glocalisation (where home-market products and services are tailored to the taste of overseas customers and innovation (where staffs lead innovation and then the company applies these new ideas to mature markets).

● Talent is a relative concept, it includes these components, such as technical specialists, especially in areas key to the organization's core capabilities, individuals with hard-to-recruit skills, bright individuals from underrepresented groups whom the positions , the best-performing graduates or school leavers and managers with the potential to move into senior management positions at the local, national or international level. However, judgement effort is the main factor to influence organizations to select individuals whose behavior and values fit with those of the organization. How performance and potential are measured is for senior managers to decide.

● In many cases, the definition of exceptional performance is explained in competency frameworks and appraisal systcms. Defining high potential can be more difficult and might include a range of assessment tools, such as development centers, psychometric testing and the personal judgement of those whose insights into talent are widely respected.

● Talent plan has three components: talent gaps mean HR works with business management levels. Once a year to identify which leadership , management and functional skills are needed, how those roles and responsibilities and whether the talent processes are producing people who will be able to solve these skill gaps; talent supply means most of the focus is on management trainees and a smaller proportion of people who are recruited mid-career; talent development means recruiting high-potential individuals at the start of their careers and taking them through a structured development program.

● Talent strategy means how senior leaders can identify the capabilities that help achieve the company's strategy strategic objectives and provide a competitive effort. These capabilities are not just tactical or operational skills, which although important, do have as much of an impact on business performance and profit. Operational management or senior levels and the talent management team then break down each capabilities into parts, such as specific skills, knowledge and expertise. They look at how these skills sets enable each business unit to deliver their part of the strategic plan.

● This analysis should indicate the roles where knowledge and expertise are needed for maximum business value. There are not automatically senior leadership or management values. They also extend to technical and specialist roles or to previously overlooked roles, e.g. positions within the organization that help sure that expertise from one part of the business. Part of review many necessitate a fresh look at knowledge management processes across the business. The HR team should also review its own ways of working and thinking o make sure that its processes for recruitment, selection, learning and development, appraisal , reward and recognition and concentrates on the skills, cultural values and behaviors most critical to business performance.

● Talent review aims to assess how well employees are performing currently in the critical roles, identified by the strategic review, and their potential to move into more demanding roles. Some of the required data will be held centrally by HR, but almost certainly, the team carrying out the review will need to speak directly to operational and line managers to get feedback about the performance and potential of key individuals.

● At part of the review, gap analysis will help identify gaps in skills necessary to carry out the business's strategy and plans and whether any critical roles are unfilled. Succession planning is a important factor here as it may well be that insufficient numbers of potential successors have been identified for certain critical roles. A talent based gap analysis main aim is to focus on hiring and/or training needs as part of a talent strategy, it is the company's strategic planning process. It draws ona wide source of data, both internally and externally. It looks at strategic needs both current and future, and makes judgements about operational needs.

● This analysis determines whether the right talented people are in the right position at the right time. These three factors will influence whether talent planning needs to be improved. For example, right people, but wrong time, it means that people who might not be being used currently because of ao downturn in markets, but who the organization does not want to lose as it takes too much time and money to replace them when demand increases. The organization must therefore determine its strategy for retaining and motivating them; wrong people means that people are not employed to perform the work .

● This suggests that a mistake is between HR processes and the business strategy, learning and development processes may not be keeped good with changing business needs. There may be needed to appraise and promote to make right decisions that are leading to a mismatch between roles and people, right people, but wrong location. It means that people who can do the work , but are in the wrong location as a result of a reorganization and constraints on mobility, make more creative use of temporary assignments and virtual working, or relocate work to where it can be done by the most skilful employees.

● Finally, once the talent review has identified any shortagesof talent, an organization has three options: either buying talent through external recruitment or building talent through tailored learning and development programmes that involve work experiences that will help talent employment development or borrowing talent by resorting to temporary workers or outsourcing.

● Buying talent is an obvious choice when a company needs particular skills or expertise that it does not have time or ability ro develop in existing staff is to buy in that talent. The task is then to source this expertise, and offer the right set of inducements to recruit and retain individuals with the desired skills. However, buying talent can be costly as the going rate for sought-after specialists is high and they are often in a strong negotiating position. For example, swift recruitment processes and flexible remuneration package can attract talent employees' applications through external recuritment seeking recritment method.

● Borrowing talent is a temporary need for specialist skills it makes sense to borrow or " rent" what is required by contracting with, for example, freelancers, independent consultants, staff on seondment or firms that will supply staff. This form of flexible labour means uncertain times such flexibility becomes more attractive because it enables firms to assemble new combinatins of skills in swift reponse to sudden shifts in their environment. It provides firms with access to wider pool of talent, especially in the case of work that can be performed in any location.

● This, building talent means that a larger firm will seek to build its own talent by creating a reliable high potential and high performing employees. The aim is to rise and train talent skilful employees' qualities and efforts and to invest in their careers in the expectation that they will progress to senior positions in the business. So, these individuals are placed in a talent pool where their progress is monitored and where they are given extra opportunities for training and development. To keep talented people to develop, there is an emphasis on performance management, so any weaknesses or developments are needed to find.

●

● sourcing staff methods

● Internal sources advantages of filling a vacancy internally, they include better motivation because employee capabilities are more ensured to promote or transfer, improved moral, performance and loyalty to the employee, lower staff turnover rate, better utilisation of employees because he/she owns more abilities in a different job or capacity , less training required, greater reliability than external recruitment because a present employee is the terms of personality, attitudes, values, work habits etc. known more, being quicker and cheaper than external recruitment.

● External source advantages when the company need to expand and growth contribute to the need for recruitment. Other factors include resignation, dismissal, retirement and relocation. Although internal recruitment has many advantages, many positions are filled by external applicants. When an internal candidate is transferred or promoted, it means that his/her position then because a vacancy, presuming that there is no reduction in staff numbers and no organizational restructuring. Hence, external recruitment can be time consuming , expensive and uncertain. However, organizations still need to conduct the external sources selecting method on a regular basis. The external recruitment source channels may include internal online or newspaper advertising, private employment agencies, professional bodies appointment services, local employment services office of government labor department, direct links with universities, colleges and schools, unsolicited applications, recommendations by present employees or by other employers' referrals.

● Talent management steps in validating a test. Test aims to ensure whether the test listening and speaking competence, he/she owns the skillful effort is enough to do the vacancy or position in the organization. The steps in validating a test is as below:

● The organization needs to analyze the job. It is necessary to conduct a careful job analysis to produce a good job description and an appropriate job specification. These requirements can then become the objectives of the selection tests. Then, it needs to choose the test from among the various testing means, choose the one that is the most valid and reliable. Next, it needs to administer the test. One can either test current employees and find out of there is any significant differences between the scores and the employees' performances , it means concurrent validation or test potential candidates before they are hired and compare their scores with their performances after they have been in their jobs, it means predictive validation.

● However, predictive validation may have disadvantages, e.g. job performance may be difficult to assess objectively, the process of validation may be lengthy, the results of the test are compared with the performance of a selected group only, it is not completely validated. Concurrent validation is quick, but its disadvantages may include standardisation is difficult, the test is validated against a non-typical group only, i.e. present employers rather than candidates for employment, the present employee may not behave normally when they do the test.

●
●
●
●
● Reference
● Marion, D. & Michel, S. (2014) the economist, Managing talent, Profile books ltd, London, UK, pp.1-2, 6.
●
●
●

-
-

CHAPTER SEVEN

● Employee engagement

●

● employee engagement aim

● What is employee engagement? The term employee engagement needs to be clearly understood by every organization. Some organizations perceive it as job satisfaction others say it's the emotional attachment towards the organization. Employee Engagement is a fundamental concept in the effort to understand and describe, both qualitatively and quantitatively, the nature of the relationship between an organization and its ● employees. An "engaged employee" is defined as one who is fully absorbed by and enthusiastic about their ● work and takes positive action to further the ● organization's reputation and interests. An engaged employee has a positive attitude towards the organization and its values.

● An organization with "high" employee engagement might therefore be expected to outperform those with "low" employee engagement. Employee engagement improves the productivity of an organization as the practice helps the employees in teamwork, co-ordination and inter-personal skills. It means that such as ● morale and ● job satisfaction. Despite academic critiques, employee-engagement practices are well established in the management of ● human resources and of ● internal communications. Employee engagement today has become synonymous with terms like 'employee experience' and 'employee satisfaction'. The relevance is much more due to the vast majority of new generation professionals in the workforce who have a higher propensity to be 'distracted' and 'disengaged' at work.

● The workplace environment impacts employee morale, productivity and engagement - both positively and

● negatively. The work place environment in a majority of industry is unsafe and unhealthy. These includes poorly designed workstations,

unsuitable furniture, lack of ventilation, inappropriate lighting, excessive
● noise, insufficient safety measures in fire emergencies and lack of personal protective equipment. People working in such environment are prone to occupational disease and it impacts on employee's performance. Thus productivity is decreased due to the workplace environment. It is the quality of the
● employee's workplace environment that most impacts on their level of motivation and subsequent performance. How well they engage with the organization, especially with their immediate environment, influences to a great extent their error rate, level of innovation and collaboration with other employees,
● absenteeism and ultimately, how long they stay in the job. Creating a work environment in which employees are productive is essential to increased profits for your organization, corporation or small business. The relationship between work, the workplace and the tools of work, workplace becomes an integral part of work itself. The management that dictate how, exactly, to maximize employee productivity
● center around two major areas of focus: personal motivation and the infrastructure of the work environment.
●
● In today's competitive business environment, organizations can no longer afford to waste the potential of their workforce. There are key factors in the employee's workplace environment that impact greatly on
● their level of motivation and performance. The workplace environment that is set in place impacts employee morale, productivity and engagement - both positively and negatively. It is not just coincidence that new programs addressing lifestyle changes, work/life balance, health and fitness - previously not
● considered key benefits - are now primary considerations of potential employees, and common practices among the most admired companies.
●
● In an effort to motivate workers, firms have implemented a number of practices such as performance based pay, employment security agreements, practices to help balance work and family, as well as various forms of information sharing. In addition to motivation, workers need the skills and ability to do
● their job effectively. And for many firms, training the worker has become a necessary input into the production process.

●
● THE PROBLEM STATEMENT
●
● The work place environment in a majority of industry is unsafe and unhealthy. These includes poorly designed workstations, unsuitable furniture, lack of ventilation, inappropriate lighting, excessive noise,
● insufficient safety measures in fire emergencies and lack of personal protective equipment. People working in such environment are prone to occupational disease and it impacts on employee's performance. Thus productivity is decreased due to the workplace environment. It is a wide industrial
● area where the employees are facing a serious problem in their work place like environmental and physical factors. So it is difficult to provide facilities to increase their performance level. Thus, effective employee engagement strategy can assist the organization's employees feel they are the organization's important members to serve their organizations to work more hardly in order to raise productivities easily.
●
● What is employee welfare mean?
●
● Employee welfare includes everything, such as facilities, benefits and services, that an employer provides or does to ensure comfort of the employees. Good welfare helps to motivate employees and ensure increased productivity.
● Providing good welfare to employees may be a costly decision, but the long-term benefits are immense. It is one way of complying with the law, thus ensuring that an employer avoids legal issues. It allows accompany to retain its good and skilled employees for long periods of time. Employees work well in workplaces where they are treated well and respected. Good welfare also helps to create a good company image for a particular employer.
●
● Employee welfare facilities in the organization affects on the behavior of the employees as well as on the productivity of the
● organization. While getting work done through employees the management must provide required good facilities to all employees.
● The management should provide required good facilities to all employees in such way that employees become satisfied and they work harder and more efficiently and more effectively.

●

● Welfare is a broad concept referring to a state of living of an individual or a group, in a desirable relationship with the total

● environment – ecological economic and social. It aims at social development by such means as social legislation, social reform

● social service, social work, social action. The object of economics welfare is to promote economic production and productivity and through development by increasing equitable distribution. Labour welfare is an area of social welfare conceptually and operationally.

● It covers a broad field and connotes a state of well being, happiness, satisfaction, conservation and development of human resources

●

● Employee welfare is an area of social welfare conceptually and operationally. It covers a broad field and connotes a state of well being, happiness, satisfaction, conservation and development of

● human resources and also helps to motivation of employee. The basic propose of employee welfare is to enrich the life of

● employees and to keep them happy and conducted. Welfare measures may be both Statutory and Non statutory laws require the employer to extend certain benefits to employees in addition to wages or salaries.

●

● Labour Welfare Measures

●

● Labor welfare includes various facilities, services and amenities provided to workers for improving their health, efficiency,

● economic betterment and social status.

● Welfare measures are in addition to regular wages and other economic benefits available to workers due to legal provisions

● and collective bargaining. The purpose of labor welfare is to bring about the development

● of the whole personality of the workers to make a better workforce. The very logic behind providing welfare schemes is to create efficient, healthy, loyal and satisfied labor force for the organization. The purpose of providing such facilities is to make their work life better and also to raise their standard of living.

●

● Measurement the level of employee engagement factor

● There are a number of external and internal factors that help measure the level of employee engagement. External factors include organization environment; its culture and values, manager-subordinate relationship, relationships with co-workers, monetary benefits and appraisals. Whereas internal factors include the personal values of employee, personality type and commitment to work. Gallup's research on employee engagement shows that there is a strong relationship between well being of an employee and the level of their engagement. An engaged employee is efficient an effective for the organizational outcomes.

● Employee engagement has direct effect on productivity and growth. If employees are engaged they will try level best to fulfill their job responsibilities which will consequently lead to not only increase in organization productivity but will also enhance the self performance of employee. In the world of globalization only those organizations which have highly engaged workers can survive and grow. But an organization can engage its employees only if the employees have the desired attitude. Therefore an organization should train its employees to change their attitudes if they want to properly manage workforce engagement.

● employee engagement survey reasons

● Nowadays, increasing diverse and geographically workforces bring global competition to live nd retain qualified employees aim. Organizations need to attract, motivately and engage employees though not only the core HR functions of compensation, benefits, performance management and talent development, but engagement programs, such as work life effectiveness, recognition and reward systems.

● In fact, one strategic employee engagement if designed correctly, is cost-effective program and valuable tools that can measured and increase employee involvement and ethusiasm in their work and contributions to their employer's goals or values. Industry research analysts indicated that companies in the top employee engagement designed program, which can brough 16% higher profits and 18% higher productivity in general. They also evaluated the relationship between employee engagement and employee turnover. Companies with light effective recognition engagement programs have 31 % lower ineffective turnover than organizations with ineffective recognition programs. However, to be most impactful engagement solutions require innovative features to enble full service, effective management of strategic engagement programs. Social communicative elements along with rich analytics and mobile capabilities that interoperate with existing HR solutions are necessary to keep more efficient and effective changing HR needs and organizational goals.

● As the economy slowly makes its way back in recovery mode and more employees are concerned with issues beyond job security. So organizations need to concern how to a focus on employee engagement and the criticial factor ithin organizations that drives performance. HR conulting forms point out a relationship between high levels of engagement and high levels of financial performance. Achieving overall employee engagement is overview to have need. For years, companies around the globle have conducted employee engagement surveys in an effort to determine why their organizations function the way they do, and how they can pull organizations to improve performance. The results of there employee engagement surveys sometimes reflect, better and accurate key business decisions and impacting the day-for-day lives of employees, shareholders and customers.

● But is that really all these is to real reflection? Should company focus on employee engagement as the key indicator of success or failure within their organization? Is high employee engagement brings some sort of better management skills? It is absolute no answer. When employee engagement should be measured as an important organizations human resource and social system, truly understanding how to optimize performance in your organization requires understanding your organization requires understanding your culture. For example, we know that with some people, we can increase their engagement and satisfaction by simply, making their work easy-opertating in a go along to get along manner and more generally encouraging passive behaviors.

● Employee engagement becomes a popular topic of the workplace instead of job satisfaction and organizational commitment which is approved to effect the organizational outcome. In HR department behaviors that affect th structured interviews were conducted in corporate HR to explore the employee engagement and techniques for improving employee engagement were recommended based on the interview.

● The quantitative research results show that job autonomy , performance feedback, challenging work, worker person fit, development support and the connection with co-workers have a strong relationship with employee engagement. And the recommended solutions like building on action team, have more team activities and develop a formal both for big team (corporate HR) and smaller team will improve their engagement over time.

● Organizations need to increase their performance by both efficiency and productivity. Managers would hardly deny that employees make a criticial difference in innovation, organization performance, competitiveness and lead to the business success. Hence, HR plays an important role in the employee engagement program with the responsibilities of the survey, providing feedback on results, prommoting communication in different groups of people, encouraging people to take action and providing educational opportunities. Employees growth, teamwork mangement support and basic needs are needed to measure by relevant questions in viewpoint survey by using five point scale. Personal growth is measured by talking about the progress and having job opportunity grow. The options count, mission and purpose fellow employees who committed to quality work and having a best friend at work and identified as the questions for measuring team work . Management support is measured by opportunity to do the best , recognition or praise care and encourage the development.

● Employee survey can reflect employees engagement , e.g. one viewpoint survey for the past three years and every time survey has chance to let employees fill the survey in, then HR managers can get the results to give scores. Managers should take get move real feedback from different department staff's positive or negative emotion or feeling aboug whose job tasks, whether they worry about any job difficulties. Hence, surveys can let organizations try to figure out of their employees are engaged and how to make them engaged by using different surveys and tools to stay competitive and improve performance.

● In survey contents, there are four main topics in the engagement survey: growth, teamwork, managment support and basic needs. The result can show the most items in engagement support were scored relatively low or high as mean of development support from manager. Hence, many organizations were focusing on designing a successful reward system to keep employees engaged and productive line or the low level managers who can serve their employees are typically the ones who work or fail the engagement tools because line managers need often communicate and contact workers when they are working. They can know what their feeling to their job tasks whether it is positive or negative emotion in order to find solutions how to raise their performance.

●
●
●
●

CHAPTER EIGHT

● What is the relationship between human resource ● strategy and corporate strategy

●

● In my opinion, it is very important how to implement one effective human resource (HR) management strategy, such as the development, award (compensation) management, learning and training (talent mangement), job evaluation (performance management review or appraisal, selection and recruitment activities. Because if the organization can achieve one effective HR strategic plan, then it will influence its organizatinal corporate strategy to achieve more successful. Otherwise, if it can not implement on effective HR strategy, then it will not influence its organizational corporate strategy to achieve more successful. I shall give my opinion to explain as below:

●

● Ong Teong, W (2010) explained that one organization hopes to acvieve corporate strategic success. It needs to implement a result-management system to achieve results through and with people. The steps include: The first step is strategic focus: product/service delivery process, operation process flow, functional analysis, performance expectations and operation manual elements. Then second step , it divides two channels. The first channel is from stragic focus to achieve employee performance result as well as the another channel is to plan the management management(expectation), it includes: keu results areas, key performance indicates and target elements of action plans.

●

● Then, it will implement the third step of performance management and review, it includes: evaluation: motivating, communication, coaching and counseling. Next it will bring two channels to the fourth step, the first channel is either it brings control to implement the performance appraisal and the performance appraisal stemp will give feedback to the first step of strategic focus again as well as the another channel is to give feedback to performance measurement second step again.

●

● Thus, in consequence, operations manual, performance measurement, performance management and review and performance appraisal four steps will need to give feedback to achieve the employee performance final result step. So, the author indicated the whole results-measurement system whether it can achieve effective or non-effective employee performance result. It depends on how its first step of strategic focus implement plan to achieve either effective or non-effective performance measurement step, performance management and review step and performance appraisal step in order to achieve an effective or ineffective employee performance result or aim. So, it seens that one organization hopes to achieve excellent employee performance result or aim, the corporate's strategic focus will influence how it can plan one good results-management system to achieve good results through and with people. Thus, the organization's first step how to plan strategic focus, this step is very important to influence how it can bring either excellent employee performance result or poor employee performance result.

●

● What is the strategic focus mean? It can be explained as to predetermine the ner term course of action and direct all business processes and functional activities to the collective priority of the organization for the year as a mangerial planning function. Expected organizational key results areas are also made known. So if the organization can predetermine that whether it ought how to do action and follow the correct directions to implement its functional activities to all business processes. It will bring effective human resource strategic plan to implement to achieve excellent employee performance result. Otherwise, if the organization cn not predetermine that whether it ought how to do action and follow the wrong directions to implement its functional activities to all business processes. It will not bring effective human resource strategic plan to implement to achieve excellent employee performance result. Thus, direct directions to strategic focus plan is a important factor to influence the organization's human resource strategic plan success in order to achieve either excellent employee performance result or poor employee performance result.

●

● How can human resource management influence to strategic focus ? HRM can be defined: hiring and developing employees, so that they become more valuable to influence the organization's strategic focus whether it is success or fail. HRM includes: conducting job analyses, planning personnel needs, and recruitment, selecting the right people for the jobs, orienting and training, determining and managing wages and salaries, providing benefits and incentives, appraising performance, resolving disputes and communication with all employees at al levels. Som these elements will influence whether the organization can bring either excellent employee performance result or poor employee performance result.

●

● Why does knowledge management can improve some organizations' employee performance to be better? Knowledge management is about developing, sharing and applying knowledge within the organization to gain a competitive advantage. It has argued that knowledge is dependent on people, and that HRM activities , such as recruitment and selection, education and development, performance management and pay/rewards as well as the creation of a learning culture are important for managing knowledge within organizations.

●

● However, knowledge is either explicit or implicit. In this classification , explicit knowledge is considered to be formal and objective, and can be numbers and specifications. It can therefore be transferred via formal and systematic methods in the form of rules, procedures. Otherwise, implicit knowledge is subjective, situational , and is tied to the knower's experience. This makes it difficult to formalize, document and communicate to others. Insights, personal beliefs and skills and using a rule to solve a complex problem are example of implicit knowlege, such as learning computer software designing knowledge is one kind of implicit knowledge. So, implicit knowledge can be shared in relational situations, such as mentorships, and coaching and through in-house trainings, where experienced employees are encouraged to share their experiences with their colleagees.

●

● In one organization, knowledge management is needed to let its employee to understand such as: what an organization knows, the location of knowledge , e.g. in the mind of a expert, e.g. computer software designing trainer in a specific computer software designing department, in old files' records, with a specific team etc. in what form this knowledge is stored, in the minds of experts, such as one computer software designing company's computer software designing trainers' minds, on paper, in notes of how to write the kind of computer software programme, how to best transfer this knowledge to the relevant people, e.g. the computer software designing trainees in order to take advantage of it and ensure that it is not lost, e.g. the kind of computer software designing skill and the need to methodically assess the organization's actual know-how versus the organiation's needs and to act accordingly, e.g. how to select to hire the most suitable employee to do the position, or how to follow the rules to promote specific in-house knowledge creation. Thus, knowledge management is useful or helping to any organization's employee skillful development because it focuses on knowledge as an actual asset, rather than as something intangible. If the organization can transfer its any knowledge to be actual asset, it enables an organization to better protect and exploit what it knows , and to improve and focus its knowledge-development efforts to match its needs.

●

● I shall indicate computer software product manufacturing industry, knowledge management is important to influence the computer software company's software sale number. For example, computer software design industy, any computer software design organization ought need have good knowledge management strategy to improve its computer software designing programmer individual skill level to be upgraded in order to raise their every one computer software design programme skill. Thus, learning and training strategic plan is very important to computer software sale company's software design programmers or trainees). The computer software design trainer need have more

● working experience to design software program and the high educational level for computer software designing program course if they want to be the trainers in any computer software companies in order to apply their computer software programming design skill or knowledge level to teach different different kinds of unique computer software design program

knowledge concepts and theories and programming skill in order to let their computer software designing program trainees who can learn how to create different kinds of new and unique computer software products to cope further unpredictive different kinds of computer software product users
● needs.
●
● Thus, such as computer software program designing organization case example, it explains that why strategic focus can influence its employee performance, such as computer software programmer. If the computer software program designing organization can have one effective strategic focus or corporate strategic plan, how to process of formulating, implementing and evaluating business strategies to achieve organizational objectives, e.g. it's human resource of computer software program designing trainee training aim is that how to apply computer software design program knowledge concept and computer software program designing trainers know how to transfer their computer software design knowledge skills to their trainees easily in order to improve their computer software design knowledge to create and innovate the unique computer software to satisfy its further computer software product buyers' needs. Thus, when it have right or correct directions , e.g. how to teach its computer software program designing trainees to design unique computer software products to cope computer software buyers' needs. Then, its computer sodtware trainees will have more computer software program designing knowledge concept thinking to solve any computer software program designing problem, doing the most right methods or decisions makings to design computer software products innovations, taking risks and facing uncertainty to adopted the unpredictive further computer software product buyer individual need more easily. So, knowledge management skill to computer software program designing trainers which is very important to influence whether the kinds of computer software products are popular to accept to use for the computer software company. Also, it implies that when the computer software company has a right or correct strategic focus implement plan, then it will bring the correct or right knowledge management training courses to suggest its computer software trainers to know whether they ought how to teach or train their computer software trainees in order to imprive their computer software program designing skills effectively in order to satisfy its further unpredictive computer software company clients or individual computer software users their needs

more attractively in the global competitive computer software sale market.

●

● Thus, in computer software sale industry, training and learning strategy is one important part of human resource strategy to any computer software sale companies nowadays. Because computer software consumers had been often changing different kinds of computer software products' demands, they need to raise their software qualities to satisfy their needs. If the computer software company has none any excellent computer software programmers to design any new and unique computer software products to satisfy further unpredictive computer software product users' changing needs. Then, they can choose to buy another computer software company's software products which can provide similar or better software functions to replace its traditional software products easily. So, the training and learning development is one important factor to influence the computer software company whether its software sale number can be increased or decreased easily. It depends on the knowledge level of its computer software programmers. So, the software designing knowledge is every software programmer individual tangible asset to influence the computer software company's any kinds of software product sale number. It assumes that the software company can increase software sale number easily if it own many number of high software program designing skillful software programmers. Otherwise, if it own less number of high software program designing skillful software programmers. it can not increase software sale number easily, even it will decrease software products sale number.

●

● Hence, it explains why some organizations need have skill satisfaction, such as computer software design organization case example, for HR to have a major role in software program designing organizational business strategy, it needs to have the kind of right software program designing skills to its different kinds of software program trainees. Highly correlated with HR's overall role in strategy are business partner skills, such as software program designing skills. Included in the scale are businss understanding, software designing strategic planning, how software organizational department's organization design and cross-functional experience of different kinds of software designing skills, e.g. who can be the kind of software designing trainer. it is harding surprising that these different kinds of software desinging skills are so strongl related to one computer software program desinging organizational HR's role in strategy. They are all critical and capability to engage in any computer software product sale organization's business decisions and to deliver organizational -level to different kinds of software programming products design method in one software product sale organization. It is consistent with the point that, to be a strategic partner to the software designing organization, such as the computer software trainers. HR needs to understand the computer software business, e.g. how to select the most excellent software designing trainers to teach the different kinds of software designing knowledge to their diffeent kinds of software designing trainees to learn in order to improve o upgrade their software program designing skills effectively.

●

● In conclusion, it explains that every organization of strategic focus is different . It depends on whether what kinds of product it sells or what kinds of service it serves. Such as computer software product sale organization, it's strategic focus is how to design the different kinds of unique software products to satisfy software product , such as company software or individual software users' needs. Hence, training and learning department is one important department to influence its software product sale number. It must need excellent software trainers to teach their software trainee individual software designing knowledge in order to improve every one software designing skills in order to cope further software product buyers' needs, when it chooses th right training and learning strategic plan to train its software designing skills. Then, they can have more confidence to design any kinds of good quality of software products to sell in global software product market successfully, e.g. the software sale company can have new kinds of software products to promote to sell every three month. Hence, it seems that right strategic focus will influence right HR strategic plan to be implement to improve employee performance or better quality of software productive result. It explains that learning and training department is needed to computer software sale industry.

●
●
●
● Effective training on employee performanc
●
● An effective training can maximize the job performance. Every organization' responsibility to enhance the job performance of the employees and certainly implementation of training and development is one

of the major steps that most companies need to achieve this. Organizations need to utilize human resources effectively. Training of human resources needs to fit into the organization's structure as this it will make the organizations achieve their goals and objectives.

●

● For telecommunication industry case example, how to carry on one effective training to raise employee efficiency. It includes these questions:

● What training programs exist on the telecommunications sector? What are the training objectives what methods are used and do these methods meet the training objectives? How does training affect employee performance? Why does telecommunication industry employees need training is better? Training is a type of activity which is planned a systematic and it results in enhanced level of skill, knowledge, and competency that are necessary to perform work effectively.

●

● In telecommunication organization, staffing needs to ensure that the right people are available at the right time in the right place. Thus involves identifying the nature of the job and implementing a recruitment and selection process to ensure a correct match within the organization. Training and development are often used to choose the gap between current performance and expected future performance.

●

● How does training and development provide performance feedback, identifying individual strengths and weaknesses, recognizing individual performance, assisting in goals identification, evaluating goal achievement identifying individual training needs, determining organizational training needs, improving communication and allowing employees to discuss concerns.

●

● There are a number of alternative source of appraisal includes to train telecommunication staffs, manager, supervisor appraisal is done by am employee's manager one level higher, self appraisal performance by the employee prior to the performance interview,

●

 ●

●

●

● Reference

●
● Ong Teong, W. (2010), Results management effective people management to acheve cxcellent results: Singapore, John Wiley & Sons (Asia) pte. ltd. pp.1-8.
●
●
●

   ● How human resource brings
● benefits to organizations
●

● Why do some organizations need human resource department(HRD)? Why do some organizations also need human resource strategy? What will occur if the organization has none human resource department? I shall attempt to explain as below:

● Torraco, R.J. & Swanson, R.A. (1995) indicated that the role of HRD in organization strategic planning. Two factors have influenced HRD toward a more active role in the formulation of busines strategy. They include the centrality of information -technology to business success, and the sustainable competitive advantage offered by workforce expertise. These two factors work together in such a way that the competitive advantages they offer are nearly impossible to achieve without developing and maintaining a highly competent workforce.

● What will be human resource department's positive influence to bring to organization's benefits? I assume that HRD is a more influential role at the point of strategy formulation and is becoming on of the key determinants of business strategy. Due to this rapidly changing business environment fator, it requires a dynamic strategy planning process and flexible use of resources . So, I assume that HRD is a formative role in both the strategic planning process and in developing innovative , competent human resources in large size organization.

● In fact, human resource department can bring various benefits to large size organizations. Some benefits may be calculated , e.g. raising productive bumber, reducing employee turnover number, but other some benefits may only be feeling, e.g. improving employee engagement performance, building positive employee work attitude, building employee loyalty and organizational warming culture. So, if one large organization has one effective HR department, it can help the organization to achieve above these any one of aims easily.

● Moreover, every human resource department ought have HR management strategy, it includes these elements: planning HR needs, staffing organizations based on HR needs, compensating and motivating employees, appraising employee behaviors, enhancing potential e.g. training and development, maintaining effective work relationships and work environment. Meeting current needs to every department staff, e.g. what are the application to the position's minimum requirement, whether the applicants need to raise skill level, knowledge, expertise, education level to apply the position. Forecasting when the department will have staff number shortage challenge ot excessive staffs number, it needs to plan when to need to reduce the staff number to some positions in the department before the deparment feels that it does not need extra employees in short time. Succession HR planning to ensure year organization can provide skillful training and learning knowledge to avoid talent employees and organizational knowledg lost. increasing maximum utilization of individuals to achieve organizational objectives, supervising employees to work efficiently and effectively in all levels.

● Hence, HR department role is advisor. It needs to provide advice and services in the following areas. On an ongoing basis: maintenance of HR records, recuitment, selection, orientation, training and development, compensation and benefits , administration, employee counselling and labour relations. All HRM functions are interrelated as well as each function affects other areas. The functions include how to manage every employee's performance, it is one goal-oriented process directed toward ensuring organizational processes are in place to maximize productivity of mployees, teams as well as how to achieve formal system of performance as team task performance, how to achieve compensation to all rewards that individuals receive as a result of their employment.

● Compensation can influence direct financial compensations, e.g. wages, salaries, bonuses and commission , indirect financial compensation (benefits), e.g. vacations, sick leave, holidays, and medical insurance, non-financial compensation , e.g. satisfaction that person receives from job itself or from psychological and/or physical environment in which person works. Employers also need to concern safety and health to its employees, such as protecting employees from injuries caused by work-related accident and freedom from illness and their general physical and mental well being: human resource activity is often referred to as industrial relations, because business is required by law to recognize a union and bargain with it in good faith if the firm's employees want the union to represent them, e.g. one airline firm's front line service employees plan to strike on job, due to they feel their salaries are below than market salary level. So, they will find union to represent them to complain the airline, e.g. stopping on continue to work in unlimited period. They will wait till to the airline management can meet them to discuss their unfair salary issue. Then, the airline needs have one HR compensation represent to be arranged on what day and time to plan how to meet them to solve their complaints. Hence, the airline labour relation represent needs have good negotiation skill to persuade them to continue to work in the shortest time in order to avoid airline travellers' dissatisfaction, due to planes are delayed to fly. So, HR department needs have good negotiation function to solve labour related issues nowadays.

● However, human resource department's function , instead of selection, recuitment, reward, training, performance evaluation etc. functions. The benefits arrangement function is also very important to influence employee individual engagement to bring positive attitude to work in the organization. I shall indicate global public service (government)'s police force organization case for example to explain why whose human resource department needs to consider policemen benefits issues. Because if the country's public service police force organization can provide excellent benefits to encourage them to do catching thiefs activities hardly. Then, I believe that the country's crime rate to itself country will be fallen down , even to the miniumal level , zero crime occurrence. Then, it will influence the country's critizen will live in safe environment and many different countries travellers will choose to go to the safe country to travel in preference when they feel the country's crime rate is low, so the crime chance will be less to occur to the traveller himself/herself. When he/she is staying in the country's journey time.

● I shall indicate Hong Kong (HK) public service police force organization example, its HR department is considering policeman individual welfare issue. It insource one welfare department to deal all policeman individual welfare needs. So, HK policemen individual welfare can include: insurance, free holiday living vacation appartment, subsidiary of travelling air ticket price allowance, HR policeman individual adult son or daughter whose overseas education subsidiary allowance, low market rate of rent private living quarters, low interest private loan , low interest education loan etc. different kinds of benefits. So, HK pubic service police force organization whose HR function is considering policeman individual welfare need. It aims to encourage every one has more engagement to catch any thiefs to achieve zero crime final result aim as well as it hope to let travellers feel safe to choose to travel to HK , this small city as well as it hopes HK citizen can feel safe to live HK to reduce emmigrant to overseas number. It seems that HK government's police force organization's welfare issue will be HR main function. It will follow different HK policeman individual beneficial nees to arrange the most satisfactory beneficial arrangement to provide their needs. So, it also seems HK policemen will consider whether HK police force employer can provide what kinds of benefits to persuade themselves to select to join to HK government police force organization to work. Hence, how to arrange different kinds of benefits to satisfy HK policemens' needs. It will be HK police force's main part of function for HK police force organization. When this organization has good benefits to satisfy HK policemens' extra need , instead of attractive salary and promotion rank chance.

● Financial and non-financial benefits will be global police force organizations which need to consider matter if they hope their country policemen can have more engagement to do catching thiefs activities in order to achieve zero crime occurence final aim. Moreover, every private or public organizations' benefit policy can influence the organization's employees performance either improve or not improve. Because nowadays employee will consider whether the organization can give provide what kinds of benefits to encourage them to stay to the organization to work longer time. If the organization can provide attractive benefits to let its employees to feel financial and non-financial reasonable reward, instead of basic salary /wage reward. Then, reasonable benefits can enourage their working performance to be improved. So, any organizations' HR department ought consider whether whose organization's employees have any benefits need in order to reduce employees turnover number and imprve working performance and efficient working productivities. So, how to choose the suitable benefits arrangement issues , it will be future HR department's one part of important function to any private or public service organizations.

● Finally, the another consideration is how to achieve HR planning. How it will provide the managerial function of an organization, such as it ensures adequate supply of human resource,, it ensures proper quality of human resource, it ensures effective utilization of human resource. However, human resource planning must incorporate the HR needs in the organizational goals, HR planning must be directed towards clear and well defined objectives. HR plan must ensure that it has the right number of people and the right kind of people at the right time doing work for which they are economically most euitable, HR planning should concern the principle of periodical reconsideration of new developments and extending the plan to cover the changes during the given long period. So, HR planning will given the organization to estimate and project the supply and demand for different categories of personnel in the organization for the years to come. For example, HRP can help the government to allocate its resources to the various sectors, e.g. agriculture, industry etc. depending upon the priority accorded to the particular sector. It can help industry sector to estimate the more accurate employee demand number and the labour market employee supply number in order to avoid employee shortage challenge or excessive employee number to the organization's different departments.

● HR planning perios can include activities planning, daily and weekly (short term) e.g. the department supervisor writes specific actions, responsibilities, cost time schedule and organizational profitability , day-to-day and week -to-week plans and work schedule decentralized throughout the firm. The intermediate range planning (3-5 years) , e.g. deployment of resources, acquisitions, divestments and internal development of product line need for employee number increasing or decreasing arrangement. The strategic planning (5 to more years) long term, it is corporate philosophy value system and policies, goals and objectives, key success factors, product market scope, competitive allocation of resources, analysis of issues raised by external factors, employment demand and manpower supply analysis, forecasting total staffing level, number of managers and personal forecasting changes in managers and key personnel, activities , e.g. planning change whose current positions to seek another firm's positions or planning to promotion for the employee's career planning.

● Consequently, HR department function will need to predict every employee individual activities and how to influence its organizational development, e.g. predicting the employee plans when to find nother employer to replace current employer, predicting when the employee hopes to earn promotion chance during he/she feels bored to do current job duties, predicting when the employee will feel his/her basic salary /wage is not reasonable and he/she needs extra welfares to be provides to satisfy his/her award needs. Hence, future HR department ought not consider how to improve group or team work performance to excite whole members' working performance. It ought serve it organizational employee individual's award needs, it seems to be one social worker role to consider whether what kinds of salary and benefits need to every employee individual who is actual hoping in order to avoide the employee turnover number increasing to bring training expenditure to need to be increased to train any new employees who replace the leaving employees. So, HR 's main function ought need to achieve to reduce the aim of employee turnover number to be increased for any organization in long term. An effective HR department which ought persuade any old employees to choose to stay to himself/herself organization to work for long term. This is HR department's one important strategic aim for any organizations nowadays because the resigning employees will attribute whose skills to another new firm when he/she chooses to leave his/her organization. Then, it means that the firm help the another competitor to raise its competitive effort from its training's any resigning employees. It will bring negative influence to replace its market position. So, how to persuade old employees to stay to itself's company to work for long term issue, it will be value to every firm's HR department to need to spend to research to solve their leaving reasons because every old employees will be any organization's assets.

-
-
-
-
- reference
- Torraco, R.J. & Swanson, R.A. (1995). The strategic roles of human resource development, HR planning, 18(4), pp.10-21.
-
-
-
-
-
-
-
-
-

CHAPTER NINE

● Solving human resource
● international organization
● strategic challenges

● When one company is one international company, it needs have offices are located in overseas. So, its staffs will be different countries' people and people's cultures are totally different. It will influence how they cooperate to work in teams efficiently together. If they feel difficult communication, then will have possible to bring poor performance or inefficient productivities. So, one firm has office(s) in overseas. The human resource (HR) department needs to consider how to deal to let every different countries' staffs feel easy communication in order to cooperate efficiently. It will increase to need for highly qualified multicultural managers as organizations globalize their operations. Therefore, a resource-based view of human resource management is needed to utilized. In view of human capital needs to provide insight into the value of managers to have unique local market knowledge, i.e. social knowledge. So, they can help organizations to develop / maintain a distinct competitive advantage in the markets they enter, if they hope to enter overseas market to sell their services to the country market successfully.

● It brings these question: How will these global population and economic change impact the HR management practices of global organizations in overseas market development? How to maintain resources in various increase competitive advantage against global competitors, when the organization needs to develop overseas market?

● I shall indicate case , such as how Japan firms can implement human resource strategy to manage their foreign employees when their organizations hope to enter overseas market? The typically Japanese ways in which Japanese companies have long arranged their human resource stragegies are certainly changing.

● However, Japan's organizational culture is different to overseas countries, e.g. US, UK etc. western countries' organizational cultures. Hence the Japan company needs to change it's culture to attempt to adapt western countries' staffs cultures, when it plans to set up office(s) in any western (countries). Because it needs to employ western staffs who owned the country's sales experiences to assist its Japanese salepsople to cooperate to sell its poducts to any western country (countries)' market more easily in possible. Alos, it means the Japan firm HR manafers or any department managers need to change whose management attitude to adapt the western countries staffs working culture to cooperate to work in order to achieve to raise performance or improve productive efficiencies.

● Hence, the Japan firm's Japanese human resource manager needs to concern how to particular qualify management system to adapt western working culture, consensus decision-making, building foreign employee loyalty to its overseas branch images and avoiding a look of gender equality in the workplace. Japan forms like to train employees, making them to own with a range of skills and abilities that they can contribute to the company throughout their career. Lifetime employment also leads to a decreased turnover rate for company. However, this kind of continue training method, it is not absolute to be adapted to some western countries because some western countries' staffs who do not accept their employers force them often need continue training courses to improve or raise their skills aim. They only like to spend time to attend one time training course finishing or sometime attend in house training courses in their companies. They feel that company is wasting their working time to learn non-essential or unuseful knowledge or skill. So, when a Japan firm needs overseas western staffs need to often be trained, it will bring the western staffs choose to leave its company earlier. So, Japan firm needs to concern continue lifetime training method whether it is suitable to any western countries' staffs to be accepted to spend working time to learn extra new skills or knowledge. For this working suitation example, if one western employee feels busy that he/she needs to finish whose current tasks today immediately, but the company will need he/she attends the training course to learn immediately. Then, it will bring he/she feels worry anout whether he/she can finish his/her tasks today to avoid whose superviser feels angry. Hence, how to arrangement suitable training time , that is imporant factor to influence the western staffs to feel whether the Japan employer really considerate their work need. Hence, Japan human resource management needs to concern how the immediate short -term training course impact will bring western countries employees' complaints and dissatisfaction. Consequently, it is important to influence western employees' performance to be poor of the Japan firm skill needs some countries' western employees often need to attend training courses to learn something immediately.

● When one firm needs to set up office(s) to be operated in overseas market. It needs to concern what is the comparative HRM between itself country and foreign countries. For example: Who is living or has lived in a foreign country? Who can speak two or more languages? Who has non-academic work experience? These comparative factors will influence whether the company ought follow what the requirement level to select the most right foreign employees to serve its overseas office organization. Becauuse if the firm can select the most right foreign applicant to do the position in the overseas office(s). It will bring positive long-term consequences: Individual well-being organizational effectiveness and societal well-being. The company needs to considerate the comparative issues, e.g. what is the recruitment and selection difference beteen itself country and its foreign coutries markets when it has no market economy link? What is the working time flexibility need between itself country and its foreign countries markets ? What is the salary level difference between itself country's staffs demand and its foreign countries staffs demand? What is the training need difference between itself country's staffs and ots foreign country staffs' needs? What is the downsizing need difference between itself country and its foreign countries organizations?

● Can outsourcing foreign human resource strategy raise foreign employee individual performance? If the company selected to find one foreign job agent to help it to select whom is the right foreign applicant to do the position in overseas office(s). The foreign job agent is located at overseas, such as US office is the China firm's foreign office . So, the foreign job agent company will locate in US. It is better than the firm's home country job agent to outsource staffing selecting job to it to do, because when the outsourcing staff selecting job agent is the firm's home town , but it needs to help the firm to select foreign employees. It is very difficult for it to contact these any foreign applicants as well as the home country's outsoucing selecting foreign employees job agent does not have same working cultural management to know how to help the home country firm to seek the suitable foreign applicants to do any positions to work in its overseas offices more easier than one foreign outsourcing foreign employees selecting job agent.

● Hence, it seems that one international organization needs to set up offices to let its different department managers to cooperate with the foreign countries (country) employees. The foreign outsourcing staffing selecting job agent can help it to select the most right foreign applicants to cooperate with the company's local manager(s) more easily. When the organization nees to employ 100 foreign employees, even 100 foreign employees, It's HR department has no enough time to select whom are the most suitable foreign employees to fill the foreign vacancies. Hence, the foreign outsoucing staffing selecting job agent will be the best choice to replace the international firm's HR department or local job agent to arrange how to select the most right foreign employees to cooperate with its local manager(s) to work in overseas office(s) in team together. The international firm's HR department can only concentrate on dealing local employees issues. All foreign employees recruitment activites which will be arranged to deal from the foreign outsourcing job agent.

● However, concerning foreign employee performance evaluation, reward management, training arrangement , benefits , promotion department's issues which will be dealed from the international firm's itself HR department. The foreign outsourcing staffing selection job agent is one assistant role. It only needs to gather all foreign outsourcing employee individual file of productivities record, performance reward record, clients complaining record, salary level record to let the department managers to know. Then all these foreign employee individual personal record information will be sent to the international firm's HR department to review at every year end. This international firm's HR department will enquire every overseas branch offices' deparment managers recommendation about every foreign employee individual performance as well as it will follow up all these foreign employee personnel data record to evaluate whether whom can be promoted or dismissed or increased salary level, or provided more benefit, or none change to the foreign employee. Hence, every foreign department manager's duty will need to supervise every foreign employee team performance to evaluate whether which is efficient or non-efficient team in order to decide whom foreign employee ought need to be promoted or dismissed or increased salary or trained to raise skills or working knowledge.

● In conclusion, it is better to any international firms to find foreign outsourcing staff selecting job suitable foreign employees to do the positions in foreign offices. It can help itself HR department to share workload definitely.

● Outsourcing HR advantages and disadvantges

● Some large organizations will choose to outsource their some HR tasks from outsourcing HR specialists to help them to do some HR related tasks, e.g. selection, performance, reward, management etc. consultant tasks. Hence, these outsourcing HR specialist will be the firm's consultant role. It needs to give recommendation whether how it ought follow which performance management method is the suitable to achieve to evaluate every employee individual performance more accurate in order to decide the employee ought need to be promoted or raised salary level, or it ought how to choose reward or benefit management plan to achieve the most reasonable and the most attractive award policy to compensate to every employee and benefit in order to let its award is fair to every need.

● It brings these questions: How does tht firm decide whether it ought seek outsourcing HR specialists to live recommendation need ? Whether which kinds of HR related tasks, it ought choose outsource to HR specialists to replace its HR department's some tasks?

● Outside resourcing or outsourcing of HR tasks is seem by manay as a future trend, which brings many benefits to the partners between the HR specialist partner and the outsourcing client. So, in long term beneficial cooperation relationship , the HR specialist will be one partner role to its outsoucing HR client. Because it hopes it can contribute to find its HR recommendation service, it will spend more time and effort to concentrate on gathering datas concern the firm's every employee performance evaluation method data or /and reward management method data whether they both are the best HR strategies to evaluate every employee performance fairly and give reward to every one fairly. If it found a few HR problems appear, due to demanding requirement of clients, or its clients feel lack of experience leading to solve HR difficulties in selecting which kinds of selection, performance evaluation, reward and beneficial methods are the best suitable to satisfy employee individual need. It will need to spend time and effort to compare different kinds of performance evaluation and award and beneficial methods to decide whether which one is the best suitable method to be used for their organizations' reward and performance strategies.

- Wilcocks, Fitzgerald, (1993) explained the following options for HR outsourcing given the multiple criteria of classification as below:
- (1) The proportion of HR outsourcing , total selective, partical.
- (2) Outsourcing can be applied in human strategy, project development management and service management.
- (3) The outsourcing contract can be general, transitional or of an economic process.
- (4) The type of outsourcing relationships can be described as: one provider -one customer , one supplier more customers, some vendors , a or several vendors, more customers.
- (5) The period of outsourcing can be on long term or short term.
- (6) Location of the supplier is local, international, offshore and regional (near shore) , closer to the customer.
- The components of an HR outsourcing strategy needs to include these elements to bring these benefits from one human resources outsourcing company. They include: on benefit administration aspect, employee insurance plans arrangement, e.g. health, dental, pension, personnel files ; on HR management aspect, HR consulting, employee communication, counsel for employee issues, training arrangement, interview arrangement; on employment law aspect, solving employee labour somplaints, dealing labour union and employee individual benefits argument issues. However, HR outsourcing also brings disadvantages to organizations. If the HR outsourcing specialist changes high service fee. It will bring high cost to the outsoucing firm. When, it can not achieve to reduce HR employement costs, improve employee individual performance, raise efficient productivities.
- So, the HR outsourcing firms ought to choose some simple HR tasks to attempt to examine the first choice of outsourcing HR specialist's effort, if it feels its service performance is not achieve its need. Then, it won't lose too much service fee. It can choose another outsourcing HR specialist to replace it. The outsourcing HR specialists' service may include as below:
- Outsourcing to improve overall cost and predictability of employee benefits. So, the outsourcing HR specialist needs to maintain the quality, options and features of suitable employee benefits. They include health care coverage, e.g. medial , dental choice health care flexible spending planning arrangement, commuter benefit life insurance and personal accident insurance, short term and long term disability insurance choice arrangement.
- Outsourcing to reduce payroll and adminitration burdens. So the

outsourcing HR specialist needs to bring a benefit to the HR outsourcing client from a decrease in time spending with payroll processing and maintaining wage records, receivable reliable assistance with tasks such as: payroll processing that export pay check preparation and delivery.

● Assistance with employer-related laws and regulation , e.g. administister people in accordance with the country's labour law, and help to the outsourcing HR firm client properly report salary tax to government administer unemployment claims.

● Helping the HR outsoucing client to reduce liability , such as solving any employee individual complaint with HR related law and dealing workers' compensation cliams support.

● Helping the HR outsourcing client to access to seasoned HR professional. It employs knowledgeable professionals who specialize in HR and can be trusted to handle issues in timely and thorough manner, including: employee liability awareness training, employee relations support, employee claiming investigation and mediation.

● Helping the HR outsourcing client to freedom to focus on core business issues, e.g. giving recommendation how to improve employee performance, raising productivities growthm, avoiding reduce non-related employee essential cost.

● HR related cost reduction aim

● In fact , many organizations choose HR outsouring. Their main aim is cost HR relation reduction. They hope outsourcing HR specialist can help them to give the best HR cost redicing recommendation, e.g. how to improve employee performance and raise productive efficiency, how to reduce employee adsenteeism number, how to reduce employee turnover leaving number, how to raise employee individual engagement, how to apply interview method to select the best employees to fo any low , middle and high level positions , how to attract talent applicants to choose to apply their organizations' any positions, how to raise employee morale. All these cost will be HR related cost, when the organization decides to seek one outsourcing HR specialist to help them to implement any HR strategies effectively.

● Hence, such one international firm which needs to set up office in overseas. It can outsources one overseas HR specialist to give recommendation and help it how to select the foreign country's the best quality of employees to serve its foreign organization, how to arrange the most suitable and the most attractive reward and welfare benefit to attract foreign employees to work for its foreign organization, how to select the best performance evaluation methods to measure every foreign employee individual performance more accurate in order to judge whom has the actual effort to be promoted to do complex jobs more accurate. Because when one international firm needs to enter overseas market to sell its products or provide service, it must not familiarize the foreign country(countries) market, it must need the foreign country's HR specialist to give its recommendation how to implement its HR strategy to adapt the overseas country (countries) employees reward, welfare etc. needs. In conclusion, whether the organization needs outsourcing HR specialist to help it to implement HR strategy. It depends on the firm familiarizes the foreign country's people whether what are their actual needs in order to attract talents to choose to apply the organization's any kinds of positions. So, in this suitation, the international firm ought choose to find one foreign outsourcing HR specialist to help it to implement any HR related strategies which is better than implementing the foreign country's HR strategies from itself. Unless the international firm familiarizes the foreign country's labour market whether whom like overseas employers can provide what award and welfare in order to attract the foreign country / countries talent applicants to choose to serve its organization. Then, it can implement HR strategy to the foreign country's market from itself.

-
-
-
-
-
-
-
- reference
- Wilcocks, L. Fitzgerald, G., "market as opportunity? case studies in outsourcing information technology and services." , Journal of strategic information systems, vol. 2 no 3. 1993 pp. 201-217
-
  -
-
- Developing countries Human
- resource development whether
- need to be improved

● Do developing countries need to help human resource development to assist their businesses development, it is possible due to staff individual lacks knowledge to do whose job in whose organization ? What is the developing and developed countries' organizational human resource strategic difference, e.g. award strategies? I shall indicate one developing country,such as South Africa's businesses' general organizational human resource strategy case to explain whether what causes their human resource strategies, e.g. award managment strategies are different to compare developed countries, such as US, UK as well as I also indicate what weak points that they ought to concern in order to improve these developing countries' businesses productivities and efficienc, if South Africa 's firms hope to raise staff performance to be better. I shall explains that South Afria country governement needs to implement human resource development strategy as below:

● In general, South Africa employers feel human resource development strategy is needed to innovate and attempt to ensure that they meet the needs of their economy. So, South Africa employers are considering whether how they ought need to improve their human resource strategies in their organizations in order to raise productive efficiencies and performance to their employees effectively. In fact, because South Africa country lacks effective human resource development to recommend to itself country's businessmen how to select the right employees to do right positions, how to evaluate whom has more effort to be promoted to do senior position, lacking fair reward and welfare to compensate to their employees. So, it brings many reasons to explain why in South Africa society unemployment and poverty still existence. Not all of the reaons have to do with the capabilities of people , may have to do with the unequal distribution of productive assets in South Africa society.

● Nowadays, the South Africa employers only feel South Africa workers are only their own labour to use or sell. Hence, they won't like to provide reasonable and fair award to compensate for their Africa employees general lack high education level and skills. So, it also influences their award will not increase. Moreover, there are South Africans who have skilled labours to sell and they can not find buyers because there are not enough jobs , their skills do not match the demands, and there is a systematic process for information to flow between government, the workplace and labour.

● Hence, many South African people are unemployed, due to their knowledge are not enough to satisfy or accept to employers' demands. It will cause South African income inequality will be continue serious. The salary range between the high education level and low education level of labours' difference is large. A cycle of income inequality, low skills and poor education have limited economic growth.

● In fact, in South Africa society, many domestic people ae skilled agricultural and fishery workers, plant anf machine operators and assemblers, elementary occupational workers, non-permanent employees. They are low education level people. Otherwise, less doemstic people are legiclation, senior officials and managers, professionals, technicians and associate professionals , clerks, service are sales workers. So, the low educational level occupational domestic people must be kept low level to compare high educational level occupational people in South Africa society. However, the high education level occupational labour shortage is serious. Otherwise, the local low low educaional level labours number is excessive to supply in South Africa labour market. It causes the South Africa labour market supply and demand is inequal between the labour supply and employee demand number in society.

● Thus, South Africa government has implemented whole country's human resource development strategy. It's key mission is to maximize the potential of the people of South Africa, though the acquisition of knowledge and skills to work productivity and competitively in order to achieve a rising quality of life for all, and implement an effective HR operational plan, together with the necessary HR need arrangement to satisfy every employer's labour need. The South Africa country HR development goals: To improve the human development and an improved basic social need for critical for a productive workforce and a successful economy, to reduce disparities in wealth and poverty, and develop a more unemployment society, to improve international confidence and investor perceptions of the economy. The actions include a basic foundation, consisting of early childhood development, general education at school, and adult education and training, securing skills, with the further and higher education and training bands to anticipate and respond to specific skill needs in society, participation in lifelong learning, an articulated demand to skills, generated by th eneeds of the public and private sectors, including those acquired for social development opportunities and the development of small business, implementing a research and innovation sector which supports industrial and employment growth policies. Hence, South Africa government is concerning itself country's young people's education policy, it ought plan how to innovate in order to improve HR development to satisfy employers' labour needs for long term economic benefits.

● This new strategy therefore recognises both the demand and supply side HR issues, acknowledges that HRD is needed to implement from the foundations of early childhood development right through to labour market entry, recongizes systemic challenges as to successful HRD policy implementation, located HRD in the development issues , such as poverty, inequality, high unemployment levels. However, instead of develop countries feel HR development need. Most developed countries are also implementing a systematic strategy for HRD in support of economic growth and developments. They both feel need. It is perhaps due to the flexibility and capacity of workforce to adhust speedity and capacity of workforce in technology, production , trade and work organizations. Consequently, the ability to respond to these changes with speed and efficiency has more becaue the area where many countries seek a competitive advantage.

● However, South Africa country feels it is very serious mismatch between the supply of and demand for skills in the South Africa labour market. So, it's HRD innovation main aim is to improve future itself country's society to reduce the mismatch problem to be serious between the supply of and demand for skills in the South Africa future labour market. So, such South Africa 's inequal supply and demand for human resources in labour market case, the South Africa government is implementing a high and intermediate level skills strategy on the supply side of high education level of labour to be provided in South Africa labour market as well as a demand strategy that is stimulated large-scale labour absorbing employment growth supported by a appropriate inputs of law-level skills training in order to satisfy future public or private organizations' labour demands.

● Hence, higher education and training development will be South Africa future educational development trend in order to raise South Africa local high education knowledge level graduates number to be enough supplied to local labour market. It does not South Africa employers need to make decision to give high reward to attract overseas high educational level job competitors to go to South Africa to do any local employers' jobs. It may raise local South Africa graduates' competition in future Soutch Africa labor market. It will bring negative raising unemployment influence to South Africa high education level local graduates.

● The developed countries , such as US, UK , they have high quality of educational enough institutions to provide local students to learn different kinds of subjects, e.g. law, accounting, engineering, science, chemical, architecture etc. different kinds of professional subjects. Thus, these developed countries can have enough universities and lecturers number to provide local students' learning needs in order to find any kinds of professional jobs in local labour market. Thus, the important difference between developed countries and developing countries' labour market is that developed countries' local high education level job applicants supply number is enough to satisfy local employers' high education level labour demand number. So, in general, the developed countries' reward is needed to compensate to graduated employees, the reward number can be lower level to compare developing countries' employers. Otherwise, developing countries' employees feel difficult to find the righ high education level job applicants to fill high education level positions , due to local graduates number doe snot enough to supply to developing countries' labour market to let employers to select whom is the most right applicants. So, they need to raise general local normal reward level to attract overseas high graduation level professions to let they can select who are the high quality applicants to work in their organizations more easily. It seems that if developing countries, such as South Africa's government can raise enough universities, high schools, primary school students number and it can train many teachers to raise their teaching effort in order to raise future new yough generation's education level. Then, when these developing countries have enough high education level graduate number to be supplied to local labour market to let themselve countries' employers to select whom is the most right job applicants in order to achieve to employ the local graduate students intention.

● When any developing countries' employers choose to employ the local graduate students to fill their high educational level positions in preference. Then, their reward must not raise in order to attract overseas educational level graduate students intention. However, if developing country, such as South Africa government hopes to have enough graduate students to be supplied to local labour market. It needs to find methods how to raise teachers' teaching effort in primary, secondary and high schools in order to train them to own enough teaching effort to teach next young generation's learning need. Then, their developing countries; high -educational level graduate students number will be raised to supply in local labour markets. It will bring benefits to local employers who can reduce wage/salary to reward overseas job applicants (staffs cost reducing benefits) to bring economic development benefit when it avoids local businesses' failure risk, due to they have no enough expenditure to employ many overseas high educational level employees to fill their organizations any high education level positons in long term.

● In conclusion, developing countries' human resource development needs to be improved or revised, if there are many employers feel need to pay very high salaries to attract and select overseas high education level job applicants to fill their organizations' any high educational level positions. However, local high education development must need to revise in order to help many local students have chance to enter schools to learn to earn high education level knowledge to prepare to do any domestic employers; high education level jobs in themselves organizations. Then they will not need to raise high salary level to compensate rewards to their countries themselves local graduate students, when themselves countries have excessive high educational level graduate student applicants number supplies to domestic labour market to let local employer to choose.

●

● The relationship between human resource department and raising employee individual productive performance efficiency

●

●

● There are one considering question to any business leaders: Does human resource department need to set up to assist them to raise themselves employee individual productive performance efficiency in order to satisfy client attitude to their performance needs as well as their managers' work efficient needs? It is one very important question to be worth to any organizations' considerations. Because if the organization's human resource department can not achieve it's aim to raise employee individual efficient aim or raise product number productive aim or improve service performance aim to let their customers or managers to earn positive emotion feedback. Then, it seems that the organization's human resource department can not bring valued attribution to let its organization to earn long term economic or non-economic positive benefits from its overall employees' performance in its organizations. So, it means that it doe not need to set up one human resource department to assist the ineffective organization's human resource department. It is one non-essential effective department to the ineffective organization, even it is wasting time and management's nervous and effort and resource to develop its internal human resource department to be grown up. Thus, it also brings this question: Does it essential to set up one human resource department in any small, medium, large organizations? I shall give some useful cases and assumptions to describe whether what factors will have possible to influence employee individual efficiency or productive performance to any organizations when they have one human resource department or have no one human resource department in their organizations.

●

● Firstly, I assume the organization's one human resource department can bring some related human resource issue related benefits or causes any one of below factors as well as the organization's human resource department can cause any one of these factors to bring any one below of human resource issue related benefits to the organization when the organization had set up one in house human resource department in its organization. Then, any one of these factors can bring benefits, such as the raising productive efficiency or the improving service performance or the raising productive number etc. different human resource related benefits to the organization.

●

● Jean, W (et al.) (pp64-65,2004) stated one case study , it concerns both organizations of Quarriers and Richmond fellowship Scotland (RFS), they have grown rapidly and diversified since the mid-1990s. For example, they are increasingly delivering services, such as support for people with learning disabilities within individual's communities rather than in large scale residential projects, key informants in both organizations felt that the organizations were now at a critical point in their organizational life cycles. However, they indicated these both organizations were encountering challenges: retaining their cutting edge innovation, when controlling the level of bureaucracy that accompanies growth. At the time of this research RFS employed around seven hundred 700 staff and Quarriers nearly one thousand 1,000. Both organizations have well –developed HRD strategies and practices, (including supervision), are recognized as investors in people and providing training for managers as developers. They also aspire to be learning organizations. It seems that both organizations therefore provided appropriate working environments to explore the development behaviors of line managers.

●

● It seems that it can explain that these both mental health service organizations had set up one human resource department, it can provide effective HRD, including raising supervision skill to mental health service managers . So, the both organizations' training department can provide any useful supervising training skill courses for managers as developers to learn how to supervise their departments to raise themselves mental health service teams' efficiencies and service performance to their mental patients. Hence, their different mental health department service managers can be trained to raise excellent supervisory skills to manage and arrange their team members how to work efficiently in order to raise excellent service performance and provide high quality services continue to be delivered in respect of individuals with mental health difficulties or learning disability. These both organizations stress the values of human-centered approaches implicit in the social care model of care. Their mission statements aim to ensure the best possible high quality services continue to be delivered in respect of individuals with mental health difficulties or learning disability. This aims to meet these individual's right aspirations and needs as well as to work together to overcome personal and social disadvantages, inspire optimism , create opportunity and offer choice to children, families and others in need of support. When, these both mental health service organizations have a clear aims, then their human resource department can know what their service needs and review their mental patients' complaints in order to find what their mental health care service needs to be improved to let every mental health service managers to know and learn from its training courses more easily. So, when they know what are their aims, then their trainers can know how to teach supervision skill to let their mental care managers know they ought how to supervise their team members to work in order to raise raising service performance efficiency to serve their mental patients more easily.

●

● Thus, due to these two mental health care service organizations had set up one effective human resource department, its in –house training courses can provide excellent training service to teach the mental health service leaders knowledge and train their mental health care skills how to let they to know how to teach their every team different kinds of mental health care workers to learn their knowledge as well as provide effective supervision to manage thcm how to allocate their time to serve every mental child or family patients in order to cure every one's mental illness effectively in short time. Thus, these two both mental health service organizations had made right decision to set up one human resource department to provide in-house supervision training service in order to implement one effective supervisory strategy to let their mental health care service mangers to learn how to supervise their mental health care service workers to work effectively in order to let their mental patients to believe their mental illness to be cured satisfactorily. It seems effective supervisory is one important factor to bring these two mental healthcare service organizations' leading efforts to be obvious raised effectively. It implies that the HRD department is real need to these both mental health service organizations. If they had not designed or set up this human resource department to arrange how to provide in-house supervisory training courses to train their mental health care service managers to learn how to supervise their mental care service workers efficiently and effectively. It is possible that their mental health mangers (leaders) can not be trained to own excellent leading or supervisory efforts to supervise or lead their every team's mental health care service workers or members to serve their mental patients to let them to feel they have efforts to cure their mental illnesses satisfactory. So, the HRD is critical influential factor to arrange effective supervisory training courses to raise every mental health care mangers' supervisory effort in order to raise their mental health care service performance to bring their every team to serve their mental patients to let they feel they can provide good mental care service to cure their mental illnesses satisfactory. Hence, the consequence of the raising performance of mental health service workers, it has relationship between the HRD and the effective training supervisory factor.

●

● Leslie, W. Rus et. al (pp.62-63 2007) stated Frederick Herzberg has developed an approach to motivation that has gained acceptance in management. They explained that his theory is referred to by several names: motivation-maintenance approach, dual-factor approach, and motivator-hygiene approach. Herzberg's approach deals primary with motivation through job design. The approach is based on the belief that the factors that demotivate employees are different from the factors the motivate employees.

●

● Herzberg maintains that the factors usually associated with the work environment. These factors include much things as job status, interpersonal relations with supervisors and peers, the style of supervision that the person receives company policy and administration, job security, working conditions, pays and aspects of personal life that are affected by the work situation.

●

● Hence, he believed that raising employee individual performance , it includes these both factors. The first is hygiene factor, relates to the working environment. It includes policies and administration, style of supervision , working conditions, inter-personal relations, factors that affect employee's personal life, salary /wage status, job security feeling. The another factor is motivator factor, related to the job itself. It includes achievement, recognition, challenging work, increased responsibility, promotion or senior position advancement, personal growth. Hence, the author feels that external working environment and the job itself to the employer personal satisfactory feeling these both factors will influence how the employee individual performance to be motivated or demotivated to influence how he/she like to put how much whose effort to be performed to finish or achieve whose every task either inefficient or efficient performance. Thus, the author felt what factors can influence employees' performance to be raised or weakened. They include job stress, motivation and communication enable them to be compared to the another working environment factor., they have more influential effort to influence employee individual performance to be raised or weakened more easily. Also, he felt the job itself satisfactory feeling factor to the employee and the organization's working environment factor both must have relationship to influence any employee individual performance to be raised or weakened.

●

● The job stress can influence employee individual performance. Job stress is produced when one can't properly coordinate available resources and job demands with personal abilities. Job stress is derived from a situation of job environment to threat to an individual. Hence , if the employee often feels difficult to work in a job stress working environment. Then, it will influence her/her performance to be weakened. Thus, employers ought need to consider how to avoid any employees feel job stress to influence whose performance in their organizations. Human resource department staff relation manger can attempt to enquiry every feeling job stress of employee when he/she begins feel job stress and he ought attempt to help them to find where the causing of job stress sources are coming from external environment factors (non organizational factor, e.g. themselves mental illness or his/her unsatisfactory salary or welfare feeling to whose employer or internal organizational factor, e.g. unreasonable policy, noise and danger working environment in order to solve their negative emotion to avoid job stress causes poor performance.

●

● Another factor is motivation to influence employee individual performance, it is defined as the willingness or desire to do something, conditioned by the activity of the ability to satisfy some needs, such as the employee needs to finish the task in order to earn higher wage/salary or promotion chance or performance appreciation. So, it seems today enterprises' HRD needs to find methods how to realized that actions of motivating their employees are crucial in order to achieve the organizations' raising efficiency or productive performance or raising profit etc. different goals.

●

● The motivated employees relate to the manners of self satisfaction, sell-fulfillment and commitment that are expected produce better quality of work. So, it seems that motivation has relationship to influence employee performance, one demotivated employee won't raise employee performance. Otherwise, one motivated employee will raise employee performance. Hence HRD needs to provide training to let the managers have chance to have been asked to know the feedback gained from the employees which probably affects their work motivation. For right time of delivering such information, this they may perform based on the messages they receive. In obtaining such as good performance, the managers must show the initiatives of developing and providing opportunities to learn new skills to their employees through the communication process. Thus, such as enhancing training and non-traditional compensation , e.g. pay for skill, bonuses, gain sharing, and profit sharing, which will affect job quality. Thus, intangible factor, such as improving workplace environment and job itself quality both factors can influence employee individual working performance, instead of tangible factor, such as raising salary level, promotion or appreciation change. These both factors can make incentive in ways that reward quality and performance improvement to frontline or back office workers, instead of increasing earnings may be significant greater factor to increase motivation and productivity. The intangible factor, e.g. redesigning of the job itself often involving both new information technology and increasing worker autonomy was resulting increase in efficiency or redesigning new method to avoid the employee to feel increased task complexity, responsibility, autonomy , training and gain sharing are interdependent and mutually reinforcing. For example, it may be far more effective both to train frontline employees in problem –solving and to permit them to solve more problems than to make either change alone. Thus, it seems that more chance to promote or appreciate or higher wages encouragement which are not the main factors to influence the employee to raise performance. Because some employees will feel bore or difficult to do the job, so how to redesign the job itself to be better or more attractive or how to reduce the employee's job stress is caused by the unhappily or feeling high dangerous working environment risk or noise or dispute with difficult cooperation relation to staffs will cause poor or negative emotion to the employee , then which will be other main factor to influence the employee individual performance to be weakened or poor in the organization.

●

● However, sometimes intangible factor, e.g. job stress , boredom, promotion chance, appreciation will have more influential to the employee individual working behavior to be better or worse more than tangible factor, e.g. raising salary/wage level , increasing welfare provision , e.g. increasing holiday days, free lunch allowance, cheap air ticket allowance, son or daughter student education allowance etc. Psychological factor is more important to influence how the employee performs in the organization.

●

● The another raising employee performance factor is performance evaluation measurement plan. It has close relationship to raise employee individual efficiency and organizational effectiveness. HRD needs have an effective strategic plan or performance evaluation plan to measure effectiveness and efficiency for every employee performance measures, the performance evaluation plan can bring these advantages to the organization , e.g. making more accurate decision whether the employee is value to be promotes to do the senior position. Efficiency is oriented towards successful input transformation into outputs, where effectiveness measures how outputs interact with the economic and social environment. Thus, HRD needs to find how and why what causes the employee work inefficiency or under (below level) productive performance in order to improve her/his performance to achieve the organization's minimum performance acceptable level. For example, how to upgrade the low talent or foolish employee job related knowledge or skill to be better or improved when he/ she feels difficult to finish the job.

●

● In effectiveness vs. efficiency view point, there are various opinions regarding valuation of any organizations. However, Chavan , M. (2009) states Frey etc. al (2009) had found the findings that efficiency information provides different data compared to effectiveness one. So the chain of effects: From efficiency information (input is the first step causes the process step), then the second process step brings the causation or consequent step , such as effective information (output causes the outcome final step). It is the chain of effects process. It explained that effectiveness oriented companies are concerned with output, sales, quality, creation of value added, innovation , cost reduction. It measures the degree to which a business achieves its goals or the way output, interact the economic and social environment. So, in the workplace may take various forms, such as relationship between leader and staff, employee's personal attitude with the organization, involvement in the decision making process, psychological feeling. So, it is possible that the causing supervisor performance is caused by the staff personal attitude towards the organization. Thus, organization needs to consider how to change the employee individual attitude when it occurs the employee the negative emotion or attitude to work in its organization.

●

● So, it seems the effectiveness vs. efficiency measurement strategy, such as hoe to measure efficiency between inputs and outputs or how successfully the inputs have been transformed into inputs, e.g. how to stable production, avoiding defects, reduced speed, minor, stoppages, set up and adjustment equipment failure. etc. issues which can influence employee individual attitude to be caused positive or negative emotion to work in whose organization. Employers can not neglect all these above issues because they will be possible to influence employee attitude to work efficiently or effectively. These input elements can bring either positive or negative output effort in either inefficient or efficient way. Thus, HRD needs to consider how to improve output efforts in order to raise efficiency or efficient performance to its employees. It seems that efficiency and effective measurement strategic plan factor will influence employees performance how performs in whose organizations. Hence, manpower performance can be increased by putting efforts to factors that enhance the employees' motivational level, creativity, job satisfaction and comfort workplace environment etc. intangible factors influence.

●

● Why does HRM department designing has relationship to raise employee performance? HRM can be defined as the process of analyzing and managing an organization's human resource needs to ensure satisfaction of its strategic objectives. It is a pattern of planned HR development an activities which affect the behavior of individuals with the intention of enabling organizations to achieve their goals. So, it seems that all HR activities are dependent upon the manager's efforts to formulate and implement the organization strategy as well as it has direct relationship for resulting and developing their employees as well as their behavior, attitudes, brings indirect relationship how to influence and performance to achieve the organization's goals.

●

● Thus, it brings this question: Why and how HRM can influence employee performance? We need to know employee performance is explained with quantity of output, quality of output , timeliness of output, presence attendance on the job, efficiency of the work completed and effectiveness of work completed. Hence, employee performance is the successful completion of tasks by a selected individual or individuals (team), it is measured by a supervisor or organization to pre-defined acceptable standards when efficiently and effectively utilizing available resource within a changing environment. In fact, performance is about behavior or what employees produce or the outcomes of their work. However, HRD needs have these duties, and duties can influence how employee performs, such as competitive compensation level, training and development, performance appraisal, recruitment package and maintaining morale. So, management ought need to consider how to design HRD these tasks duties or functions issues, what factors will influence how employees choose or decide to perform their behaviors to do their tasks in organizations. It seems that how to design or arrange HRD 's functions which will influence how employee individual performs to do whose tasks daily. Thus, if the organization can design its HRD has effective functions, then it will influence its employees to do more effective performance or better or improved behavioral performance in their organizations. Otherwise, ineffective HRD functions, it will influence how every employee decides or chooses to do ineffective behavioral performance or inefficient productive behaviors easily in their organizations. So, any organizations need to concern how to design their HRD's functions to be useful in order to achieve more effective consequence.

●

● Finally, I states the tourism service industry case to attempt explanation why and how HRD is needed to set up in order to raise service performance in this service industry's organizations. How to raise tourism industry service performance? For tourism industry example, this service industry will combine with many other industries, such as food and beverage, transportation, sight-seeing, health and beauty and hotel industry. However, all these industries are service nature provision, e.g. how to increasingly improve in the hotel management, service quality and work efficiency in order to increase the customers' level of satisfaction. The superior service performance issues will be the important factor to influence whole tourism industry and related tourism industries client numbers to be raised, e.g. modern international attractive airport can attract overseas travelers to visit the country's airport for their aim instead of travelling aim, beautiful sea port design and high class hotels and restaurants design, offering the best location, best service and food to let travelers to feel. So, the country's hotels themselves service quality need to be improved to attract many overseas travelers to select to visit the country when they need to live in the country's any hotels anyway, they are first time to visit this country or repeat visit to this country.

●

● Thus, when one country's any related tourism industry's service level is unsatisfactory to let it travelers to feel, then it will bring negative influence to them to choose to travel this country again. For hotel case example, how to excite the country's hotels employees' performance raising? In fact, the work performance of hotel employee is to important that the success of the hotel may depend on it highly satisfied employee will produce high quality of service and results in highly satisfied customers.

●

● I believe that how to teach hotel frontline employees to use of equipment, e.g. how to improve coffee making frontline service staffs, how to use coffee machine to coffee making knowledge, skill and positive attitude to serve the hotel clients when they have needs to buy coffee to drink in the hotel. So, the frontline hotel coffee service staffs need to be trained to apply the coffee machine how to make good taste coffee to let hotel guest to drink, or how to train the hotel frontline room booking service staffs' skill to operate the computer system to help any hotel guests to book any rooms to live or check who is the pre hotel room booking guests to avoid them to waste time to wait their rooms to live. So, the hotel training courses need have good trainers to teach any departments how to learn hotel computer system to be operated in efficient proficiency way. Because many hotel guests do not like to waste time to wait their service when they feel need to find their help. They hope that they can serve them immediatcly.

● The another factor is that hoe to let hotel frontline staffs to feel job satisfaction , it means that how the employee feels joy and happiness result from doing the job descriptions, such as joy to work with the co-workers, satisfy with the income and rewards from doing the job or good attitude towards the job, satisfaction is good attitude towards work, value of work, challenge od work , freedom of is the feeling of the work which is like or not like in the areas of job description, compensation, rewards benefits, relationship with others in the organization, such as hotel. So, hotel needs have good reward plan, performance evaluation method, job designing strategy, promotion chance in order to encourage every hotel staff to work efficiency in whose departments.

● The final factor to influence hotel employee personal working performance, it is work motivation, work motivation means something in a person to motivate them to work, to move and finish any task within the goal. Work motivation means the ability to motivate a person to work hard to achieve the objective of the work of the organization within his / her volunteer of without force. Work motivation is important tool to positively push the employee to love their work, willing to work hard to finish the task with high quality and work hard to achieve the high level of effectiveness and efficiency.

● In tourism industry, airline service and travel agent which are the prior contact travelling service providers to travelers. So, the airline attendant service will influence the travelers' choices to find the travel agent or another travel agent to buy air tickets to catch the airline's air plan or another airline. For airline service attendant performance case example, airlines feel airline attendant age will influence every service performance. Why does airlines do not permit their frontline airline passenger attendant individual age can not above 50 age or between 45 to 50 age? The reason is simple, because airline frontline passenger service attendants, they need often fly to different countries, but their working time must not fix, they have no stable working hours and time to fly. They sometime need to catch air plans in continue several nights, then they will be possible to sleep one night to continue next morning flying or night flying. Even, they have no one day sleep, they only have more than three hours or less than three hours to sleep in busy seasonal travelling periods. Hence, they will have no enough nervous to serve their airline passengers in possible. In long term lacking enough nervous air plane working environment, it will possible to influence their performance to serve their air plane passengers to be poor in possible. Thus, it explains why airlines usually do not permit their frontline airline attendants to prolong their service period to serve their airline passengers on air planes. Because airlines usually assume that they must lack enough nervous to serve their airline passengers when they need often fly overnight flying planes to arrive different countries in their frontline airline attendant career.

●

● However, many airlines do not plan to encourage them to leave their airline career early. They will choose to change their positions in house training department. So, they have enough airline passenger service working experience, they can attribute their airline passenger service knowledge to teach the junior airline attendants how they ought serve their airline passengers to let them to feel more service satisfactory feeling form their performance on air planes. SO, these airlines won't lose these old age talent airline attendant employees. Their passenger service experience can assist the new young age airline attendants to learn that whether how they do the best decision to deal any passenger complaint or sudden accident occurrence in any sudden difficult predictive flying environment in order to protect their passengers' safety or solve their reasonable or unreasonable complaints more easily. Even , if the new young age airline passenger attendant can perform very excellent to let any passengers to appreciate often. Then, the old age attendant trainer and the young age attendant both will have chance to be promoted to senior position level or raising their salary level fairly, when the HRD training department believe the excellent performance airline attendant is taught from the old age airline attendant trainer. SO, how to design the training courses quality which will have direct to influence the attendant trainers to teach their trainees to be better or worse.

●

● IN conclusion, effective HRD designing functions will bring long term economic and non-economic related benefits to raise service performance. Otherwise, ineffective HRD designing functions will not bring long term economic and non-economic related benefits to raise service performance in possible in any organizations.

●

●

●

●

●

●

●

●

●

●

●

● Reference

●

● Chavan, M. (2009) The balanced scorecard: a new challenge// Journal of management development. Vol. 28, issue 5, pp. 393-406. www. Emerald insight.com/0262.17111.htm < ziureta2011.02.24>

●

●

● Jean, W. & Monica Lee & Jim Stewart (2004). Routledge Studies In Human Resource Development: London and New York. Routledge publish, pp. 64-65.

●

● Leslie, W, Rus & Lloyd, L, Byars (2007), Supervision:

● Key Link To Productivity: America, The Mc-Graw-Hill companies Inc. pp. 62-63.

●

●

●

● Source: adopted from Frey and Widmer (2009)

●

-
-
-
-
-
-
-
-
-
-
-
-
-
-

● Human resource assists ● organizational development

●

● Human resource assists change management strategic development

●

● When on firm sets up one human resource department, whether it can assist itself organization to implement change management strategy more easily? What is change management mean? Change management is a critical part of any project that leads, manages, and enables people to accept new processes, technologies, systems, structures and values.

●

● It is the activities that helps staffs to adapt good change management from present way of working to the desired way of working. So, change management is the continuous process of operation an organization with its marketplace in order to achieve more responsively and effectively than competitors.

●

● In fact, any organization's change, it must strat with a vision. Anyway its changing need is from external environment factors influence, e.g. economic, social or technological or internal factors, e.g. policy, systems or structure , creating a vision wil clarify the direction for the change. In addition, the vision will assist in motivating those that are impacted to take action in the right direction. So it ensures that vision can assist change management more easily. However, whether human resource department strategy can follow the organization's vision to assist change management to implement more easily, when the organization feels need to change.

●

● In fact, a strategy(HR) will ensure the vision is achieved more easily when the organization needs to change, it can provide direction for achieving the vision when its organization needs to change. Without a strategic plan and vision, the change effort will not be successful easily. Hence, when the organization decides to change, it also neds to change HR strategy, e.g. how to match the best employee to change his/her old position to do the right new position from company's internal staffs choices when it needs to change , how to redesign reard o compensate new staffs when they replace the old staffs to do the the old staffs' positions. It seems that HR strategy will need to change, when the organization needs to change its internal organizational structure.

●

● However, the HR department needs to implement how to change some issues related to human resource matters, such as solving these HR problem when the organization needs to change, e.g. employee resistance, solving different communication breakdown, insufficient time devoted to training, reducing staff turnover during the organizational changing period, reduced costs exceeded budget. The change obstacles of employee resistance include solving the staffs relationship with the different department leaders' team to satisfy employee concerns on s personal acceptable level, asking for their feedback and responding to their concerns honestly and openly. The communication breakdown obstacles include communicating key information to employees on an on-going and consistent basis. Staff turnover obstacles include engaging the leader's team by involving them in the initiative, coaching, mentor and enriching their new roles.

●

● Thus, HRD needs to particular the organizational change tasks, such as needs to know what the changes, their impact, rationale and benefits are, it needs to explain them to anyone to believe the chane in worthwhile, how th change is impacting the old staff individual existing workload, or it needs to communicate the need for change to explain the first steps, how the changing position staffs need to be supported and when they have achieved quick to gain benefits to themselves, it needs to explain how the changes impact the same group, what changes will happen and when, explaining the change leaders what know their responsibilities and the commitment expectations to their team memebers, describing what change has successfully occurred in these groups in the past, explaining how and why these changing staff can learn from what work did or did not well.

●

● Hence, in the whole changing steps, HRD needs to participate every team through each stage of the change effort. The step one, it needs to assist organization to change urgent message to let staffs to know. The step two, it needs to buid a guiding team to help departmental staffs to adapt to changing tasks more easily. The step three, it needs to choose the right vision to give right direction to let organizational change method is implemented in a correct way. The step four, ot needs to commicate every for one-by-one to do empower action clearly, the need of help of changing staffs to create short -term wins in every changing process. Moreover, the HRD needs to consider thee matters do not work, such as focusing on building a rational business case, getting top management, approval, and ignoring all feeling, that are blocking change, ignoring a lack of urgency and immediately to create a vision and strategy. The HRD can not misunderstand the difficulty of driving people from their comfort zones. Hence, it needs have enough staffs number to already to replace the low skillful of employees when they can not adapt change to do the new tasks. Then, they will need have highly attractive people to be chosen to replace them to do the new changing of natural characteristic task to satisfy different department's needs after organization had changed its internal structure. Thus, HRD has responsibility to arrange enough staffs number and explains what the new changing tasks to let the changing task need of employees to know whether they ought how to do in order to adapt to do new changing of tasks more easily. Hence, it seems that HRD can assist organizatonal development when it decides to implement changing strategy in the organizational restructure changing period.

●

● HRD (human resource deapartment) assists training management strategic development

●

●

● Does HRD assist training strategic arrangement more easily? When one large organization needs to spend too much expenditure for training and development. If it had not set up one human resource department to control its cost spending, it will be possible to implement poor trainings to cause failed training. Hence, if one HRD could help every different knids of training course to focus on issues, such as training methods, selecting the most right trainer to teach different training courses, program design and following trainee characteristics to choose the most right training courses to let them to learn. Then, it will be more easier to implement every training chouse to let trainees to learn successfully.

●

● In fact, when one organization has none one effective Human resource department, it will bring high change of training failure. So, it seems that training failure has relationship with poor HRD, include: unskilled practitioner provides invalid training , skilled practitioner provides invalid training or valid training but learning does not transfer of valid training, learning transfer , but hierarchical level, organizational (dominant) is too much limited to grow up its human resource department to develop, lacking effective characteristics of human resource development, e.g. poor performance appraise standards, restricted standardized training.

●

● All of these above issues will have relationship to HRD. HRD includes psychology, sociology, managment and adult education. This is not a comprehensive review of related to training effectiveness, HRD and organizatonal culture, but is intended to be representatives. HRD needs to know there is no single measure of training success, such as productivity or job satisfaction. There are numerous qualitative and quantitative evaluation, approaches useful in determining training effectiveness.

●

● However, successful training depends on the benefits of various groups including: organizational leaders, supervisors, trainees, HRD managers and training facilitators. So, organizations need have one good HRD plan (human resource development) plan in order to train every training teachers to provide effective training courses to let every trainee to learn in order to apply to work to raise efficiency or improve performance successfully. So, HRD is important to influence every training whether it is successful or failure training course.

●

● Thus, any large organization needs have one effective HRD strategy in order to provide enough number of excellent training teachers (trainers) to assist its different departments to provide useful training courses to let every trainee to learn. Every trainer individual knowledge, skill, working experience will help his/her organization to train the new employment staff to learn their knowledge, skill effectively. So,, it seems that one effective HR department can assist its organization to develop HR (trainers) to be excellent training teachers to teach their traineers (new employment staffs) to absord their knowledge, skill to prepare to do their new position more to avoid none training cost waste successfully.

●
●
● HRD (human resource department) assists
● diversity in the workplace to be benefits
●
●

● Nowadays, globalization requires more interaction among people from diverse background. So, large organizations will need to consider when they have need to develop overseas markets. Their offices will have different countries' staffs to cooperate to work together. For this reason, profit and non-profit organizations need to become more diversified to remain competition. Maximizing and capitalizing on workplace diversity is an important issue for management. It brings this question: Can human resource department assist the organization's diversity development in order to let continue people to cooperate to work in order to raise performance or productivity or efficieny easily. For example, if the organization's HRD is effective, the interviewers can ensure to help their organizations to select whether what countriess' applicant whom is the most right applicant to do the departmental tasks, one China company's finance department needs one applicant who familizes US accounting/ finance policy knowledge and owns US related finance and accountinr working experience to do this fiance manager position. Then, the China fiem needs to decide whether it ought to select the foreign US country's domestic applicant who owns many years of finance and accounting working experience and US accounting/finance university subject knowledge to do this finance manager position or select itself country's China domestic applicant who owns US finance/accounting related working experience and familizes US accounting/finance subjects knowledge. Although, if the China company selected the local applicant who owns finance/accounting knowledge and US company finance/accounting related working experience to do this finance manager positin. The advantages are that the finance manager and whose finance team staffs who can speak fluent chinese language. So, the finance manager and his/ her finance department staffs can communicate to bring easier cooperation. But, it does not guarantee that he/she must lead or supervise his/her finance deparment staffs to raise peformance or efficiency daily. Otherwise, if the China firm select one foreign US applicant to do this finance manager position. Although, this US foreign finance manager can not speak fluent Chinese languare and he/she can only speaks American language. It is possible that the finance department staffs who all are Chinese. They can not understand English language easier. It is possible to bring communication difficult problem between the US foreign finance manager and his/her finance department staffs. But, the US foreign finance manager who has competitive effort is that his/her local US finance/accounting related working experience and university graduation of finance/accounting subject knowledge is better to compare to all China applicants whose own similar accounting/finance knowlege and related working experience in China. It seems that the foreign US finance manager applicant can perform more excellent to compare all China domestic finance manager applicants. If the finance manager's duty needs to familiarize US acocunting/finance policy to calculate tax and profit for US government tax department , due to this firm needs to sell products to US market often. It is possible that the foreign US finance manager applicant can lead or supervise whose finance department staffs to raise efficiency to work more easily, due to his/her familiar US accounting/finance policy and working experience is useful more than the China local applicants who owns more China accounting/finance knowledge and China accounting/finance related working experience.

●

● Due to this finance manager position needs the applicant must own many years US firm accounting/finance working years and US education is prefer. Hence, HRD needs to consider diversity of workplace problem when it decides to employ one US foreign applicant to do this finance manager position to replace China local applicant to supervise or lead all Chinese staffs to work in finance department. So, knowing how to supervise finance staffs to cooperate to work efficiently and raise performance which will be the applicant's strength to do this position to the US applicant. However, the US foreign finance manager' s language and culture , education level, related finance and accounting working experience must be different to all Chinese finance staffs. Hence, workplace diversity issue will be this organization's HRD which needs to concern hoe to let different Chinese finance staffs and the American finance manager to easier adapt to work together in this company's finance department.

●

● The best method is that this company's HRD needs to employ both Chinese and American people who can cooperate to work in human resource department together. The advantage is that when this company's HRD has these two countries' people to work, they can apply themselve countries' HR working experience and HR management knowledge to choose the most right applicants to do the positions, e.g. the finance deparment needs one finance manager, the US HRD manager can give better recommendation to know how to choose the best US finance manager.

●

● Hence, in any diversity organizations, supervisors and managers need recognize the ways in which the workplace is changing. Managing diversity is significant organizational challenge. So, the diversity organizations' HRD needs to select the applicants who own more different countries' working experience and managerial skills in order to adapt to accommodate a multicultural working environment. The department manager applicants need have different countries effectively manage diverse workforces. It provides a general definition for workforce diversity, discusses the benefits and challenges of managing diverse workplace, and presents effective strateges for managing diverse workforce. Moreover, the diverse organization's HRD needs have effective performance evaluation strategy to review manager individual management practices and develop new and creative approaches to managing people. They aims to bring positive changes will increase work performance and customers service to let their organization can develop in diverse organizational working environment.

●

● Why does diversity in the workplace need to occur to satisfy future some organizations' needs? Significant changes in the workplace have occurred , due to downsizing and outsourcing, which has greatly affected the organization's human resource management needs to be changed also. For example, globalization and new technologies have changed workplace practices, and there has been a trend toward longer working hours. Generaly speaking, organizational restructuring usually results, in fewer people doing more work. So, some organizations' HRD needs to select the efficient workers to continue to serve their departments.

● Whcn they need to discuss the non-efficient or below productive workers, again recruiting the new efficient working applicants to replace them. It is future organizational restructuring tend. So, any organization's

HRD needs to concern how to devise to keep the most efficient workers to continue to serve for their organizational departments and how to select the most efficient applicants to do the jobs after the organization restructures.

●

● What benefits of diversity in the workplace are bought to the diverse organizations? Diversity is beneficial to both employees and employers. Although, employees are interdependent in the workplace, respecting individual differences can increase productivity. Diversity in the workplace can reduce lawsuits and increase marketing opportunities, e.g. foreign sale market development, recruitment of the most right overseas applicants to do the jobs which need overseas educational learning knowledge and overseas working experiene, creating and building good business image to overseas market. When flexibility and creativity are keys to competitiveness, diversity is critical for a organization's sussess. Also, the consequences of loss of time and money should avoid.

●

● Hence, future department managers need to own managing a diverse work population working experience when their organizations are international. Training department also needs to provide training courses to train new employing managers to learn how to deal more simply acknowledging differences in people. It involves learn how to teach every team's staffs to accept recognizing the value of differences, learn how to deal combating discrimination, and learn how to make reasonable decision to select whom can be the right staff to be promote as well as learn how to deal complaints an dlegal action against the organization. Due to different countries people work together to non necessary cause argument.

●

● However, HRD and department managers need to know negative attitudes and behaviors can be barrier to organizational diversity because they can harm working relationships and damage morale and work productivity. Negative attitudes and behaviors in the workplace include: prejudice, discrimination, which should never be needed by management for hiring and termination practices, it can lead to raise organizational cost in long term , because the organization will have many overseas staffs choose to resign, if they felt discrimination is serious. Then these organizations will have lost any talent overseas staffs , due to their designation, any team efficiency will reduce, even performance will be poor when any team lacks talent overseas or different countries staffs and itself local staffs to work together. Hence, management level to staffs, e.g. supervisors, managers need to be trained to learn how to avoid to bring negative attitudes and behaviors to let overseas foreign countries staffs to feel unhappu to work together.

●

● Training needs to be provides to train managers to be effective and are aware that certain skills are necessary for creating a successful , diverse workforce . For example, managers must understand discrimination and its consequences. Also, managers must recognize their own cultural biases and prejudices. Diversity is not about differences among groups, but rather about differences among individuals. Each individual is unique and does not repesent or speak for a particular group. Even, managers also need be willing to change organization of necessary. HRD also needs to provide training to let organization leaders , e.g. The lacking overseas working experience of CEO needs to learn how to manage diversity in the workplace to be successful in the future. So, training needs concentrate on teaching high, middle and low management level staffs' managerial skill how to corporate with different countries' staffs or lead or supervise them to work efficiently, happily, unfortuately. It is not easy to train these management skill to them. It mainly depends on the manager's ability to understand what is best for the organization based on teamwork and the dynamic of the workplace.

●

● In fact, managing diversity is a process for creating a work environment that everyone. When creating a successful diverse workplace, an effective manager should focus on personal awareness. Both managers and team members need to be aware of their personal biases. These organizations need to develop , implement and maintain ongoing training because a one day session of traing won't change people's behavior. Managers need to concern these issues in diversity working environment: social gatherings and business neetings,where every member must listen adn have the chance to speak, are good ways to create happy working environment, managers need implement policies, such as mentoring programs to provide different countries staffs access to information and opportunities.

●

● In conclusion, HRD needs to concern how to let a diverse workforce environment to implement effectively, how to let diverse work teams bring high value to organizations, how to let individual difference to bring benefit the workplace by creating a competitive effort and increasing work productivity, how to lead or train diversity management benefits every team by creating a fair and safe workplace environment where everyone has access to opportunities and challenges. Finally, HRD will need to train management leve staffs, e.g. supervisor, manager, CEO in a diverse workforce, it should be used to to educate every team members about diversity and its issues, including organization policies and regulations. Most workplaces are made up of diverse cultures, so organizations need to learn how to adapt to be successful. This is important successful factor to a diverse organization.

●
●
●
●
　●
●
● Effective human resource department characteristics
●
●
● What is the strengths and weaknesses between owning human resource organization and lacking human resource organization? How to achieve more effective human resource department development on organizational raising productivity? In fact, effective human resource development can enhance productivity in order to reduce poor performance in organization. For example: enhancing the efficiency of human resource training to train many excellent performance staffs aim from the human resource training function. It brings this question: Whaat factors determine and identify to affect human resource development and organizational productivity and changing positive attitude of the senior management to raise their managerial efforts successfully?
●
● Human resource development is the engagement of people to work in order to achieve sales growth and profitability. How to make sure that the effort of employers are appraised from time to time to find out how they contribute to the achievement of organizational goals, and also raising educational qualifications for recruitment, selection, promotion and placement of workers more effective.
●

● I assume that effective human resource management enables employees to contribute effectively and productivity to overall company direction and accomplishment of the organization's foals and objectives. If every human resource related tasks or functions , such as recruitment, selection, orientation, training, appraisal, motivation functions can achieve perfect aims in the shorten time efficiently, then the organization will have implement one effective human resource department.

●

● This effectice HR related functions will ensure its stable continuity and achievement to the organization. However, I believe personal element is the main factor to raise organization's effectiveness to compare other kinds of factors, e.g. good machine facilities , good working environment, good employee morale and organizational policy etc. factors. If the organization has good qualities of personnel element. Consequently, the organization should prioritize the development of the human element to maximize talents, skills and ability which will automatically reflects on the company's profit. So, it seems that company's profit raising up or falling down , it has relationship to good or bad personnel element. One firm seems to be an auto-mental machine factory, it needs to employ some people , through a conventional plant with similar capacity might require more people. So, the company (factory) needs good personnel element for proper HR planning to employ the suitable workers to do the right job positions, it is known as a "manpower planning".

●

● Hence, training is one important function to some organizations, when the organization needs to train lacking technicians or raise to improve their modern skills of improve upon their talents and educational qualifications when it selects to employe these low skillful employees to do its any departments' high technical skillful jobs when the organization needs to change. Thus, the technical workers need to be equip themselves skills which will boost quality product and profit making of their organization.

●

● If focuses on raising raising productivity through improved quality, efficiency , cost reduction, and enabling customers concentrate on their core business activities, such as one vehicle manufacture factory needs have one effective training deparment to train whose vehicle manufacturing workers to learn how to apply artificial intelligence (AI) technological robots to manufacture good quality vehicles number to supply to overseas markets to sell in short time efficiently. Thus, the vehicle factory focuses on raising vehicle number productivity through improved artificial intelligence and skillful workers' skills to achieve raising vehicle quality in efficient way, and reducing employee number and salary cost and satisfying vehicle customers' different kinds of new vehicle design driving needs from artificial intelligent technological manufacturing.

●

● However, some business is full of uncertainty and understanding of labour contribution or human resources development to training / raising management level staffs' managerial skills of boosting organizational productivity and as well as its profitability . I believe raising managerical skills to managers, which will assist to whom to raise effective productivity or efficiency to different departments. Why can training raise or improve managerial skills to managers ? The reasons are that the challenges of lack of skilled labour, heavy competition among firms, technological problem, low productivity and then rate of poor performance and poor product implementation when placing a serious limitation on product expansion and increase increase in productivity. If the organizatin has no enough high managerial skillful level of managers to know why and how to manage their team members to work efficiently in the organizational structural high technological changing working environment. Then, the poor skillful employees won't adapt to work in high technological changing working environment, such as artificial intelligence manaufacturing working environment. Then, it will be reduce productivities inefficiently, due to lacking high level owning managerial skillful of managers to supervise or lead them to work in one high managerial efficient way.

●

● Hence, future HR development to train or raise managerial skills to different department managers. it seems to need have one essential HR training policy to any organizations if they hope to innovate to rsise productivity and efficiency successfully. I assume that the effective human resource development can enhance productivity in order to avoid poor performance as well as efficiency of human resource training to managers can result in organizational growth.

●

● An effective HRM involve maintaining and improving all aspects of a company's practices. Hence, HR manager must devise the most efficient and cost -effective means of hiring, e.g. advertising and recruit for vacant positions. HR management team must devise and implement the selection procedures to choose the mot suitable candidates establish paying welfare and salary policy efficiently.

●

● What factors can influence employee performance appraisal system? Has it relationship between good employee performance appraisal system and raising productivity or improving efficiency? One effective employee performance appraisal system can let human resource department to raise service efficiency to assist the organization to raise whole human resource long term development (human planning). An effective performance appraisal system can meet targets to acceptable quality standards and benchmarks as determined in each category of human resource service delivery. One effective employee performance appraisal system should be supported by training of staff, particularly those with managerial and supervisory responsibility , and the process should be regarded as interactive for multural agreement between supervisors and appraisers.

●

● In fact, if one organization has one effective employee performance appraisal system, it can encourage employees to work hard, raise efficiency and productive performance more easily. It is one good tool for human resource management and performance improvement. The process of performance management involves the identification of common goals between the appraiser and the appraisee. It must relate to the overall organizational goals. To test each employee performance, such as if a process is conducted effectively. It will increase productivity and quality of output when the department(S) staffs who had ever participated the process. Hence , the performance appraisals , accuracy and fairness in measuring employee performance is very important. Performance management is a control measure used to determine which work tasks with a view of taking corrective action. It is also used to reflect on past performance as the organization plans ahead. So, provision of feedback on the required corrective action to let every employee to know whether why and how he/she has done error in order to let he/she to revise whose error is critical in the process. For the appraisals to be effective, the top management must be supportive in providing information, clear performance standards must be set, the appraisals must not be used for any other purpose apart from performance management and the evaluation must be free from any rating biases. However, comparing the employees' performance from the performance appraisal is important in making future improvement. The performance appraisals are supported to be conducted at least twice annually to be better than once annually. The annual performance appraisals also need to help in determining how every employee fits into the organizational development and efficiency in performing all the assigned tasks and responsibilities. Moreover, it also needs to help in determining the training needs of the employees in planning future job schedules.

●

● Additionally, the kind of working environment that is needed to be created by the performance appraisals optimizes the employees' work performance. Then, departmental and individual objectives are needed to formulate which will be consistent with the organizational objectives. In fact, training is one method to raise employee performance. The raters should be trained on various aspects, like supervision skills, conflict resolution, coaching, setting performance standards, linking this system to pay, and how to provide employee feedback. The training will equip ratees with expertise and knowledge what they need in making decision in the course of the process.

●

● What factors will influence employee performance appraisal system successfully? They include formal meetings factor, individual performance should need be discussed. The performance review may include the actual performance, the tasks that are completed and areas that need improvement. It aims to achieve " action inquiry" to let employee individual or every team has chance to enquire whether how to improve productive performance questions in order to earn more effective recommendations. The another factor is feedback, it is an important part of one effective employee performance appraisal systems. The feedback should be specific and timely and be against the predetermined performance expectations. So, every employee has right to know how who are progressing in performing the assigned tasks and to receive feedback. However, feedback should need to be provided on a continuous basis, e.g. daily, weekly or monthly more better than two weekly or half year period.

●

● In conclusion, poor performance evaluation won't havve the desired effect. There should be a proper development of the appraisal to remove subjectivity and bias in the ratings. Because the appraiser's subjective bias will cause the inaccurate measurement to every staff individual actual performance to decide whether he/she ought need to be promoted or not. Hence, removing subjectivity and bias in the ratings of appraiser personal poor performance evaluation factor will be very important to achieve one effective employee performance appraisal plan to bring either positive efficient method.

●
●
●
●
●
● Effective training on employee performance
●
● An effective training can maximize the job
● performance. Every organization's respensibility to enhance the job performance of the employees and certainly implementation of training and development is one of the majoe steps that most companies need to achieve this organizations need to utilize human resourcee effectively. Traning of human resource needs to fit into the organization's structure as this it will make the organizations achieve their goals and objectives.
●
● For telecommunication industry case example, how to carry on one effectively training into raise employee efficiency. It includes their questions: What training programs exist the telecommunications section? What are the training objectives? What methods are used and do these methods meet the training objectives? How does training affect employees performance? Why does telecommunication industry employees need better training? Training is a type of activity which is planned a systematic and it results in enhanced level of skill, knowledge, and competency that are necessary to performance work effectively.
●
● In telecommunication organization, staffing needs to ensure that the right people are available at the right time in the right place. This involves identifying the nature of the job and implementing a recruitment and selection process to ensure a correct match within the organization. Training and development are often used to chose the gap between current performance and expected future performance. How does training and development provide performance feedback, identifying individua

strengths/weaknesses, recognizing individual performance, assisting in goal identification, evaluating goal achievement, identifying individual training needs, determining organizational training needs, improving communication and allowing employees to discuss concerns?

●

● There are a number of alternative sources of appraisal includes: Training telecommunication front line staffs, supervisors, managers appraisal are done by an employee's manager one level higher, self appraisal performance done by the employee prior to the performance interview, subordinate appraisal: appraisal of a supervisor is by an employee, which is more appropriate for developmental than for administrative purposes. Peer appraisal is by follow employees for use in an interview conducted by the employee's manager, team appraisal based on total quality management concepts, recognizing team accomplishment's rather than individual performance, customer appraisal that seeks evaluation from both external and internal customers.

●

● Training is a planned and systematic modification of behavior through learning events, activities and programs which result in the participants achieving the levels of knowledge, skills, competencies and abilities to carry out their work effectively. The main purpose of training is a acquire and improve knowledge, skills and attitudes towards work related tasks. It is one of the most important potential motivators which can lead to both short-term and long-term benefits for individuals and organizations. It can raise high morale, employees who receive training have increased confidence and motivations, lower cost of production, training eliminates risks because trained personnel are able to make better and economic use of material and equipment thereby reducing and avoiding waste, lower turnover, training brings a sense of secutiry as the workplace, reduces labour turnover and absenteeism is avoided.

●

● Change management, training helps to manage change by increasing the understanding and involvement of employees in the change process and also provides the skills and abilities needed to adjust to new situations, providing recognition, enhanced, responsibility and the possibility of increased pay and promotion, helping to improve the availability and quality of staff.

●

● An effective training needs to focuse on workers' performance, improving certain: working practices, this focuses on improvement regardless of the performance problems and changing or renewing the organization situation, which may arise because of innovations or changes in strategy. When the organization feels training need, it needs to create , develop maintain and improve any systems relevant in contributing to the availability of people with required skills. Moreover, training programs should be designed to carter for the different needs.

●

● Furthermore, HR , the training programme, content and the trainees' chosen depend on the objectives of the training programme. There are two different methods that organizations may choose from for training and developing skills of its employees. There are on-the-job training given to organizational employees then conducting their regular work at the same working venues and off-the -job training involves taking employees away from their usual work environments and therefore all concentration to the training. Examples of the on-job training include but are not limited to job rotations and transfer, coaching and/or mentoring.

●

● On the other hand, off-the job training examples include conferences, role playing. Different organizations are motivated to take or different training methods for a number of reasons for example: depending on the organization's strategy, goals and resources available, depending on the needs identified at the time and the target groups to be trained which may include among others individual workers, groups, teams department or the whole organization.

●

● Job rotation and transfers is as a way of developing employee skills within organization involves movements of employees from on official responsibility to another for example taking on higher rank position within the organization, and one branch of the organization to another. For transfers for example, it would involve movement of employees from one country to another. These rotations and transfers facilitate employees acquire knowledge of the different operations within the organization together with the differences existing in different countries, where the organization operates.

●

● The knowledge is acquired by the selected employees for this method is beneficial to the organization as it may increase the competition advantage of the organization. In every training, trainees are provided with some information related the description of the roles, concerns objective, responsibilites, emotions.

●

● In conclusion, effective training needs have these requirements, identifying and defining training needs, defining the learning required in terms if what skills and knowledge have to be learnt and what attitudes need to be changed, defining the objectives of the training, planning training programs to meet the needs and objectives combination for training technique and locations, deciding who provides the training, evaluating training amending and extending training as necessary.

●

●

●

● Designing effective pay for performance compensation system

●

●

● One effective pay compensation system can give fair rewards to encourage employees hard to work, including front line employees and top level managers to individual , team and/or organizational achievement, short term or/and long term goals, efforts or outcomes when external constraints exist. Employees can be rewarded by one time cash bonus, increase to base pay or combination. So, effective pay reward system will improve performance evaluation process. For example, rewarding individuals who generate the greatest amount of output may be appropriate in some organizations that are very production-oriented.

●

● It could be problematic in an organization whose work demands closed attention to how results are achieved particularly, in regard to matters , such as quality , safety or teamwork. A performance system can only be effective if employee is value the pay or recognition that the organization offers in return for high performance, understand what is required of them, believe that they can achieve the desired level of performance, and believe that the organization will actually recognize and reward that performance.

●

● How to design fair reward measurement? For example, supervisors will need training in designing performance measures and providing performance feedback , a performance evaluation system that enables them to accurately distinguich among levels of performance, and guidelines for determining pay increases or performance bonuses. A fair pay reward system will have these characteristics: performance goals and measures are relevant, reasonable and usable, employees understand and participate in the performance evaluation process and performance is evaluated fairly.

●

● However, an effective pay reward system can help employees to understand what is expected of them, to choose wisely among various courses of action, and to identify, seek and obtain the resources (such as training and equipment that they need to succeed). A pay for performance system can not have these desirable effects unless employees understand the organization's goals, their role in achieving these goals and how the pay system works.

●

● How can be a pay for performance system? Outstanding performaners will receive the greatest reward , to acknowledge their supervisor contributions and to motivate them to continue high performance. Average performers will receive substantially smaller raises, which may encourage them to work harder to achieve larger raises in the future, poor performaners will receive no increase, which is intended to persuade them to improve their performance or leave.

●

● How to implement an affective selection? Effective selection process which needs assessment to determine the current and future human resource requirements of the organization. If the activity is to be effective, the human resource requirements for each job category and functional division/unit of the organization must be assessed and a priority assigned, identification within and amends are be valued the employees, the awards are often to be given, how often the rewards are reviewed, the award is long or short term.

●

● Legal framework for reward system, such as payment of wage, restriction on wages deduction, minimum wage, benefit, such as share options o housing benefits. Major benefits plans include: retirement benefit schemes, personal security , e.g. healthcare, dental , hospitalization, accident or life insurance, financial assistance, e.g. mortgage interest subsidies, rental subsidies, staff discount, education subsidies, personal needs, e.g. holidays and leave pay, child care , fitness and facilities, use of holiday house etc. employee shares purchase plan, company car, identification within and outside the organization of the resource pool and the likely competition for the knowledge and skills resident within it, job analysis and job evaluation to identify the individual aspects of each job and calculate its relative worth, assessment of qualifications profiles, drawn from job descriptions that identify responsibilities and required skills , abilities , knowledge and experience determination of the organizational ability to pay selection and benefit within a defined period, identification and determination of the actual process of restructure and selection to ensure equity and the equal opportunity. Hence, all of these will be on effective recruitment process factor to choose the most right applicants to do the positions method.

-
- ? How to Judge whether the training is effective?
-
- Effective training can raise employee individual
- performance and efficiency. Otherwise, inefficient training can increase cost, and waste time and trainer individual resource as well as it can bring negative reducing efficiency and poor performance and poor morale to employee individual negative emotion influence. Hence, organizations need to consider whether the training can bring positive influence to satisfy employee individual raising skills and knowledge level need to be applied to do those tasks. If the training seems that it is ineffective. I recommend that organization ought not to spend time, resource to implement the training.
-
- Daniel G. (2015, pp.79) states that if a company hires correctly, workers will want to be super performers, and they can be managed through honest communication and common sense. Most companies focus too much on formal policies and at the small number of employees whose interests aren't fully applied with the firm's. Hence, the author believes that super performance employees do not need their organization's formal policies to manage them. They must communicate to their team supervisors honestly. Because they hope their employers believe their efforts to feel they ought increase salary to earn fair rewards due to they are superior performance employees. Hence, it means that whether the training is either effective or ineffective, it is not important to train the super performance staffs. If the ineffective training is provided to the superior performance staffs (trainees) to learn. It will bring negative influence to reduce their effort to

do the tasks because they feel their employers do not believe they are super performance staffs. So, it is not important to train them, it means that what training must not need to be provided to train all these owning superior performance employees. The training is time waste, resource and money to teach them if their new hired workers can own good knowledge and skill to do their tasks.

●

● So, the company ought not decide to implement training to teach them when they are recruited in beginning, due to it feel they are foolish, unskillful and lacking knowledge workers to do their tasks. It ought spend time to wait, e.g. spending three month or more time to wait in order to observe their behaviors when their efficiency and performance can improve to satisfy it's the least task requirement. Then it can make more accurate or right judgement to find whom will be the super performer worker(s), who do(does) not need to be trained.

● In general, one company implement formal policies to aim to manage small number of employees more effective, due to it feels they are difficult communication employers. But, another feels it is not effective to improve their performance. Daniel, G. (2015, pp.79) explains that solution is that hire, reward and tolerate only fully formed adults. Tell the truth about performance. Make clear to managers that their top priority is building great teams. Leaders should create the company culture, and talent managers should think like innovative business people and mot fall into the traditional. human resource mindset.

●

● Hence, raising rewards is not effective method to encourage workers to work hardly. Companies ought not only concentrate on raising reward to employees in order to feel it can excite their productivity and raising efficiency. It is very wrong decision, companies ought design any actual effective training courses to raise every team leader or department leader individual managerial skills or efforts and knowledge level in order to manage himself/herself team members to work in order to improve performance or raise efficiency more effectively.

●

● Hence, any training trainee target and training course designing need must be chosen how to implcment carefully in order to avoid to implement the wrong or ineffective training course to let the wrong training target trainees to learn, e.g. if the different team or department supervisor or leader individual skill and knowledge need is more important to be trained more useful than their staffs' needs. It means that the different department or team manager individual managerial skills is more needed to be raised or improved to achieve the raising efficiency or improving performance consequence or aim to compare to train every staff individual skill and knowledge level. Then, the organization ought concentrate on designing any useful managerial skill training courses in order to raise their managerial skill and knowledge to know how to achieve to manage themselves' department or team 's workers or staffs to do their tasks more efficient or more performance improvement effectively.

●

● In conclusion, effective training implement is depended on whether the course's choice learning target trainees whom are right learning target trainees or not as well as how to design the training course's teaching contents whether it is actual useful or help in order to raise the trainee individual efficiency and improve performance effectively.

●
●
●
●
●
● Reference
●

● Daniel G (2015) . The definitive management ideas of the year from Harvard business review, HBR's 10 must reads . Boston , US, Harvard business school publishing, pp.79.

●
●
●
●
●
●
●
●

CHAPTER ELEVEN

● How human resource development ● assists organizations to ● raise productive efficiency

●

● In any organizations, instead of their human resource department function includes: interview, selecting, training, peformance evaluation management, reward management etc. based human related responsibilities. Can human resource department assist any other departments to raise employee individual productivies and efficiencies? Although, it has only indirect relationship to productivity and efficiency issue. It does not represent that it can not assist any departments to attempt to raise employee individual productivity and efficiency. I shall indicate evidences to explain how it will possible occur.

● How to impact human resource (HR)management on turnover productivity and corporate financial performance? I believe that HR development has an economically and statistically significant impact on both intermediate employee outcomes (turnover and productivity) and short and long term measures of corporate financial performance.

● In fact, the impact of human resource management policies and practices on firm performance is an important topic in the fields of human resource management. The high performance work practices may include comprenhensive employee recruitment, selection procedures, incentive compensation and performance management system , and implementing employee engagement, training strategies, which can improve the knowledge, skills, and abilities of a firm's current and potential employees.

● However, arguments made in related research are that a firm's current and potential human resources are important considerations in the development and execution of the firm's strategic plan. It brings this question: How and why organization's human resource development plan which can assist to raise employee individual productive efficiency. I shall assume that one organizational human resource policies, if it is effective, then it can bring properly contribution to provide a diect and economically significant contribution to the firm.

● An organization's effective HR department development is needed to support by the development and vaidation of an instrument that reflects the system of high performance work practices adpted by the firm's employees. Then, if the organization has high performance work practices, it implies that its all employees had adopted its working environment to do every task efficiently. The reasons include as below points:

● The first point, their employees must add value to the firm's production processes from effective training methods to achieve raising levels of individual performance successfully.

● The second point, the skills to the firm seeks must be rare. So, the firm's employees can have rare skills to contribute to their organization to compare the other similar industry's organizations, their owning general ordinary skills of employees. So, rare skillful employees and effective training both methods which will be important factors to assist different departments to improve performance and raise productive efficiency more easily. Also, it implies that an effective Hr department will have above characteristics when the organization's human resource department owns above these competitive advantages. Then, achieving the raising productivity and efficiency aim will achieve more easily.

● The third point, the human resource department needs to have long-term human capital development to invest to the firm's employees to continue to train them to improve their hard and soft both skills. Investments in human resource development, they are similar to organization's equipment or facilities investments. So, they both are such as to invest in the firm's specific human captial, which can further decrease the probability of such imitation by qualitatively differentiating between the firm's specific talent employees and the other same industry firms' employees .Thus, it means that the firm's employees' skills and efforts will be better to compare its same industry competitors' employees, if the firm has long-term human resource talent development strategy to its different departments' employees to prepare to raise heir skills and efforts level.

● The final point, a firm's human resources must not be subject to replacement by technological development, e.g. artificial intelligence, computer, information technology, internet or other substitutes of they are to provide a source of competitive advantage. Although, when the organization can choose to apply technologies investment to replace all employees or many employees to do their tasks in order to manufacture any products. However, the labor saving technological method is not suitable to half-service industry. For example, a restaurant can use robots to replace waitors to deliver food to clients to eat. It is simple food delivery tasks. But it is not good to apply robots to replace cookers to do their cooking tasks, because robot cooker's cooking skill, it is difficult to imitate human cooker's cooking skill in order to make same or similar ,even better food taste to let restaurant clients to feel better food taste. For the restaurant's cashier task example, because casher;s calculation ability will be netter to compare (AI) 's calculation ability. Human cashier's calculation error chance will be lesser to compare robot cashier's calculation skills. So , if the restaurant's all cookers, waiters and cashiers whose tasks all are replaced by robots. It will bring under utilized consequence because robots can not perform above their maximum potential more easier than human employees in the restaurant's long term working hours every day, because the restaurants employ more than one staff to prepare to replace the staff when he/she feels tired to need rest. Otherwise, these all restaurant positions , it has only one robot to do its position in the restaurant. I believe that these three cashier and cooker and waitor robots will be used to the maximum of utilization , then they will be older and calculation, walking and cooking speed and effort will also be slow and poor when they are used long hours every day to serve clients in the restaurant.

● Thus, when one service organization, it can not only concentrate on robots to replace human employees to do their positions' all tasks. It will perform worse than the service organizaion , it only uses robots to replace some employees to do some tasks and some positions still use human employees to do themselves tasks. Otherwise, one manufacturing organization, e.g. car manufacturing organization, it may apply robots to participate some part of human employees' manufacturing tasks in the car manufacturing process. It will help human empoyees to manufacturing can productivities and efficiencies more than the another car manufacturing firm only employs human workers to manufacture all cars in car manufacturing process every day. When the later car manufacturing neglects to apply robots to participate the whole car manufacturing process to assist human workers to manufacture cars. Then, the later only applying human workers' car manufacturing firm which will have worse productivities and inefficiencies to compare the prior car manufacturing firm to apply both robots and human workers to manufacture any kinds of cars in whole car manufacturing process. The reason is because human workers must feel tried when they need concentrate their nevous to manufacture many cars every day. If robots can participate their car manufacturing tasks to share work load to assist they to finish some more difficult or complex part of tasks, then they will feel less nervous and they reduce pressure to manufacture the complex part of car manufacturing process. Then, their efficiency and productive performance will be raised in possible.

●

●

●

● Can HRM practice influence employee individual skills through the HR development of a firm's human capitals in organization?

●

● It will need long time to implement HR development in any organization, if the organization decides to implement long term HR development strategy, e.g. it can provide formal and informal training experiences, such as basic skills training, on-the-job experience, coaching, mentoring, and managemet development can further influence employee individual skills to be improved in other to achieve raising productive efficiency to every department.

● Other raising productivity and efficient method is that employee psychological method. The HRM practices can attempt to encourage employees themselves motivates to work both harder and smarter. So, when some employees have higher skills, they can do tasks more better , but these igher skillful employees limit their effort to work in lazy. So, their productive efficiency can not achieve the best performance. The question is concerned how to persuade or encourage them to motivate and perform work hard? The solution may be performance appraisals that assess individual or work group performance, linking these appraisals to incentive compensation systems, the use of internal promotion systems that can focus on employee merit, e.g. the performance evaluation may have three levels:excellent performance, good performance and poor performance three levels. Thus, the oftenhigh performance employees can earn more reward to compensate their efforts or promote them to higher positions in short time in order to persuade how they perform their tasks to improve their productivities and efficiencies in short time.

● The another raising productive efficient method is to change organizational culture to be better. It seems that organizational culture can influence turnove. I shall assume that it has relationship between productivity and organizational culture. For example, if the organization's culture or policy is not one punishment method. Then, it can enourage the lazy workers to apply many leaving pay holidays and the lazy workers will be encouraged to absence and the absenteeism number will increase. It needs to change its traditional organizational culture in order to threaten the lazy employees need to hard to work. When the firm changes punishment method to treat these often absent employees, then these lazy workers number will be possible to reduce, due to they do not want be punished. When the organization has punishment method and disciplinary actions to treat the employees who have higher absenteeism, due to they feel afraid to be punished. Thus, the positive consequencey may be increasingly product quality and direct labor efficiency, lower absenteeism, and labor high teams increased productivity.

● In conclusion, it seems that when one organization can achieve to implement one long term human resource management development strategy to its any departmental employees, it have more chance to bring long term raising productivities and efficiencies and improving employee individual behavioral performance consequence.

●

●

● Human resource raising productive

● efficient factors

●

● Why some organizations' productive efficiency can be improved? Otherwise, why some organizations' productive efficiency can not be improved? Does it has relationship between the organization's efficiency and effective human resource (HR) strategy? I shall indicated some cases to explain why it is possible that an ineffective HR department strategy which will influence inefficiency and low productive performance to the organization in long term.

● How to achieve efficienct organizational behavior, it depends on many factors. However, effective training can raise employee individual efficiency, due to the effective training can raise the employee individual confidence to do whose task.

●

● 1.0 Effective training preparation

● Stephen, P.R. & Timothy, A.J. (2018, pp.108-11) suggested that self-determination theory and goal-setting theory are well supported contemporary theories of motivation, he/she is capable of performing a task. The higher , the staff self-efficiacy, the move confidence the staff has in whose ability to succed. So, in different situations, staffs with low self-efficacy are more likely to lessen whose effort. Self-efficacy can create a positive working attitude in which those ith hifh efficacy become more engaged in their tasks and then , increase performance, which increases efficacy further.

● However, it brings one question: How to increase the staff's confidence to reaise whose performance? I believe that if the HR organization can provide effective training to any skillful shortage of staffs number to satisfy to different departments' efficient performnce needs. The effective training can be the best method to assist unskillful staffs to raise whose task effort. The effective training programs can often be made use of enactive training teaching materials by choice of the most suitable teaching materials and building the confidence to staff individual skill. In fact, one reason training works is that it increases self-efficacy, particularly when the training is interactive and feedback is given from the trainees. So, the trainer can know whether every trainee feels what difficulty to understand whose feeback in every training course. Individuals with higher levels of self-efficacy also appear to bring more benefits from training programs and are more likely to use their training on the job. So, effective training teaching material arrangement and enough time feedback in every training course will be one imported factor to raise staff individual efficiency to whose goals.

●

● 2. Developing people through effective delegation skill

● Delegation is one important method to raise staff individual efficiency and productive performance. In fact, it has relation to effective HR department's decision. For example, if one poor management skillful manager who is selected to employ to do the manager position in the organization's one department. If his/her managing skill is poor, he/she doesn't know how to arrange different kinds of tasks to delegate to whose department's different positions of stafss to work. If his/her judgement of arrangement task's skill is poor. He/her delegates the urgent or important tasks to one low skillful or low effort staff to attempt to do the tasks, then, it will bring raising task difficulty to the low skillful or low effort staff. He/she won't improve whose performance , even it will bring pressure to the low skillful employee to work inefficiently.

● Bernard, M. B. & Bruce, J.A. (1994, pp.11-13) explained that developing people's skill, it can through delegation. Because of such influences are downsizing, restructuring and greater informational competition for products and services, organizational leaders need have rethink rapidly to know how to manage their people and organizations. With fewer employees required to share greater work loads, also many of these leaders need to raise capacity of their human resources to keep competition with rapid changes in the market.

● In fact, one common way for organizations to train potential leaders to development opportunities is through rotating job assignments, often these assignment are in highly visible positions in different departments across the organization and ususally for a specified period of time. The purpose of such assignments is to test the capabilities of the leader in an attempt to improve potential, perhaps talent into actual talent. The costs of such programs, however are considerable.

● However, if the HR department makes judgement to select on poor managing skillful and less mangement working experience's manager to manage whose department. He/she is the poort delegation skillful manager to know how to arrange the urgent or important tasks to whom to do. Then, the relocation expenses, salary increases, losses in efficiency an derrors during the learning process, and the cost of failure is a new assignment all contribute to the high price of development. Hence, every manager needs to learn and know how to use job rotation for development in short term or long term urgent or important tasks' finishing assignments in due dare to avoid organizational inefficient consequence occurrences or caused, due to the manager's poor delegation skill.

● In fact, delegation is a way or method to solve how to deal any important or urgent tasks to be finished before due date. Defined simply, it is the assignment of responsibility or authority to another, it is a frequently used management tool in organizations around the world. Delegation has been conceptualized as a time management tool, a decision making process or a way of getting more things, dome through others. However, if the manager delegates one urgent or important task to one neglect or careless staff to attempt to do it. It is possible to bring inefficiency or poor performance.

● Although, delegation can ease the job og managing and increase the effectiveness of the manager, this is a relatively narrow view point of delegation. However, it is not absolent sure or guarantee to any managers can develop right or reasonable delegation or how or why some leaders seem to be able to develop the potential in others when other leaders can not . Hence, it implies that if the HR department can select the best managing skillful manager to attempt to do the position. Then, his/her wrong delegation possible occurrence chance will be reduced to the minimum level to avoid inefficiency and low productive performance causing chance to be raised to the organization.

●

●

● 3. Predictive analytics when the organization feels its human resources need to be changed.

●

● The third point to raise efficiency and improve productive factor is that the organization feels need to know how it ought need to spend time and human resources to gather external environment and internal data to predict when the suddent environment changes to influence insufficient productivities and poor performance is caused from unpredictive poor environment change factor influence.

● Jac, F.E & John, R.M. (2014, pp.13-16) explained that if any organizations expected they can adapt any external poor economic environment as well as organization's weakness causing changing factors to bring their organization's inefficiencies and poor productive performance causing in long term. They need to know and learn how to predict their HR needs when their HR is needed to be changed in order to adapt the sudden external economic environment changing and organization's weakness to cause its inefficiency and low productive performance consequence.

● Any organization needs to gather datas concern: What will be needed to be lead potentially? What are the future market demands? What are the leader's changing managing attitude to let whole company's staffs to adapt easily in order to encourage they raise efficiency and improve productive performance more easily? It also needs to predict when the external forces drives will occue to cause how it's human resource strategy needs to be changed to adapt or fight the sudden external forces drives influence in order to avoid inefficiency or low productive performance consequence. The external force drives may include: Slow encourage growth, technological labour shortage, customer complaints number increasing, new competitors' products existing or enter the market, government regulation prohibition. Then, the organization gathers all these external environment forces drives datas to predict when these poor external environment changes will occur.

● On the one hand, it can implement human resource changing strategy, such as reducing workforce, new skills needed, increasing training, focusing on service, informing employees new benfits regulations. On the other hand, it needs to change the internal drives factors, due to the external forces drives sudden change influence that it feels it needs to change its human resources strategy in order to avoid inefficiency or/and low productive performance causing. However, it also needs to find whether its organizational internal drives factors also need to be changed to avoid inefficiency and/or poor productive performance causing. The internal drivers factors may include: Whether the company itself needs to change new company vision, due to external environment changes, whether it needs to change its leadership gap to adapt sudden external environment factors influence, whether its organizational culture and brand image and finances sources and expenditure controlling need to be changed , due to external environment changes influence factor.

● However, when the organization discovers that it needs to change its human resource strategy in order to adapt the sudden economic environment poor changing influence. Then, it needs to explain to let its employees to know whether why and how and what aspects, it needs to change, how to implement accelerate development to adapt the possible sudden economic environment poor changing occurrence, when it is the right time to begin transformation, reimplement to wage/salary payment policy and evaluation performance method, due to the possible sudden poor economic environment changing influence. Hence, when the organization can predict when the external poor economic environment changes influences to cause the inefficiency and poor productive performance consequence, then it can know how to change its human resource strategy in order to adapt the possibe sudden poor economy environment changing influence to cause inefficiency and poor productive performance causing consequence in possible.

●

● 4. Good working place environment and no sex labor different treatment factor

● One good working place environment is another important factor to influence employee individual performance and efficiency to be improved. I assume that selected the best skillful workers to do the tasks, but it is not represent these best skillful workers must raise efficiency to do their tasks .

● Fiona, M.W, (2004, p.79) indicated one case to explain why skillful working won't be possible to raise efficiency to work , if the organization's workplace environment is poor and it implements unfair sex treatment to employ workers between male and female sex and different country. The case concerns one factory employed over 2,000 workers, women made up nearly two-thirds of these workers. Nearly, half the workers were other country, e.g. Asian. The division of labour was clear, when the Western country, e.g. US men were knitters, mechanics, dyers and top managers. The Asian women workers in the finishing process in personnel, and white collar jobs.

● The finished jobs women did-were low paid, repetitive and based upon piece production, which is conceived of as a natural attribute, not a skill, they joined fabric together, bar-tasked herms, and operated button-sewing machines. An Asian woman might sew side seams all day, every day, for weeks at a time, unlikely the assembly line that controlled the flow of work, the machinist wzs dependant on the supervisor to bring work to her. This could be caused frustration to the factory's women labour. The individual worker had no control over what she would do not tried to boost her speed on each operation in order to secure the highest rate for the job. The women disliked bring moved between jobs , but management looked for flexibility in the use of their labour power.

● However, the work environment was physically tiring, noisy and monotonous. This was a common response to the job . The Asian women were expected to meet targets of production each day and had to work under pressure to earn a bonus. Monotony was eased through conversation, jokes. The Asian women's work was domesticated by them. For example, the factory manager feels the female workers seem to be very machine and tells them you are my machine. So, it causes the factory Asian female workers feel angry and complain the Western , US manager's verbal joke behavior is poor to cause the Asian women workers have negative emotion to do ths factory job often.

● Hence , it explains that why this factory Asian female workers won't raise efficiency in possible, due to its unfair job treatment, the factory management high level positions are selectcd to US male applicants to do. So, the Asian female workers will feel unfair position treatment and they feel they won't earn promotion chance, even they have effot to do any managment positions to replace these US male managers in this factory . Morevover, their factory managers' attitudes are poor to let them to feel often. The US managers often speak to them, such as my machine. They have not said high value Asian female workers to let them to feel they are important employees in this factory 's manufacturing deparment. Hence, their emotions will be influenced to be poor and spend less effort to hard to work to raise piece productivity in order to earn bonus , due to they feel tried to work , because they have no rest time in this factory. Finally, the poor working environment , it lacks good air condition facilities to let them to feel more cool feeling to comfort to work in summer or warm heater facilities to let them to feel warm feeling to comfort to work in winter. Moreover, machines' sound cause noise pollution to cause them to feel ear listening physical illness when they need to work in noisy workplace workplace in long term in possible.

● All these poor psychological and physical both factors will influence the skillful Asian female workers to perform poorly. Hence, it seems this factory needs to change its employment strategy to let the Asian female workers have fair employment chance to apply the manager positions in this factory. It aims to let the Asian female workers feel they have promotion chance to promote to do any low, middle and high level of management positions and attempt to manage the Western male workers to do the hand-needed productive tasks.

● This factory may arrange one training department. For example, the training department can provide factory manager's managing skillful training courses to teach the high potential Asian female workers to be promoted to do the management level positions. So, they have chance to be promoted to the high level management position from the middle level and low level management position in this factory. So, the fair position promotion , salary reward and improved factory's facilities, e.g. increasing factory spaces, increasing machine number, increasing warming heaters and air conditoners number these factory facility management issues will influence the Asian female worker individual efficiency and productive performance to be improved in possible.

● However, this factory management will need to solve the most important influential poor performance or inefficiency workplace environment facilities problem in the factory, the organization must need to change in order to let these Asian female workers feel comfortable environment to work in this factory. The maintenance system to improve the factory's workplace environment to be felt more comfortable to these female workers. The type of tasks may include: Inspection for leaks in hydraulic system, predictive maintenance, scan all electrical connectons with infrared, cleaning and removing debris from machine, taking reading rcord of machine operating every day time, scheduled replacement and removing replace pump every three years, interviewing the operator to enquire how machine is operating, carrying on analysis concerns how a type of machine performance history analysis. So, these factory's facility management tasks are important factor to let these Asian female workers to feel safe to work in this factory,when this factory female workers feel this workplace environment is improved to be more safe and comfortable as well as their illnesses are reduced and promotion. Ths another review point is that many Western male manager individual behavior and attitude is changed to let them to feel better and the training course is effective to let them to feel skillful level is raised . Then, the skillful Asian female worker individual piece productive number will be raised as well as the low skillful Asian female worker individual productive performance will be improved, due to the organization has effective training courses to let them to learn how to raise their skills to produce every piece of product in efficient way.

●

● 5. How can school's human resource bring educators' teaching efficiency?

●

● These are considered questions concern school organiations : Must school's training deparment need to be arranged? How can school organizations' human resource department help educators determine cost (efficiency) , how to define student performance (effectiveness) and how to compare cost to raise high quality of teaching performance to teachers? Has it relationship how to guide policy and allcation of resources between school organizations' human resource strategy and the structure that produce the greatest improvement to teacher individual teaching behavior for the least cost to satisfy student's learning need?

● I beleive that school's human resource deparment has relationship to influence teacher individual teaching performance and student's individual performance in eduation industry. The teaching effect to teacher's performance includes: high cost and high performance or high cost and low performance or low cost and high performance or low cost and low performance.

● However, these unpredictive variable factors will bring above these teaching effect to be changed, even the school's human resource department had selected the teacher who owns more years teaching experience and high level of qualification to teach the subject. It means that the high level qualification and owning more teaching experience's teacher can teach whose students in poor teaching performance to bring poor learning effectiveness to whose students. The unpredictive variable factors may include socio-economic make up of student high populations, so the prior excellent performance teacher needs to teach 30 students in one classroom in prior. Currently, he/she needs to teach 50, even more tham 50 students number in one classroom, due to the shortage of teachers number and/or increasing students number to the school , size of school, e.g. classroom number is no increasing change, but the students number is increasing to the school, teacher turnover ratio increases, it is possible that many teachers feel pressure to teach many students in one classroom. They want to change career development, they feel unfair salary and benefit treatments, they are complained by students of student's family, they feel themselves teaching studetn's learning performance, it can't improve and examinatons results are worse. They teachers concrn themselves' teaching responsibilities more than students themselves learning responsibilities as well as the mobility of students, e.g. many students often change different subjects to learn or many students are leaving this school and they change to another new school to learn. So, the teacher needs to spend much time to teach the new students , due to they are replaced to the leaving old students as well as the teacher needs to spend much time to teach the new student swhen he/she is studying this new subject and he/she is the another old subject student. So, these unpredictive variable factors will cause the owning past excellent teaching performance's teachers feel pressure to teacher his/her students currently. If any one of above these unpredictable factors influence to his/her teaching behavioral needs to be changed to in order to adapt this sudden new and complex's teaching workplace or learning environment. Then, it is possible that their teaching performance will be worse, due to they feel pressure to teach their students in classroom every day.

● So, it seems that it has no relationship between the effective human resource department's application selection process and the training course' content and the teacher's teaching performance because all of above these factors can not predicted when one of them will occur in order to find solutions to solve these problems in prior. Moreover, it also explain that teacher individual teaching performance has no direct relationship to human resource department, because one excellent teaching performance teacher will have possible to be influenced his/her teaching performance to be poor, due to any on of above these factors influence.

●

●

● How can school teaching training influence to teacher individual teaching performance?

●

● Has any school training necessary to train every teacher individual teaching skill to be raised? It depends on these factors to judge whether it is that all schools have necessary to arrange any training courses to achieve to raise whose teacher individual skill aim. These factors may include: Whether the junior or high school teacher had been trained whose teaching skill in prior of another old school, before he/she had not employed to teacher this school's students? Whether the junior or high school teacher has good teaching efficiency of career development or owning more years of teaching experience before? Whether the junior or high school teacher had attended relevant research of career development education before? Whether the fresh teacher, experience teacher, and teacher with master or above educational background, he/she has the best overall teaching efficiency of career development before? Whether the junior or high school teacher with higher teaching faith of career development, he/she will be higher teaching efficiency career development before?

● Hence, any one of above factors will influence that whether the teacher must be necessary to be trained to raise the teaching skills when he/she changes to this new school to teach his/her students from another old school. Unless the teacher is one new teacher who lacks more years of teaching experience and/or lacks any training courses to be taught to prepare to develop his/her teaching career from prior another old school. It is possible that thi new teacher will face how to adapt the change of educational environment, understanding the importance of career development to teach whose students in this school. Then, this school ought spend time and effort to arrange different kinds ot training courses to re-establish the own teaching faith environment to let this new teacher to learn how to adapt whose teaching career in development in this school and keeping up to train this new teacher to learn how the teaching ethusiasm and ideal are the initial motivation to develop whose teaching career development in this school successfully. Hence, it seems that must be necessary to set up training department to any schools. If the school's all teachers who own more years of teaching experience and all they had been trained how to develop theor career in order to teach their students more understanding. Otherwise, if the school has many new teachers who lacks more years of teaching experience and they had not ever trained to develop their teaching career from other schools before. Then, this school ought set up one training department to arrange any training courses to prepare how to design different kinds of training course materials or contents to teach them in order to achieve to raise the new teachers' teaching skills more succedsfully.

● Hence, it seems that education organization's training cause is only necessary to be arranged as well as the training department is also needed to set up, it is based on whether the school had how may new students number who are studying in the school.

●

●

● 6. Can tourism industry's human resource management influence to improve productivity in airline, travel agent, hotel tourism sectors?

●

● In tourism industry, measuring productivity froma HRM prespective is extremely difficult and has proven to be a limitation within the tourism sector. Due to the customers are not tangible. For example, how can the travel agent measure its travel consultant individual service performance to evaluate whether the travelling customer feels or does not feel satisfactory loyalty from his/her service? How can the airline measure its pilot , airline front-line travelling passenger service attendant indiviual service performance to evaluate whether his/her travelling passenger feels or does not feel satisfactory to whose service performance?

● However, the complaint number whether it is more or less to the airline or travel agent's service behavior , it does not represent whose service attitude or behavior or performance is poor absolutely because there are many travelling consumers whose complaints are unreasonable , although they feel satisfactory to the airline attendent or airline front -line service staffs individual service performance, but if they feel unhappy to be caused by the airline or travel agent service staff. They will still compain their performance. For this suitation example , it is possible that the travelling passenger is delayed to catch the airplance to fly, due to the country's sudden worse weather influnce, he/she will complain the airline fron-line counter travelling customer service staffs, it concerns when the air plane will arrive the airport, if the airline counter service staff's feedback is that the airplane needs long time arrival. Then, the travelling passengers will complain to the airline counter service staffs in angry. But in fact, the air plane delays to arrive the airport, the airline counter service staffs ought not need responsibilitie to explain the reason why they can not assist the delayed air plane to arrive the country in easier. Furthermore, thy will be complained unreasonably. Hence, it is difficult to measure tourism sector's service staffs ' performance, also the complaint exact number is not one judgement factor to measure their service performance absolutely.

● I assume any tourism industry's front -line service airline staffs, they must attempt to serve their travelling passenger in positive service attitude and behavior. So, any tourism industy, how to improve their front -line service staff performance in order to let they to know how to deal unreasonable complaints in sudden unpredictive suitation. Their training materials or contents my include: Teaching them how to provide positive feedback to treat any travelling passenger individual difficult problems or unreasonable complaints in order to reduce their psychological pressure to unknown how to treat these passenger individual related problems when they are facing in airports or travelling agent workplaces. The travelling agent or airline travelling service organizations can attempt to collect measures of employee performance from customers , for example, comment cards in hotel rooms, airplane, travel agent's workplace, mystery shoppers etc. more focus shouls be pleased on this form of evaluation. In order to evaluate the actually place value on the customer ratings to every employee. The all every day, the form of evaluation concerning the actually value on the customer ratings , will be gathered to strategic , it has how many customers feel good or bad ratings to every employee individual performance when every one's tasks are finishing. Due to one month, it can make statistic report to calculate how much performance marks to give to every employee in order to evaluate whether every one's performance is satisfactory to be accepted to the lowest level. If the employee's marks rating is low, his/her department manager can arrange a time and day to meet him/her to discuss whether which aspects of problems who feels in order to give recommendation how to improve his/her service attitude to let customer to give higher marks rating to him/her next time.

● Hence tourism industry's service sector organizations need to have one training department to arrange courses how to improve employee service performance in order to let customer to give higher marks rating to very one as well as finding methods how to excite every front line service employee individual loyalty , they can increase their confidence to know how to deal sudden unreasonable complaints in effective and efficient positive attitude.

● In conclusion, how to improve employee service performance issue will be any tourism service organization's HRM concerning problem. HR department needs to know how to find the most effective methods to solve how improvement of front line employee individual performance problem in order to raise the airline or travel agent's quality of service to let itself further customers to feel its service performance is better than others.

●

● How can HR improve public sector efficiency?

●

● Any country's public service organizations will concern how to improve service servants' service performance in order to satisfy itself country's citizen's needs. Any public service organization's HR department needs to concern how to decentralize of political power and spend responsibility to sub-national government, arrange appropriate humwn resource management to any departments in the public education and health sector, there is evidence tht increasing the scale of operations may improve efficiency.

● However, some important factors to any publis service organizations, they need to concern: thre is no one model of performance budgeting comtinue need to adapt their approach to the relevant political and or institutional content. A fixed common whole-of-government planning and reporting framework importance to any country's public service organization, every country's public service organization's HR department ought design itself government wide systems that can automatically link performance results to resource allocation should be avoided, because they may distort incentives and because it is difficult to design systems that take chance to avoid to cause of poor performance to any country's orgnization public service absolutely independent assessments of performance information should be carried out, the support of political and administratoin leaders is vital for implementation , the staff and resource capacity of the ministry of finance and spending ministries is critical, reform approaches need to be adapted to evolving circumstances . It is also important to develop incentives to motivate civil servants and politicians to change their behaviors, learning -by-doing process is important to influence every country's public service organization's success, e.g. learning to make the budget process more responsive to priorities, learning to make management, practices more flexible , such that defined priorities are easier to achieve, learning how to strengthen competitive pressures among providers of public services and where not incompatible with equity considerations, containing the demand for public services . Hence, all above of any one issues which will be public service organization's solve consideration issues if they expect public servants can raise service performance to let themselves citizens to feel in themselves countries.

● In conclusion, any public or private organizations need have on effective human resource management strategy to raise employee individual performance efficiency. In summary, these several aspects, they need to consider that they many include: avoiding to lack of continuous training and education , when the organizaton's top manager feels to consider investments in itself human assets. It trends to see human expenses as something which needs to be minimised. For example, lack of continuous learning opportunities is because the organization only consider to devolve to bottom line profit award aim in short term. In general, leaders have not consider how to develop talent employees in their organizations. They have mistakenly highly consider they need to truly reward the qualities that provide for long term stability. If their organizations failure, it is due to lacking skill development is appropriate when they believe performance can be important of the employees acquire or refresh job related skills from himself/herself job related learning effort every day as well as increasing job responsibility to him/her. However, effective training arrangement can bring fresh job knowledge and learning job related practice chance to raise every employee individual confidence and skill or effort to learn whethe he/she ought need how to do himself/herself daily simply or complex tasks in right or correct attitude in order to minimize mistakes chance occurrences, even avoid mistakes occurrances again in possible . Hence, effective training courses arrangment will have necessary to some organizations,wheh they had have many new employees are working in their organizations.

-
-
-
-
-
-
- Reference
-

- Bernard, M.B. & Bruce, J. A. (1994) Improving organizational effectiveness through transformational leadership: US. Sage publications, Inc. pp. 11-13.
- Fiona, M.W. (2004). organizational behavior and work , a critical introduction, 2 ed. : New York, US, Oxford university press, pp.79 .
- Jac, F.E.& John , R.M. (2014) predictive analytics for HRM:US Pearson Education pp.13-16
- Stephen, P.R. & Timothy, A.J. (2018). Essentials of organizational behavior, 14 ed.: US. Pearson Education, Inc. pp.108-110

● Facility management raises ●

productive efficient research

● Facility management can reduce ● maintenance service expenditure

●

● Facility management provides a variety of non core operations and maintenance services to support any organizations' operation. For logistic organization example, it is possible to provide effective maintenance service to warehouse in order to reduce warehouse facilities to be damaged to bring to spend to buy any new equipment facilities expenditure. So, when the logistic company's warehouse facilities can be maintenance to be the best quality. Then, they can be used these warehouses' machines facilities again. Their performance can assist workers to manufacture any products to keep the most efficiently an raising the best production performance in whole manufacturing process. Then, this logistic company's facility management department can bring to avoid purchase any new machine facilities expenditure spending. One to these warehouses' production machine facilities are kept in the best production performance environment even in long term production need.

● The logistic industry's facility management department can create cost savings and efficiency of the warehouse's workplaces. It's machines facilities (production machines) are dealt with the maintenance management of the physical assets maintenance service. FM (facilities management) has been being applied to industrial facilities in logistic and warehouse industry long term as well as maintenance plays a significant role to ensure the full service and the warehousing system, including both building components and equipment in warehouse.

● Maintenance service is needed to bring a certain level of availability and reliability of a warehouse facilities system and its components and its ability perform to a standard level of quality. So , it seems that logistic industry's warehouse asset cost reducing. It depends on whether it has one facility management department to provide maintenance service to itself warehouse workplace's production machine facilities and warehouse building itself in order to let workers t feel the manufacturing machines can bring good manufacturing performance to assist them to produce any products in one safe warehouse workplace environment. Hence, the performance measurement of warehouse maintenance issue will be valued to be consider to every warehouse manager and facility manager in logistic industry.

● In logistic industry, (FM) works at two level on the one hand, it provides a safe and efficient working environment, which is essential to influence warehouse workers whether how they perform to do their manufacturing tasks or logistic goods delivery tasks in warehouse. When they feel the warehouse is safe environment to work. They will not need to consider anywhere has risk to cause they die by accident in warehouse. Hence, they can concentrate on doing their every tasks . On the other hand, it can involve strategic issues, such as property (warehouse workplace and management, strategy property decision and warehouse facility, e.g. manufacturing machine, facility maintenance and checking planning and maintenance planning development.

● However, reducing the operating expense issue will be the main aim when the logistic company feels that it has need to set up one in-house facility management department to carry on any maintenance service for its warehouses' any workplace property and manufacturing machines facilities. So, when the logistic company decides to implement one facility management department, it needs to ensure its facility management department can bring the minimum level of keeping manufacturing performance and efficiency to its warehouses' any manufacturing machines and warehouses' property to avoid to be damaged in short term, such as loss of business due to failure in service, provision of project to customer satisfaction, provision of safe environment, effective utilisation of workplace space, e.g. warehouse effectiveness and communication between the workers and the logistic managers in the warehouse workplace , due to the warehouse's space is not enough maintenance service reliability to the logistic company's warehouse, responsiveness of the warehouse's worker individual negative emotion problem, due to he/she often feels need to work in one unsafe warehouse working environment. Hence, it seems that poor or unsafe warehouse working environment can influence workers feel negative emotion to work to bring low efficiency (inefficiency) or under productive performance in warehouse. It has relationship to influence they to bring psychological negative emotion feeling to work when the organization lacks one effective warehouse management repairing service to be provided to the warehouse's facilities and properties' maintenance needs in order to avoid incffective measurement and misleading of performance.

● Hence, the logistic company's facilities management department often needs to be reviewed whether its maintenance service level is passed to achieve the lowest repair (maintenance) service standard to its warehouse itself property and manufacturing machine or warehouse delivery tool facilities or warehouse lamps' light whether is enough to let workers to see anything clearly to avoid accident occurrence or see anything to work clearly or the warehouse space areas are enough to let they can have enough space to walk or communicate to their team supervisors or deliver any goods more easily in the short distance between the worker's sending goods location and the delivering goods destination in order to avoid because the lacking enough space to cause the accident occurrence , due to the space is not enough to let they deliver their goods to any locations in warehouse.

● Hence, it seems logistic company's (FM) department can contribute to the organization's mission, such as avoiding warehouse accident occurrence, inefficiency, not enough and unavailability of the facility for future needs when the warehouse lacks enough space areas to bring poor performance of facility and dangerous warehouse itself property in warehouse, e.g. safe and reliable operations of material handling equipment and maintenance of warehouse facilities, grounds, security system, utilities, plumbing, heating , enough lighting system, air conditioning, warming heater, fire protection, security system alarm etc. facilities in warehouse.

● Hence, it seems that if the logistic company expected to reduce to spend lot of excessive manufacturing machine purchase expenditure, lose of workers' life or bring workplace accidents , due to poor warehouse workplace environment, even bringing lawsuit compensation claim loss , due to the worker individual accident or death is caused from the poor warehouse facilities, or bring negative emotion to let the workers feel they are working in unsafe warehouse workplace environment. Then, it ought choose to set up on facility management department in order to provide enough maintenance service to its warehouse to avoid these non essential expenditure causing , due to these poor warehouse facilities factors.

● Hence any logistic company ought choose to set up one itself in -house facility management department, it be better than outsourcing its all facilities service to one facility management (maintenance service provider) to help it to deal any kinds of maintenance service in warehouse. Because it is long term maintenance need to its warehouse's any machines and warehouse itself properties. If it chose to find one outsourcing facilitiy management maintenance service provider to replace its in-house facility management department to deal all related facilities maintenance tasks in warehouse. Then, it is possible that it needs to pay long time facilities maintenance service fee to its outsourcing facility management maintenance service provider more than itself facility management maintenance service provision department.

● In conclusion, to decide whether the company ought need or not need facilities maintenance service or either set up in-house facility management department or outsource one facility management maintenance service provider. It depends on whether its organization has how many facilities are used in its workplace, how many staffs are working the workplace, how much size of its workplace, its workplace is office or warehouse or factory, how long time of its facilities' useful time etc. factors , then it can decide whether it needs or does not need one facility maintenance service department or outsourcing facility maintenance service provider to help it to deal any facilities management problem in its organization.

●

● Facility management role in

● organization

●

● When one company feels that it has need facility management service. It can choose to set up either in-house facility management department or seek one outsourcing facility management service provider to help it to arrange any facility management service need. However, this facility management role is only one for the organization. It concerns this question: What facility management maintenance function can bring the benefits to the organization?

● It can define that all services required for the management of building and real estate to maintain and increase their value, the means of providing maintenance support, project management and user management during the building life cycle, the integration of multi-disciplinary activities within the built environment and the management of their impact upon people and the workplace. In traditional, (FM) services may include building fabric maintenance, decoration and refurbishment, plant, plumbing and drainage maintenance, air conditioning maintenance, lift and escalator maintenance , fire safety alarm and fire fighting system maintenance, minor project management. All these are hard services. Otherwise, cleaning , security, handyman services, waste disposal, recycling, pes control, grounds maintenance, internal plants. All these are soft services. Additional services, might also include: pace planning, things moving management, business risk assessment, business continuity planning, benchmarking, space management, facilities contract outsourcing service arrangement, information systems, telephony, travel booking facility utility management, meeting room arrangement services, catering services, vehicle fleet management, printing service, postal services, archiving , concierge services, reception services, health and safety advice, environmental management.

● All of these services will be every organization's in-house facility soft or hard services needs. So, it explains why some large organizations feel need one effective facility management department to help them to arrange how to implement facility services efficiently in order to achieve cost reducing, raising efficiency and performance improvement aims because one effective facility management control system can influence employee individual productive effort to be raised or reduced indirectly.

● However, (FM) can be selected either setting up one in-house (FM) department or outsourcing its services to one facility management service provider to help the organization to solve any kinds of facilities maintain service problems. One on-house (FM) department is a team, it needs employees to deliver all (FM) services. Some specialist services are needed to be outsourced, when the service is on expertise in the company. The no expertise services will be outsourced to simple service contracts, e.g. lift and escalator (FM) department will have direct labour, but it can outsource some specialist to help it to do some complex facilities management service. So, the team leader can of can manage whose team staffs, such as maintenance technicians run low risk operations . Otherwise, the outsourcing facility management service provider needs to help it to operate high risk operations or maintenance vital plant facility management service. Anyway, it can set up in-house (FM) department to arrange specialist direct labour and outsourced (FM) services to more than one facility management service providers to do different kinds of (FM) services. One of these outsourcing (FM) service provider, who can arrange sub-contractors to assist it to finish any (FM) services of it's outsourcing (FM) services are more complex to compare the other sub-contractors (third parties).

●

● What is a facility manager's role to provide quality service to satisfy its user needs?

●

● We need to know how quality can be defined in facility management and why it should be defined by the customer? How facility managers can find out customer (user) needs? What are the difficulties in finding out users' needs and in delivering quality services? Whether improving quality always means requiring higher cost?

● In general, facility manager's major responsibilities may include these major functional areas: longer range and annual facility planning, facility financial forecasting, real estate acquisition and/or disposal, work specification, installation and space management, architectural and engineering planning and design, new construction and/or renovation, maintenance and operations management, maintenance and operation management, telecommunications integration, security and general administrative services. When the facility manager had implemented any one of these FM services for those user. How does he/she provide excellent (FM) service quality ot let whose users to feel satisfactory?

● In fact, quality issues can not be considered without customer-oriented perspective service quality involves a comparison of expectation with performance. (FM) service quality is a measure of how well to service level delivered matches customer expectation. So, these issues are (FM) service user's general measurement level requirement. The (FM) manager needs to achieve these the minimum performance measurement level to satisfy whose (FM) user's needs.

● However, (FM) service quality has three characteristics: Intangibility, heterogeneity, inseparability. But in fact, (FM) service delivered may be through tangible physical aspects, e.g. factory plant workplace building, machine equipment maintenance, intangible (FM) services, e.g. managing space moving in plant to let staffs to work, managing outsourcing cleaners to clean factory equipment. However, all (FM) service performance often varies, due to the behavior of service personnel. Hence, a well developed job specification and training can help to improve the consistence of services of (FM). Any (FM) production and consumption of many services may are inseparable and they are usually interactions between the (FM) client and the contact person from the service provider.

● Hence, it seems that service quality is considered as hard to evaluate. In (FM) service quality, it includes physical quality and interactive non-physical service quality. Physical quality is tangibles: The appearance of the physical facilities, equipment, personnel and communication materials. Non-physical services quality means reliability: The ability to perform the promised service dependably and accurately; responsiveness means the willingness to help customers and provide prompot service to let user to feel; assurance mans the competence of the system in its credibility in providing a courteous and secure service and empathy means the approachability, ease of access and effort taken to understand customers' needs.

● Hence, a good performance of (FM) manager , he/she ought satisfy the user's tangible and non-tangible both service quality needs. I recommend that he/she can attempt to predict what are the (FM) customer expects in each (FM) service needs. Then, it can make decision what aspect(s) will be the (FM) users major (FM) service need and what aspect(S) won't be the (FM) users major (FM) service need. Then, he/she can make more accurate decision to arrange time, human resource , cost spending amount arrangement whether when it ought concentrate on finishing the (FM) major service tasks as well as whether how he/she ought finish the major (FM) service tasks to be more easily, e.g. how to arrange staffs number to finish, how many the minimum staffs number is needed to be arrange the major (FM) service tasks, time arrangement is important factor, because it can influence whether he/she ought finish the major (FM) service tasks today or tomorrow or later in order to have enough time to finish other non-major (FM) service tasks. Instead of time management, staff number arrangement is also important factor , if he/she arranged the excessive staffs number to do the (FM) major services tasks, then it is possible that it will have shortage of staffs number to finish the non-major (FM) service tasks on the day. So, avoiding either major or non-major (FM) services can not finish on the day. The (FM) manager needs to predict when the major (FM) services and the non-major (FM) services which are necessary to be finished in order to have enough time and staffs to assist him/her to finish every day major and non-major (FM) service effectively. Then, the achievement of his/her (FM) major and non-major tangible and non-tangible services , it will have more chance to be performed efficiently by his/her managed staffs.

● In conclusion, in any organizations , (FM) manager needs have good predictable effort to evaluate whether when his/her managed team need to finish the major and/or non-major (FM) tasks as well as whether how he/she ought arrange the accurate time and staff number to finish any major and/or non-major (FM) service tasks on the day. Then, his/her leading of (FM) service team can be managed to work more efficiently in order to satisfy her/his (FM) service user's needs.

●
●
●
●
●
●

CHAPTER THIRTEEN

● How (FM) space moving management ● can bring valued add to organizations

●

● There are interesting questions: How (FM) can bring value-add to avoid loss or earn more profit to the organization? Can it influence employees to raise performance and improve efficiency ? Some organizations' (FM) service need which is necessary in order to let employees can raise productivity.

● It is based on these assumptions: I assume the organizations have completely either outsourced or in-house their (FM) facility management departments will gain more effect on added value than they have no (FM) function as well as organizations have a strong coordination with the (FM) department will gain more added value than organizations with a weak coordination. Organizations in the profit aim can gain more added value than organizations in the not for profit aim sectors.

● In fact, any organization is difficult to confirm it has relationship between improving performance, raising efficiency and owning (FM) function in its organization. (FM) could have to do with the attraction of easy but incomplete indicators of efficiency rather than the necessarily and less direct measures if the effectiveness and the relevance of space moving useful management, e.g. whether building has the enough space to let employees to move to work easy in order to raise efficiency, whether the building has excessive furniture and equipment number and they are putted on wrong places to be caused employees move difficulty in the building in order to influence productive performance.

● However, how to arrange space moving management to equipment, e.g.

copying machines, faxes, productive machines, they are putted on the locations where have enough space to let employees to move to another locations. For example, the building floor has more than 50 employees, but its space is not enough to let these 50 employees to move to any locations to let them to feel easily often. Then, it is possible to cause they feel nervous pressure and they can feel difficult to work , when they are working in a small office space or factory space or warehouse space. Then, the consequence will be under-predictive efficiency or poor performance to any one of these 50 employees in this office or factory or warehouse.

● " Facility management is responsible for coordinating all efforts related to planning, designing, and managing buildings and their systems, equipment, and furniture to enhance. The organizations abilty to compete successfully in a rapidly changing world." (F.Becker)

●

● The author explains equipment, workplace internal space designing, furniture space putting location arrangement will have possible to influence employee individual productive performance or efficiency to be raised or reduced in the workplace. Hence, it seems that, in the value chain (FM) belongs to the activity part of the firm. To make the facilities cooperation with each office or factory or warehouse using space moving facility management. Facility space moving management must be linked strategically, tactically and operationally to other support activity to add value to the organization's office or factory or warehouse space moving management arrangement more effectively.

● Thus, how to arrangement space moving management issue it will have possible to influence the organization's employee individual productive performance and efficiency in whose workplace. It seems that (FM) space moving management arrangement have indirect relationship to influence the organization's employee individual performance and efficiency , due to they need often to work in the workplace, if they feel moving difficulty , or excessive equipment , furniture number is putting into the small office, factory or warehouse locations, or they feel the office or factory or warehouse has excessive (a lot of) staffs number to work in the small space of office or factory or warehouse. Then, they can not concentrate nervous on finishing every tasks in possible. In long term, their efficiencies will be poor or inefficiencies or their performance won't be improved or causing poor performance in possible.

● Instead of the not enough space moving and excessive staffs number factor, it will bring another question: Can enough information systems equipment cause a more efficient and improved performance to the organization staffs in the workplace?

● I assume that the office has 100 employees and it has only ten copying machines. So it means that ten employees use one copying machine. Hence, it brings this question: Is it enough to provide only ten copying machines to average ten employees to use? It depends on other factors, e.g. whether any one of these 100 employees needs to print how many documents per day , whether the five copying machines' locations are far away to separate different locations or they are stored in one printing room in the office, whether the day has how many staffs are absent, whether the day has how many printing machine(s) is/ are broken to need to be repaired. Hence, these unpredictable external environment factors will influence whether the five copying machines number is enough to let these 100 employees to use in the office every day. Hence, facility manager ought need to spend to observe average their copying behaviors every day in order to make data record. Many employees need to use copy machines to print documents, average how many document's page number, they need to print, how much average time spending to print their documents, average how many staff absent number on the day. Even, if the all five copying machines are stored in the printing room, calculating the staffs number whether how many staffs need more than five minutes to walk to the printing room to print their documents many staffs need to spend five minute to walk to the printing room, and they have other urgent tasks to wait to finish. It is possible to influence their efficiency, due to they often need to spend more than five minutes to walk to the printing room to print documents. If there are many staffs need to often to print documents, but their printing task will have many time, e.g. 20 separate printing tasks. Then, they need to spend at least (20x5) 100 minutes to spend time to walk to the printing room to print their documents. It must influence that they should not finish the other urgent tasks on the day. If there are many staffs to spend much time to walk to the printing room in the least 20 separate printing time or more on that day. All the facility manager needs to evaluate whether all the five copy machines are stored in the printing room whether it is the best location decision or they ought need be separated to put on different office locations in their workplaces, even he/she ought need to evaluate whether it is enough copying machines number, when the office has only 5 copying machines. He/she ought need to buy more copying machines number to satisfy any one of these 100 employee individual copying task need.

● In conclusion, effective office or factory or warehouse space moving facility management will be one part task of (FM) function. If the office or factory or warehouse can have accurate equipment, machine , furniture number to avoid excessive or shortage number problem to cause employees often feel moving difficult problem in their workplace when they need to move to another location to work in office or warehouse or factory as well as whether the staff needs often spend time to wait the another employee to use the copying machine to print whose document or fax machine to deliver whose document. Then, it is not that fax or printing machines number is not enough to provide the employees to use in the office or warehouse or factory workplace.

● Hence, (FM) includes space moving facility management to equipment , machines, furniture number as well as choosing anywhere is(are) the suitable location (s) arrangement to putting or storing these facilities in workplace as well as decision of the staff number and the workplace area size whether it has excessive staffs number to cause these staffs need to work in the small area size of office or warehouse or factory workplace. So, the organization ought need to decide whether it needs to reduce the office's staffs number to let them to work in another more suitable locations in another workplace. Hence, all these facilities space moving management and staffs and workplace size issues will be (FM) manager's consideration issues, because these external environment factors will influence employee individual efficiency and performance to be poor to cause low valued to its organization in long term in possible .

●
●
●
●
●

● Reference
● Becker, F. (1990). " Facility management : a cutting edge field?" property management 8 (2): 25-28.
●
●
●

● Predictive the choosing right
● data asset and (FM) analytics

- solutions to boost public
- transportation service quality
-
- Can gather the choosing right data public transportation service station facilities asset and analytics, it can give recommendation to help any organization to boost service quality? (FM) analytics data can be applied to public transportation service industry to be supported how and why the train, train, ferry , ship, air plane, underground train public transportation tools' time arrival and leaving information notice board and automated ticket paying machines facilities are putting on or stored any where locations in order to boost passengers to feel their facilities locations are convenient to let them to buy tickets and see the arrival and leaving time for the next public transportation tool from the information notice electronic board machine. So, it seems that these public transportation tools' station facilities locations can influence passengers to feel the public transportation service company how to consider to its passenger's buying ticket needs and next public transportation tool's arrival and leaving time information needs in order to boost its passengers use service quality and let them to feel better service reliable performance in any train, tram, ferry , ship, underground tram, airplane stations.
- As these public transportation service organizations need to learn data analytics represent an opportunity for its ticket paying machine equipment facilities as well as the next transportation tool arrival and leaving time information notice board electronic equipment facilities anywhere the locations are the most suitable to put on or store these equipment to let passengers to walk to the ticket paying machines to buy the ticket to catch the train, tram, underground train, ferry, airplane, taxi, ship more easily. So, they do not need to spend more time to find these facilities locations and spend more time to queue to wait to buy ticket to catch the public transportation tool in stations conveniently. Instead of where is the seeking ticket paying machine location, where is the next public transportation tool arrival and leaving information notice time , these both issues will be any public transportation tool's passenger's main needs.
- Hence, how to spend time to seek where the next public transportation tool's arrival and leaving time information electronic notice machine location and where the ticket paying machine location , these both factors will influence any passengers' positive or negative emotion causing. For example, if the passenger feels difficult to find the ticket paying machine

in the large area size train station or /and he/she feels difficult to find the train time arrival and leaving information to let him/her to know when the next train will arrive the station. Due to he/she feels difficult to find the train ticket paying machine, he/she needs to spend much time to find any one ticket paying machine in the train station. Then, it will influence him/her to choose another public transportation tool to replace the train public transportation tool, e.g. he/she can choose to catch tram, underground train, taxi, bus, ferry, taxi, ship to replace train. So, it seems ticket paying machine and time arrival and leaving information notice electronic equipment 's location putting or stored choice will be one factor to influence the passenger to choose another kind of public transportation tool to replace train at the moment. When, he/she feels that he/she arrives the destination in the most short time. Then, the public transportation service organization (FM) manager has responsibility to evaluate whether there are enough ticket paying machines number to let passengers do not need to spend more time to queue to buy tickets to catch the public transportation tool in short time as well as there are enough time arrival and leaving for next transportation tool to let passengers to know. It will be their concerning issues when they arrive the public transportation service tool's station.

● Hence, predictive passenger individual walking behavior can help the public transportation service organization to choose whether where are the most convenient and attractive locations to let the ticket paying machines and the arrival and leaving time information electronic board machines to be putted on or stored in the suitable station positions in order to let many passengers can find these essential facilities in stations very easily. So, gathering data concerns passenger walking behavior in the public transportation service any stations, which can help the facility manager to make more accurate evaluation to attempt to predict whether where the locations are common places to let passengers to choose to walk daily or where the locations are not common places to let passenger to choose not to walk daily in general. Then, he/she can apply these data of different locations in the stations to evaluate whether anywhere they will have many passengers to choose to walk or whether anywhere they won't have many passengers to choose to walk in order to make more accurate decision whether anywhere are the most suitable locations to let the ticket paying machines and the time arrival and leaving information electronic board equipment to be putter on or stored in order to let them to feel it is so easier to let them to find.

● Anyway, calculating each station's passenger number per day issue is important to predict whether where , there are many passengers choose to walk or where, there are not many passengers choose to walk in these different public transportation service stations in order to evaluate whether where the stations' different ought put on paying ticket machines or time arrival and leaving information electronic boards in order to let they feel very easy to buy tickets and seeing the next arrival and lcaving time information for the kind of public transportation service tool conveniently in the different stations. Moreover, if the station has no enough ticket paying machines number to be supplied to let passengers need to spend more than ten minute time to wait to buy ticket to catch the kind of public transportation service tool in every queue every day. Then it will cause them to choose another kind of public transportation tool to catch go to working place or entertainment place to replace it to on that day. Then, it will cause these passengers who often do not like to queue in the kind of public transportation service tool's any stations, who will not choose to go to anywhere of this kind of public transportation service tool's any stations again. Hence, in long term this kind of public transportation service tool will lose many passengers. Thus, calculating each station's busy time of passengers number , which can predict when it is the busy time and it can make more accurate decision whether the station has need to increase enough ticket paying machines number in order to bring enough supply number to satisfy passengers' ticket purchase need in the busy time.

● In conclusion, gathering above all stations' public transportation service equipment facilities number, storing positions data and every station's passenger walking behavior data, they are necessary to any public transportation tool service industry, because these equipment number and storing locations will influence them to make decisions to choose another kind of public transportation tool to replace it's transportation service if they often feel difficult to find these facilities in its different stations. Thus, it is part of task to facility manager's responsibility if the public transportation service organization expects it won't lose many passengers , due to these external environment factor influence and it also implies cheap ticket price does not guarantee the passengers will choose to catch this kind of public transportation service tool to go to anywhere.

●

CHAPTER FOURTEEN

● The relationship between facility ● management and productive ● efficiency

●

● It is one interesting question: Can facility management function bring benefits to raise productive efficiency to organizations? I shall indicate some cases to attempt to explain this possible occurrence chance as below:

● Facility management benefit to office workplace

● In private organizations, when the firm has facility management department, whether it can bring efficient administration to influence clerks to work efficiently in office, e.g. reducing administrative time or shorten time to work in administrative processes, in order to achieve minimizing clerk number labor cost. How to design office facilities to let office staffs to feel comfortable to work and reducing their pressure to work. It seems that office working environment will influence office staff individual performance. If the office working environment could improve efficiency and creativity of services to satisfy office workers' comfortable working environment needs. It will reduce every administration manager's working pressure when he/she needs often to find methods to attempt to encourage whose administrative clerks to avoid to waste working time to do some non-major administration tasks.

● Hence, how to design or allocate or arrange office any facilities' stored locations or whether how many equipment number is the enough to store in the locations, which will influence office employees' working attitude in order to raise or reduce their administration tasks efficiency indirectly, e.g. the office is clean or dirty, whether office reception has enough information telephone switchboard operation facilities, whether every clerk's table has enough computers number to supply to every to use, whether internet speed is fast or slow in order to let any employees can send and receive email to communicate or download any document from internet in short time, whether data processing and computer system maintenance service supply is enough to be repaired to employees' computers immediately when their computers are broken to wait repair, whether website editing facilities operation whether is enough to link to office every staffs in order to let any office staffs can apply internet to do their tasks conveniently in short time.

● Hence, all of these general office equipment facilities whether they are enough supplied and their stored positions anywhere are the suitable to assist any clerks to work conveniently, they will influence every office employee's administrative and productive efficiency indirectly as well as all faxes, copying machines, computers, whether internet linking maintenance service time is short or long to prepare to any office employees to use conveniently any time, these different issues will also influence every employee individual efficiency in office. Hence, it concludes that office working environment, facilities supply number, facilities maintenance service and facilities location storing both factors will influence employee individual administrative productive efficiency in office.

●

● facility management benefits to service working environment

●

● Can effective facility management improve service working environment to raise employee individual work performance? It is a concern about the quality of service to its customer question. The term" standards and goals" are often used to measure staff individual service performance whether he/she can serve to customers to let them to feel this staff's service performance or attitude is good or bad.

● Is the service workplace working environment facilities enough, it will influence customer service staff individual performance.

● For shopping center service industry case example, for this situtation, e.g. shopping center's facilities are enough or are placed to the suitable locations in order to let the shopping center's customers to feel comfortable to shopping when they enter this shopping center as well as whether the shopping center's facilities can influence the customer service staffs to serve whose shopping customers easily or difficult, due to whether the shopping center's facilities whether are adequate supplied or their locations are the best suitable positions to influence their service performance to let them to feel easier or comfortable to serve their customers in any large size shopping centers. For example, whether the lamps' lighting energy is enough to let the shoppers to feel safe to walk to visit any shops when there are many shoppers were walking to cause crowd and they feel difficult to walk to avoid any body contact to any one in busy time when the shopping center has no enough lights to let them to see anywhere in the shopping center's dark environment. Then it will influence customer service staffs to feel difficult to find any shopping center customers, e.g. when two shopping center customers are fighting in one location where is far away to the shopping customer service staffs and securities in the shopping center, because the shopping center is large and it has no enough light to let the customer service staffs and securities to find their frighting location to deal their fighting behavior and other shopping center's shoppers will feel very dangerous to walk their fighting location to avoid to close them. Then, it will has possible to cause death or hurt to any one of these two fighting shoppers ,even other shoppers' life. Because the shopping center's securities and customer service staffs who need to spend much time to find their fighting location, it will delay they can bring the policemen to their fighting location when they arrive this shopping center's destination in short time in order to solve their fighting behavior to influence all shoppers' life in this shopping center. Hence, the shopping center whether it has enough lamps number and the lamps' light whether is enough, these lighting facilities will influence any shopping center customer service staffs and securities who can spend less time to arrive any locations to deal any urgent matters.

● For another situation in shopping center, if the shopping center has no enough paying telephone service facilities to supply shoppers to phone to anyone when they feel need to phone to any in the shopping center. Then, it will lead to some shoppers decide to find where the shopping center's reception's telephone to supply to them to phone call to anyone. If they are ten shoppers are waiting to use the shopping center's reception telephone to phone call to their friend or family within one minute. Thus, it will influence the reception customer service staffs feel difficult to arrange how to distribute the only one telephone to these ten shoppers to use to phone call their friend or family when they are queuing within their one minute waiting time in the shopping center's reception. If these ten shoppers can not use the reception telephone to phone call anyone. hen, they will feel dissatisfactory and complain to the reception service staffs politely. So, lacking enough facilities in the shopping center's any where, it will possible to influence their shopping centers' shoppers to feel all shopping center's service staff individual performance to be poor. It means that if the shopping center expects to improve customer satisfaction to its customer service staff's behavioral performance, it meets have enough facilities to be supplied in the shopping center to let its shoppers to feel it is one comfortable and safe shopping center. In conclusion, shopping center's facilities will have possible to influence shoppers' feeling to evaluate its customer service staffs to evaluate whether their service attitudes are good or poor indirectly.

●

● Can facility management improve productivity

● The productivity means resources (input) is therefore the amount of products or services (output), which is produced by them. Hence, higher (improved) productivity means that more is produced with the same expectation of resource, i.e. at the same cost is terms of land materials, machine, time or labor. Alternatively, it means same amount is produced at less labor cost in term of land, material, machine, time for labor that is utilized. So, it brings this question: How can facility management improve productivity? I shall explain as these several aspects, it is possible to be improved productivity from (FM) successfully.

● Improved productivity of farm land: If the farming land has better facility management to bring advantages by using better seed, better facilities of cultivation and most fertilizer. It is in the agricultural sense is increased (improved). So, facility management can bring benefits to any land resource to raise productivity in possible. It implies that the productivity of land used for better facility management of industrial purposes is said to have been increased if the output of products or service within that area of industrial land is increased output aim.

● Improved productivity of material: If the factory has improved better equipment by facility management method to assist skillful workers to raise the manufacture cloth number, then the productivity of the cloth number is improved by (FM) method.

● Improved productivity of labour: When the factory has good manufacturing equipment facilities to be supplied to improve methods of work to product more producing number per hour, then (FM) improved productivity of worker. Hence, in any workplaces, when organization has good facilities, it will influence employees to raise productivities in possible, because they need often to improved equipment facilities manufacture products to achieve higher production number aim.

-
-
- Can facility management raise bank employee
- productivity
-
- Bank workplace environment is busy, the bank counter service staffs need to contact many bank clients to help them to serve or withdraw money from bank's counters. Whether does the quality of environment in bank workplace will influence the determination level of employee's motivation, subsequent performance productivity in bank working environment. For example, if the bank's staffs need work under inconvenient conditions , it will bring low performance and face occupational health diseases causing high absenteeism and turnover.
- In general, bank size is usually small, it will have many bank clients enter bank to contact counter staffs to need them to help them to save or withdraw money. So, it will bring air pollution the crowd queue in every bank counter challenge when the bank has many people are queue waiting in counters to queue. So, bank working condition problem relates to environmental and physical factors which will influence every bank counter staff individual working performance to serve bank clients satisfactory. However, bank staffs need to deal many documents concern every client personal data every day. So, they need to spend much time to use computer and painting machines. This is particularly true for these employees who spend most of the day operating a computer terminal in bank workplace. As more and more computers are being installed in workplaces, an increasing number of business has been adopting designs for bank offices installment. So, bank needs have effective facilities management design because of demand of bank staffs for more human comfort.
- An good equipment facility management for bank staffs to use conveniently, it is assumed that better workplace environment can motives bank employees and produces better productivity. Hence, bank office environment can be described in terms of physical and behavioral components to influence bank staffs to work inefficiently. To achieve high level of bank employee productivity, bank organizations must ensure that the physical environment in conductive to bank different department organizational needs, facilitating interaction and privacy, formality and informality, functional and disciplinarily, e.g. house loan or private loan

departments, counter service department, visa card application department.

● Thus, in a high safe privacy facility management working environment will let different department bank staffs feel safe to worry about privacy loss in possible. So, the improving bank facility to bring safe and high privacy to avoid bank client individual loss in working environment issue, the facility management can be results to bring these benefits, such as in a reduction in a number of complaints and absenteeism and an increase in productivity.

● Can (FM) create value to organization?

● (FM) can reduce managing facilities as a strategic resource to add value to the organization and its overall performance, e.g. saving the energy in building and take care of shuttle buses and parking facilities space management for , on economic efficiency and effectiveness, or good price and value for the organization.

● If the organization expects to apply (FM) process to save energy, it depends on possible input factors, i.e. interventions in the accommodation facilities services. So, it seems that the organization expects to save its energy consumption in its building. It needs have good space management facilities between parking its shuttle buses in its property's car park.

● Why does space facility management is important to influence efficiency and productivity. For one school's building example, when the school decides none of the two gymnasiums student sport entertainment centers to be built in order to reduce financial cost and higher benefits. Remarkably, the use of space with the school overall strategic goals , such as creating spaces that better can support the teaching, motivate students and teachers, attract more students and increase the utilisation of existing space to accommodate an increasing number of students.

● If it hopes to make high quality teaching facilities on student's choice where to study. The school will need to choose to build either one comfortable and new design facility teaching accommodation or build two gymnasium sport entertainment centers in its limited land space either for students' learning or sport aim. Due to it feels new teaching accommodation can make more attractive to increase students numbers to choose it to study more than building two new gym sport centers to let them do sport in school.

● Hence, space choice (FC) management strategy will be one important considerable issue, when the organization has limited land space resources to make choose to build any constructions in order to increase many clients number. Such as the school organization has limited storage land resource to let it to build either two gymnasium sport entertainment centers or one new teaching accommodation in order to attract many students to choose it to learn. Hence, it needs to gather data to make more accurate evaluation to decide how to apply its space facility to choose to build these both kinds of buildings in order to achieve the attractive student learning choice aim, so whether the two sport entertainment activity centers or one new teaching accommodation choice, it needs to gather information to decide whether the school ought to choose to build which kind of building in order to achieve the increase of student number aim, so space facility management will be this school's land shortage problem.

-
-
-
-
-
-
-
-
-
-
-
-
-
-
- Chapter Four
- The relationship between facility
- management and consumer
- behavior
-
- How and why shop facility management can influence consumer individual shopping behavior? If it is possible, what shop facility management factors can influence their consumption decision when they enter the shop to plan to buy anything. I shall indicate some shop case studied to explain whether how and why every shop's facility management can influence consumer individual consumption desire when any one consumer enters any shops.

●

● Shop's low ceiling height location (FM) influence consumer behavior

● Can the shop's ceiling height influence shoppers' shopping behavior? Can the shop's variation in ceiling height can influence how consumers process information to decide to make purchase decision in the shops, e.g. for this situation, when the consumer enters the shop, he/she feels the ceiling height is low and it has a lamp will contact his/her head in possible. So, he/she chooses to move far away from the low cciling location in the shop. It is possible that shop's ceiling low height and the lamp locates at the ceiling low height position will influence many customers' choices to leave the low ceiling height and lamp location, then the shop's low ceiling height will have possible to influenced many customers to choose to find the another shop to buy the similar kind of products , due to the lamp locates in the low ceiling height, so this lamp and low ceiling height will be possible factor to influence any shoppers who won't choose to walk to this dangerous location in the shop. If the shop's all spaces are ceiling height and it has many lamps are located at the low ceiling height spaces. Then, it will be serious to cause many shoppers do not want to spend too much time to choose any products in the shop because they feel dangerous to walk to the any low ceiling height lamps' locations in the shop.

● Hence, hoe to design the different concept may be activated by the showroom ceiling if it were relatively high, as it tends to be in mall stores, versus low, as it is in most strip mall shops and outlet centers. Relatively high ceilings may bring safe shopping emotion to let any consumers to feel thoughts related to freedom, whereas lower ceilings may let consumers to feel dangerous to walk the locations in any shops. Hence it seems any shops ought not neglect whether their ceiling height is tall and the lamps ought avoid to locate in any low ceiling height locations in order to influence consumers number to be decreased.

● Can house facility management influence consumer individual purchase intention?

● When one new property is built, whether the property consumers will consider how the new property is facility to influence their purchase intention to the property will the new property's (FM) influence buyers in real estate markets' preferences choice and living interest. Any new property's internal characteristics of the house unit itself , such as rooms available, when example, of external are location, accessibility to utilities services and facilities will have possible to influence the property buyer's final property purchase decision, so it seems that even the property price is cheap, it is not represent the property buyer will choose to buy the property, if he/she feels the property's facility management is poorer to compare other similar kinds of properties.

● So, it can help real estate analysts better explain and predict the behavior of decision makers in real estate markets. Property consumers will search for property information, concerns the property's quality, price distinctiveness, ability, facility management, service of the property's external environment to decide whether the property is high value to choose to buy to compare other kinds of properties.

● However, the external environmental forces, such as limited resources, e.g. time or financial will influence whose property consumption choice and living the property's satisfaction feeling (represent) a feedback from post-property purchase reflection used to inform subsequent decisions. The process of the property buyer's leaving experience will serve to influence the extent to which the property consumer how to consider future next time property purchases decision and new information methods. Hence, when one property consumer chooses to buy a house, it refers house features are house internal attributes , such as quality of building, the design as well as internal and external design, which are important factors for a property consumer when he/she needs to select and purchases one house.

● The other (FM) factors which can influence the property consumers' needs, include living space as features, such as the size of kitchen, bathroom, bedroom, living bath and other rooms available in the house. The environment of housing area is also important factor, e.g. the condition of the hood, attractiveness of the area, quality of houses, type of houses, type of houses, density of housing, wooded area or free coverage, slope of the attractive views, open space, non-residential uses in the areas vacant sites, traffic noise, level of owner-occupation in , level of education in level of income in, security from crime, quality of schools, religious of , transportation , shopping center, sport entertainment can be supplied to close to the house area. All these human related issue of the property's location will also influence the property buyer's living location selection. Hence, above (FM) influence property consumer purchase behavior, it is based on the relationship behavior. The consumer's house purchase intention and house features, living space, environment and distance to recreation center, supermarket, library etc. public facilities variable (FM) factors.

● In conclusion, the house internal space facility management and external environment facility management factors will influence property consumer individual house purchase intention.

●

● The effects of in-store shelf design facility management factor influences consumer behavior

● Can every store retailer's shelf design influence supermarket and large retail stores shoppers' behaviors when they visit the stores? Howevcr, currently many stores tend to build on traditional and repetitive design for their store shelf layout, it brings results in outdated store layouts.

● Another important store shelf layout design aspect, retailer should consider carefully is the allocation of products on shelves. So, it seems that efficient shelf space allocation management does not only minimize the economic threats of empty product shelves, it can also lead to higher consumer satisfaction, a better customer relationship.

● Why does supermarket shelves design is important? Any retail tore will sell product category within a shelf. They can use the same nominal category , e.g. crisps next to light crisps, same food product shelf. Anyway, a goal-based shelf display can contain several product, that determine a common consumer goal, e.g. fair trade. Hence, these two categorical product structuring methods are also described in terms of how to put product, or food on shelf benefit and attribute -based product categories.

● These shelf design food or product storing method will have more influence consumers to choose to buy the supermarket or retail store food or products more easily , due to products, or food put on their shelf very convenient and systematic to attract consumers' shopping consideration to the supermarket or retail store.

● Music (FM) environment influence consumer consumption desire

● Is it possible that shop music (FM) environment can raise consumer purchase desire? In one shop or supermarket, it can provide soft music (FM) equipment to let consumers can listen soft music or songs in the supermarket or retail shop when the are staying to spend more time shopping and whether soft music facility can be expected to raise customer individual value-added options to the music facility shop in the supermarket or retail shop.

● Can the music facilities prolong consumers to stay in the store? It is possible that tempo soft music can influence consumers to stay longer time in restaurants and supermarkets and retail shops. It is possible that the different types of music (FM) in any supermarket, restaurant, retail shop owning music listening facility shopping environment. It will have possible to influence consumers to prolong staying in their shops. For example, one wine selling retail shop has classical music (FM) listening equipment to let consumers to listen when they enter the wine shop, it is possible to cause consumers to choose to buy more expensive wine products. Some researchers indicate when the wine shop owns classical music facility to let all consumers can list classical music when they walk in the wine ship, it can evoke the wine consumers to choose to buy purchasing higher prices wine products in the long term classical music listening environment. Otherwise, in a fitness sport center, musical fir and excite or popular music (FM) environment can attract fitness sport players' emotion to play and kind of fitness sport facility longer time. Also, in one supermarket, the soft music facilities listening environment can persuade or attract food consumers to spend more time in the mall consuming food or beverage also purchase other products more easily, due to they will listen soft music to be influenced to choose to prolong staying time in the supermarket. It seems that it has relationship between retail shop's music facility environment and consumer's emotion will be influenced by these different kinds of soft music or songs to raise consumption desire in the supermarket, if some consumers like to prolong to stay longer consuming time in the owning music facility environment's retail shop.

● In fact, some researchers indicate the owning background music facility selling environment's ship , it can affect consumer decision making, memory, concentration consumption desire. So, classical , jazz soft music facility ought be installed in restaurants, retail shops, restaurants' environment. Otherwise, popular , exciting, noise, pop music facility ought be installed in fitness sport centers, theme park entertainment parks business places in order to influence fitness sport players or theme park entertainers to prolong playing or entertaining time to feel real sport or entertainment theme park playing machine facility's entertainment enjoyable feeling as well as attracting restaurant or supermarket or retail shop's consumers to prolong their staying time to make consumption decisions. Hence, it seems that music facility environment can raise consumers' consumption desire in possible.

● University bookstore atmospheric factors how to influence student's purchase book behavior?

● Any university bookstore how to do international control and structuring of book internal environment to raise students' purchase book desires in university itself school's bookstore, it will be one popular question to any universities. Hence, whether the university bookstore internal (FM) factors include: lighting, music, colors, scents, temperature, layout and general cleanliness as well as university external factors include: the university bookstore shape/size, windows, university parking facility for students availability and location, which can play an influential role of the university bookstore image in order to influence the university itself students to choose to buy books from themselves bookstore or university outside bookstores.

● Whether the university student needs to spend how long individual learning time and how much learning nervous to spend time to choose any kinds of book in the universiity bookstore or outside bookstores, this issue , he/she will consider. Because he/she does want to expect spend much time and nervous to choose to buy books in any bookstore. If the university's bookstore physical location and internal (FM) image can let its target student customers to feel it's all book products are stored in any attractive internal book shelves places, e.g. the cheapest and the most expensive different subjects of text books are stored in one system method to bring the positive image of value and quality in order to let university target student customers can find their books' choice location to spend less time to search any books to read in the unviersiity bookstore easily.

● However, due to learning time is shortage to every university student of the university's book shelves can display all text books in the attractive right locations in the university bookstore as well as the university's bookstore ought has an adequate space to let university students to walk to anywhere and find any subjects of text books and compare their book sale prices in the bookstore's any shelves' locations easily when they walk to the subject of book shelf location, then they can make accurate decision either to buy the right kind of subject book or not buy it to read in the short time. They will feel their book choice purchase decision making process won't influence their learning time in themselves universiity. Then, the university students will be influenced by themselves university's bookstore's attractive external university facilities in the university's any teaching places and the university's bookstore internal attractive environment facility image which can influence the students to make final choices to buy their liking books to read from their university's itself bookstore. Hence, the university's bookstore internal and external building environment (FM) design factors will influence its students whether choose to buy from themselves bookstore or another outside general bookstore.

● How and why does retail atmospheric environment influence consumers behavior in retail shop?

● Any shop's internal facility management design can influence atmospheric environment to influence consumer individual shopping desire, e.g. colour, lighting, music, crowding, design and layout factors, which internal shop (FM) environment can influence the first time shopping visiting client ' cognitive process how to feel the shop store image. Such as if the store's (FM) environment can bring enjoyable and fun and happy image to let them to feel shopping's enjoyment.

● In conclusion, when consumers will like to stay longer time in the store. Due to the store's internal (FM) atmospheric environment can attract them to stay longer time in the store. Then, the customer's shopping value will raise and it can bring purchasing intention and shopping satisfaction. How can (FM) influence retail atmospheric physical (FM) environment ? Can (FM) bring indirect relationship to influence how the consumer individual causes positive or negative purchase intention when he/she has influence to prolong staying desire in the store, when the shop has good (FM) , it will bring long time to make consumption chance in the shop.

●

  ●

● Facility management influences
● consumer satisfactory service
● level
●

● Can facility management (FM) quality influence consumer satisfactory service feeling? Any organization's facility management can improve the effectiveness of the maintenance organization. It can provide improved operational and maintenance functions to maintain the physical environment to support the overall mission. However, any organization will consider whether it improves its facilities, it will raise consumer satisfactory feeling when it provides the service to them, e.g. education service industry, when students need to often to attend any school's classrooms or lecture halls, computer rooms, libraries, all these facilities will be student's learning environment. If these school facilities can be maintenance to let students to feel comfortable to enjoy to study in their schools' any learning locations. Then, it has possible that to bring their enjoyable learning feeling in theirs schools.

●

● How school's facility management influences student's learning satisfactory feeling.

● However, in education industry case, the school's facility management has those criteria can be used to measure effectiveness. Student individual response time between the student's request for computer use service in school computer rooms, library reading service in school library , classroom computer facilities and tables, chairs etc. furniture supplies service and the facility management supply number and available to useful time. If the student believes that the response time is too long when he/she feels need to use any school facilities, the actual number of seconds or minutes, he/she needs to wait how long time to queue to use his/her school's any facilities in library, classroom, computer room. So, the student's queue waiting time to use any his/her school's facilities, it can measure the school's facility management effectiveness.

● Scheduling of preventive maintenance activities.

● It schedules of any maintenance activities are not arranged effectively to the school. Then, it will influence students' poor learning facility service to their school. For their situation, when the school's first floor has two men toilets are damaged. They are needed to be required. However, it is one week period, the first floor 100 students can not use the first floor men toilets. Hence, in this week, all 100 students need to go to other floors toilets to often use. They will feel busy and time is not enough when they need to attend to any classrooms to listen the first floor classrooms teachers' lesson. If he/she arrives the first floor classroom too late, due to he/she needs to go to another floor male toilets to queue to use. Then, he/she will feel angry and worries about whose absent or late attending classroom behavior when the lesson's teacher has attended early in the first floor classroom , and he teacher will need him/her to explain why he/she will go to this classroom lately, if his/her explanation won't be accepted to attend to the first floor classroom too late in the week. So, arrangement maintenance schedule to any school's facilities issue is importnt to influence student's satisfactory feeling to the school. Also, lacking of preventive maintenance activities will bring results in unscheduled shutdown of critical equipment can have an unrecoverable impact on the school's good learning environment providing to student's mission.

● In fact, however in any organizations, such as school, ship, office etc.

organizations, achieving balance of effectiveness and efficient difficulties and takes time and effort on the part of management and staff. It is not enough to establish an optimal relationship between these two parts. It has another factor that organizations need to consider costs. In today's budget tightening environment, decreasing expenses requires accepting a lower level of efficiency and effectiveness. The goal is to determine the point at which decreasing efficiency and effectiveness is no longer acceptable before that point is reached.

● It brings this question : How to apply facility management knowledge to rise efficiency and effectiveness in order to improve quality standard of service to satisfy consumers' needs in short time? Such as school's facilities service case. What factors can influence student's level of satisfaction with regards to higher educational facilities services? It seems that any school's facilities will influence its students how to satisfy its education service indirectly. Because they need often to go to school to learn. So, any school's facilities, e.g. classrooms, computer rooms, libraries, toilets, lecture halls, canteens, sport and entertainment centers, research laboratories, school car parks, student enquiry counters, all these places to the school's any students will attend. So, how raise schools' facilities improvement to satisfy students' learning needs in the school's any locations which will have help to influence it student individual satisfaction level to the school's service, instead of every teacher individual teaching performance service to the school's students.

● For any service organizations , such as hotels, restaurant, financial institutions, retail stores and hospitals etc. The physical environment can influence how customers' evaluation of their service. Due to service has intangible nature, so customers will rely on evaluate service quality.

● Any higher education institutions are education service providing organizations. They need have comfortable and enjoyable educational environment to be provided to the students to attend the school's any places in order to meet whose learning expectations and studying experience needs. So, the school's facility management will be one factor to influence student's learning satisfaction when they expect to attend the school's any locations or places to let them to feel the school's learning environment have good facility management feeling.

● In fact, if the school has comfortable classrooms or lecture halls educational environment to let its students to feel, it will bring assistance to raise their learning satisfactory feeling. So, comfortable learning facility management environment is one kind of school's facility service characteristics, it includes intangibility, perishability, inseparability and variability. So, they are every student individual learning feeling when they are attending to the school's any learning locations. So, school's facility management service feeling will influence whether they expect to choose this school to study. If the school's facility management learning environment is more comfortable and teaching facilities are better to compare other schools' facilities. Then, it will have possible to attract many students to choose this school to study. Such as any educational organizations, instead of the teachers (lecturers and professors) whose educational level is influence students number. The university's building environment will influence students' learning feeling, when they attend in the university. The facilities include laboratories, lecture theatres an offices, but also residential accommodations, catering facilities, sports and recreations centers because university students need have university life feeling to let them to fell the university can give welfare services , e.g. medical services, career guidance, sport entertainment, residential accommodation etc. service, instead of educational learning service in classrooms and lecture theatres. Hence, university's diversification facilities services are needed to satisfy university students to choose it to study, instead of university teacher's educational performance.

● When one student can enroll the university to study from secondary education institution. The admitted student will usually consider two aspects to decide to choose the university to study. One aspect is the academic programs, of sequence of courses choices and the another aspect is the university's facilities whether they can satisfy their university life need, e.g. library, dorms, bookstore, food canteen , gym's sport entertainment, education technological facilities in the classrooms and lecture theatres to let the students to feel the university's teaching facilities are achieved his/her learning demand.

● So, these two factors (teaching and learning and facilities) are linked to each other to influence student's total school learning experience and attitude towards a particular institution and this is termed as value chain in the student's learning process in the university. Hence, student individual evaluation variables will include teaching staff, teaching method, enrolment and facility enough supply actual service need.

● However, the university's facilities, such as any residential accommodation, canteen, library , classroom, lecture theatre, sport gym, entertainment center will be their useful facilities need to satisfy their learning, entertainment and eating ,even living need in residential accommodation in the school's learning life experience every day. If one student chooses to live in the university residential accommodation . All of his/her learning and eating and living time and spending will be calculated to the university's any facilities to let him/her to feel it can provide enough facilities to let him/her to enjoy.

● Hence, the facility management factor, such as overall campus environment, library, laboratory, classroom, lecturer theatre size and facility supply of on campus accommodation, welfare right service, parking areas, cafeteria , sport center etc. They will be every students facilities service needs from the university supplies choice. So, any university ought not neglect how to improve itself university's space area facilities to achieve satisfy their needs after they choose this university to study. Hence, any university's facility management will influence how the student's satisfactory learning service feeling when he/she chooses the university to study.

● In conclusion, better facility management will attract more students to choose the university to study. Otherwise, worse facility management will not attract more students to choose to study the school. Hence, it seems that the school's facility management factor has relationship to influence student's satisfactory feeling, instead of teacher individual teaching performance factor to the school.

● Property facility management influences householder buying behavior

● One new property's low price is attractive factor to influence property buyer individual preference choice. Does the new individual's facility management factor influence the property buyer's preference choice decision, if the property buyer feels its facility management is better than other similar properties, even it's price is higher than other properties. I shall indicate some cases to analyze this possibility as below:

● Some properties' facility management service quality has possible to create true value for any property buyers when they consider the calculation ingredients to make decision whether to new property has higher value to choose to buy. The factors may include: price, natural environment, transportation tools convenient available, shopping centers supplies, the neighour quality, and the property's internal facility management etc. factors.

● In fact, car or house purchase buyers, they have similar behaviors. It is that car's buyers will consider the car's machines whether they are safe to drive on roads, instead price, manufacture loyalty factors. It is possible that the car's machines quality factor will be preference to any car buyers when they make preference decisions to choose which brand its cars are the suitable. However, if the car's brand is famous and its appearance beautiful and price is cheap. But the car consumer feels its machine qualities are unsafe to let the driver to drive on road. Then, the car's poor machine quality factor will influence the car buyer's decisions to choose to buy this car. It can influence the car buyer individual car purchase decision.

● The car buyer's behavior is similar to property buyer's behavior. Although, the new property price is cheap, good neigh ours are living near to the new property's location, shopping centers and transportation tools are available to near to this new property's area. But if the property buyers' feels its facility management is poor quality to compare other similar properties. Then, the poor quality of facility management factor will have possible to influence the property buyers whose final buying decision to choose to buy this new property. It brings this question: How and why can the facility management poor quality factor influence property consumers' preference choice?

● In general, all property consumers won't know whether the new property's facility management is good or bad quality , they need to spend time to visit to the new property in order to observe whether its internal facility is satisfactory to his/her acceptable level. In simple, their purchase decision will regard to how to allocate household budget, how the household's economic resources are influenced, e.g. for travelling, visits to restaurants, comparing the different similar types of property product groups, e.g. apartments or houses or houses of a givn size data. For example, if one property's room(s) size is (re) small to compare other kind similar product type of room(s) size. Although the prior property's price is cheaper to compare to the later properties. But, if some property buyers hoped the property has large room(s) size, then the later larger room(s) size which will be possible to some property buyer's preference choice. Even, their property price is more expensive to compare the smaller room(s) size of properties. Thus, the property's room size which will be one major factor to influence property buyers' purchase decision. room's size had relationship to facility management issue. Moreover, if the room's quality and design is attractive, then it will bring more attractive to persuade some property buyers to choose to buy them to live in preference.

● Hence, whether the new property is good durable product feeling which will influence householder's choice. If the householder feels the new property has long term durable life to avoid to spend much maintenance expense when they have been living in the new property for a long term period. They will believe it has better facility management, quality to let them to live longer time and the most importance is that they do not need to spend any maintenance expense , due to the property 's any internal facilities are damaged easily.

● The external factors may include: culture, reference groups, family, social class and demography of lifestyle as well as internal factors may include: feelings, past property buying and living experience , property knowledge, motivation of the property buyer individual psychology. These both factors can influence any property buyer individual decision making process to do final house purchase behavior. However, internal factors, such as: property knowledge of facility management and property living experience, e.g. how to evaluate to choose to buy the property , due to the property buyer's past living experience for the past property's facilities whether its facilities can satisfy its property buyers' comfortable living needs. This internal factor will be more important to influence any property buyer's property purchase final decision. If he/she feels whose prior old property's facilities are satisfactory. Then, he/she will compare this new property and old property's facilities to decide whether this new property is value to buy. So, the old property's facility will be the measurement standard to compare his/her next new property purchase choice. So, the property purchaser will compare these new and old property's property facilities product knowledge to similarities among property alternative which will influence his/her final decision to choose to buy the new property to live.

● It seems that property low price factor must not guarantee to attractive many property buyers' choice. Otherwise, it is assumed that many property buyers like rent or buy to live the property for themselves for long term intention. There are less property buyers expect to sell the first property to earn profit intention. So, they will usually consider whether the property is long term durable product to avoid to pay maintenance expense when they had been living in the property in long term.

● Some factors that taking consideration are proximity to the specific location, housing prices, developer's brand, the payment scheme, reference group, which are not the main factors to influence any property buyer individual choice. Because property buyer's need is that the property has good facilities to supply to them to live, e.g. good heater equipment can provide hot water to them to bath in winter or good air conditioners can provide cold temperature to let them to feel cool comfortable feeling in summer in their homes. Good electric tools facilities , when they have need to use electricity in safe environment at home, e.g. car park accessibility facility , level of security facility , surface area facility and housing types, bedroom, bathroom facilities, quality of housing manufacturing raw material, house design , house durable guarantee, speed of complaint responsiveness, specification accuracy, confirmation of building plan service, showing legal file property purchase process service, finance instalments process assistance, speed of responsiveness, officers' skills of presentation. All of above these concern property facility management issues will influence any property buyers' final choice to decide whether the property is value to buy. So, facility management will influence property purchaser individual final decision in possible.

● Hotel facilities influence hotel consumer choice

● Travellers choose hotel to live. They will consider price, room comfortable feeling, hotel location , gum sport or entertainment service facility supplies , hotel room booking service etc. factors to decide whether the hotel can achieve every traveller individual minimum living need. However, whether hotel facilities factor will be the main factor to influence travellers' living needs. How and why do travellers consider hotel facilities whether are enough supply or facilities of quality to satisfy their demand to cause their living choice to the hotel final decision.

● Usually, hotel's customers won't plan to live too long time, e.g. more than three months in the hotel. Because they are travelling aim. It will bring this question: Does hotel facilities quality consider to influence their hotel living choice if the traveller is short-term traveller to the country? However , some travellers who have effort to spend money to live high class hotels, even their journey is short trip. Hence it seems that short trip , hotel living reason can not influence the high class hotel travellers' living comfortable demand to the high class hotel room. Hence , the high class hotel room's facility management quality is also needed high performance. Even, when they need to eat breakfast, lunch , dinner in the high class hotel canteens or playing any sport equipment, or gum equipment or watching movie in the hotel's small cinema room . They must need high class hotel can supply more entertainment, restaurant , sport facilities to satisfy their comfortable needs in the high class hotel. Moreover, they must consider safety issue when they are living in the high class hotel. So, thy must demand the hotel have enough five fright equipment in their rooms, or corridors and the stairs to let them can leave the dangerous locations to arrive the most safe locations immediately when the hotel has fire accident occurrence in any where . So, it ensures that the high class hotel's customers must ensure the high class hotel's facilities can satisfy their any one of above these needs before they decide to live this high class hotel.

● In fact, high class hotel's room price must be more expensive to compare the low class hotel. So, it explains why high class hotel's consumers will need the hotel has safe and good quality of facilities to let them to feel it is one reasonable price, safe , good service and good facilities' high class hotel to live. Usually, when the traveller arrives the country to travel, the travelers chooses the hotel to live, it is whose first time visit in common. So, he/she ought consider that the hotel environment seems it is good or bad to let the traveller to select to live. If the hotel's facility environment is new and beauty and design colorful to let the first time travellers to feel. Then, it is possible that good facilities environment can influence the first time travellers to select to live, even the hotel's room price is more expensive to compare other similar hotels in the travelling living places. Hence, it explains why hotel facilities can influence traveller individual room booking choice. When he/she is the first time to visit the hotel to select whether to live or not.

● How and why facility management can influence workplace productivity to bring customer satisfaction

● Facility management is one part of manufacturers or retailers as their productivity in workplace as their input and functionalistics within physical environment. In fact, facility management in workplace may include: site selection, property disposal, site acquisition, workplace space allocation, space inventory, space forecasting facility management, interior furniture change planning, interior furniture installation, moving maintenance, inventory, design evaluation, employment satisfaction evaluation plan, external maintenance and breakdown maintenance, preventive maintenance, landscape maintenance, energy space facility management, hazardous waste disposal, capital , operating furniture budgeting. So, it seems that one workplace considered whether the workplace's facility is enough to let employees to work in order to raise efficiency and improve productive performance more easily. Then, it will bring this question:

● How and why workplace facility management can influence consumer individual satisfaction?

● Strategic FM delivery is essential for business survival. I shall explain why for delivery is important to influence customer satisfaction. In business process view point, an effective and meaningful service to their customer , i.e. the user. For logistic industry, the product's delivery time will influence when the product can be sent to the user's arrival destination. If the product is delayed to sent to the user's home or office or any location destination. The reason is because the logistic product sender has no efficient facility management (FM) arrangement in its warehouse . Then, its warehouse lacks efficient (FM), which will cause users to feel its delivery service is poor and they will complain its delivery service staffs. Then, they will find another delivery service company to replace its service. So, it explains that logistic industry's warehouse (FM) service arrangement can raise efficient time to send any products to their customers in order to let they feel satisfactory service. For example, Amazon online logistic company's warehouse has applied artificial intelligence robotic tools to assist warehouse workers to arrange the different kinds of products to deliver to the right shelves . Then, the warehouse robotics will follow their right product shelves locations to follow the right products to deliver to US domestic or overseas product buyers in the short time and it can avoid the wrong products to deliver to the wrong buyers' risk. Also, the (AI) delivery tools can raise time efficiency to assist Amazon warehouse workers to reduce their work load, and tried to work in large warehouse environment. Although, its warehouse's area is large, the (AI) tools facility can help them to deliver the different products to different shelves in the right locations , e.g. exact product number and the kinds of product to be delivered to the right country' client's shelf location in the warehouse. Also, it implies FM is very important to influence Amazon warehouse delivery efficiency and avoiding delivery wrong occurrence chance. For example, the shelf location belongs to US domestic customers, or the shelf location belongs to Japan customers, or the shelf location belongs to Hong Kong customers, or any other Asia or Western countries' different customers' locations. The warehouse's facility needs have different countries' shelves enough space to put and it also need enough space to let the (AI) tools, robotic delivery workers and human workers both to walk to different shelves locations easily and the different countries' shelves number needs to be calculated accurate. For example, it has how many client number will buy Amazon's the kind product per day. If it has above 5,000 to 10,000 China clients to buy the kind of product. Then, it will need to make judgement how many shelves are placed in the warehouse. So, it can avoid to lack enough shelves to put any different kinds of products to prepare to delivery to China clients in efficient time and it won't avoid to delay to deliver to their homes or offices or any locations in China.

● Hence, such as Amazon logistic case, it explains why warehouse's space shelves number and area or locations facility management can influence workers or (AI) delivery tools how to move convenient and avoiding the delivery to the customer's wrong destination chance occurrence and shortening time to deliver products to its clients efficiently. Then, due to the delivering time is shorten and the wrong delivery destination's occurrence chance is also reduced , even it can avoid to deliver the product to wrong client's destination occurrence. Then, the logistic firm's clients will feel more satisfactory to its product sale delivery service and their complaints will be avoided. Hence, it explains effective warehouse (FM) space management service arrangement is essential to any logistic businesses nowadays.

● Facility management brings departmental benefits

● Why do organizations need have facility management (FM) service? As above examples indicate that (FM) can improve workplace environment facilities, e.g. warehouse environment to let workers to raise efficiencies or improve performances, even it can influence consumers to raise satisfactory to it's services indirectly, also it can help organizations' equipment to be used long term to cause old and are needed to spend expenditure to maintenance or change new equipment in order to improve better quality . So , it can assist organizations to avoid to spend more expenditure for new equipment purchase or maintenance. All these issues will be facility management service's benefits to an organizations, which can concern raising customers' service satisfaction, raising efficiency or improving productive performance, raising productivity, reducing equipment or property maintenance or new alternation much of expenditure spending, office or warehouse or any workplace space planning arrangement .

● However, every organization will need a facility manager or manage whose team effectively . When a facility manager begins to apply FM techniques to solve business problems. The case for FM is made. It is a simple matter of demonstrating a qualified return on the investment required. Every organization's success, FM operation of three key activities: they include: needing a proper understanding of the organization's needs, wants, drivers and goals and knowing when needs to review its changing circumstances, developing an effective facilities solution o support the organization's needs, wants , property drives and contribute to achieve its goals both short term and long term, achievement of reliable delivery of that solution in a managed, measured manner.

● So, it bring one question: What are the influential factors to be followed the right direction to FM manager's strategic FM operational decision? The influencing factors may include: ownership, governance sector, complexity and perhaps of most significant, the size of the organization's property portfolio.

● In fact, major occupiers feel FM service need, they are large corporate organizations and public service organizations. Their aims usually are to raise. The most marginal improvement in efficiency or effectiveness, these aims are the great significance. Major property occupiers will already have a facilities department or individuals performing the FM function with another department like property, finance or human resource, sale and marketing's facilities.

● Usually these FM need occupiers who will encounter this problem: How can apply FM service systems and processes to be developed to improve reliable service delivery making use of the economies of scale, not suffering because of the size of the problem. This question will be facility manager individual concerning question: How to apply (FM) technique to solve the improvement reliable service delivery making use of the economics of scale problem for whose organization?

● In reality much of external facilities management benefits to organizations, instead of raising efficiency, improving performance, raising productivity, reducing maintenance expenditure, e.g. energy saving, reducing natural resource waste, increasing local employment, improving supply chain management are all elements of the FM contribution to every organization's need. Hence are the work life balance argument and provision of an effective and safe working environment that supports why some organizations feel need (FM) service to support their organizational development.

● Moreover, on cost benefit of space saving efficient view point, space service cost reduction is a key driver for all organizations and the medium, or large sized players will benefit directly from a well coordinated facilities strategy. For example, application FM technique to help warehouse or office space area to save 50% space vacancy to let employees can move easily or putting enough furniture or equipment or many stocks can be putted in warehouses . So, paying more rent expenditure to rent or purchasing another new warehouse or office to satisfy workers or employees' working environment to be better need. If the organization has effective (FM) technique, then it has enough space vacancy to supply to the increase stocks number to be putted inside in warehouse and it can let workers to move safety in available to let staffs to move easily and equipment have enough space to be stored in the limited warehouse space problem.

● For greater space savings benefits will bring either long term renting or buying of increasing offices or warehouse number expenditure problem to any organizations, when the organizations' cost or renting or buying accommodation probably accounting for 60 to 70% of total occupancy cost . So a strategic program to release space or the prevent the acquisition of moves can be the most significant consideration to any facility manager, with between 40% and 60% of the workplaces are unoccupied in most offices or warehouses at any given moment in time.

● Hence, how to apply (FM) technique to save space occupied areas for employment moving or stocks or equipment saving need in offices or warehouses. This issue will be any facility managers' seeking methods to solve problem. However, the important major advantage of facility management to organizations is that the application of management principle to keep the organization's property assets with the aim of maximizing their potentials. Thus, any organizations' facilities have become important, due to the property facilities' worth will increase if the organization's facility management technique can protect the organization's facilities have good performance. Then, the organization's maintenance expenditure will reduce and it won't need to spend expenditure to buy any new facilities to replace old facilities , due to they often damage factor when they are used old.

● In conclusion, it explains why effective FM combines resources and activities can raise work environment improvement, which is essential to the raising employee performance aim. For hotel living service case example, this industry must need have good facility management service because hotels must need to fully equipped in term and facilities for effectiveness to satisfy hotel living clients' demand , hotels ought need good facilities asset management style lead to effectiveness in service delivery, there are benefit derivable from the adoption of facilities management from which other hotels can learn from for their effective operations. Hence, it explains why effective FM can bring benefits to hotels' properties to be more comfortable, beautiful appearances to attract many hotel customers to choose to live the hotel. Because hotel's building industrial kitchens, rooms facilities, equipment , halls of categories, restaurant facilities, gum sport entertainment centers' facilities, fans, elevators, lifts, electrical installation, escalators, baking equipment, recreational facilities, including golf courses which will be important factors to influence hotel clients' comfortable living feeling, if the hotel can keep its all facilities in the best living environment often. Then, it can raise chance to attract many hotel customers to choose it to live. So , hotel industry has absolute need to implement effective FM strategy to keep its properties more attractive to satisfy its clients' living needs.

● Instead of hotel industry, logistic transportation industry also needs effective facilities management in warehouse, because of the logistic company's warehouse 's facilities are good, then it will assist to raise employee individual efficiency in the safe and system shelve stored facilities in workplace environment and improving performance.

● Consequently, it will bring the shorten time to deliver any products to clients to avoide the delaying time delivery in order to let customers to feel more satisfactory to their services. In simple, it seems that some industries need have effective facilities management techniques to help them to bring long term customer satisfactory feeling, worker individual efficiency raising and performance improvement benefits. Hence, it seems facility management techniques' demand will be increased to some industries in popular in the future because it has help to raise employee individual efficiency , productive performance and client individual satisfactory level consequently.

●

● Psychological methods raise ●
productive efficiency

● How to impact of workplace ● management on well-being and ● productivity

● In facility management strategy, design can lead promotion, the value of offices that are enriched, particularly including warehouses, shopping centers to raise their market value. Moreover, effective organizations, such as raising powering workers when giving the effective design of office space. I assume that a good design of an interior office workspace environment seems a psychological department to influence staff individual emotion to bring positive power in order to raising productive efficient influence, such as in a commercial city office. So, it brings this question: How workspace management strategy can impact on staff's working behaviors in office.

● In fact, office tasks general include various forms of productivity, e.g. information processing, information management and any clerical tasks by computerization. Hence, office productivity concerns how to influence each office white color worker applies computers to work in office. The office space can impact on white color workers' performances in these several aspects: feeling of psychological comfort, organizational physical comfort and job satisfaction and productivity, efficiency. So, it seems that office workspace design strategy can influence white color workers' working behavior and attitude and performance indirectly.

● The office space management includes: how to removal from the workspace of everything except the materials required to do the job at hand, how tight managerial control of the workspace, and how to implement standardization of managerial practice and workspace design. So, these key ideas will influence how each white color worker's efficiency and productivity in office working environment.

● For this office space design situation, a large unseparated small space size's space design can accommodate more people and so brings itself to economies of scale. As a result, space occupancy can be centrally managed with minimal disruptive interference from office workers. Indeed, many businesses now adopt a clean and fresh air office working policy because they have more employees than they have spaces at which they can work. This desks are either taken on a first -come first -served basis. (hot desking) or can be booked in advance. So , when a company has many employees need to work in a small space working environment. It must concern how to let staffs to feel more comfortable in order to reduce high psychological pressure to work in this uncomfortable working environment. Hence, it explains why workspace design can impact on office workers' performance in some offices. All these issues are assumed that empowering workers to manage and have input into the design of their own workspace, then the effective office or any working places space management will enhance wellbeing to bring workers' positive emotions and improving productivity. I also assume the space working environment design have relationship of these depend variable factors to influence office worker individual productive efficiency. The variable factors may include psychological comfort, organizational comfortable, job satisfaction, physical comfort and productivity.

● However, office furniture , facilities will influence office white color workers' performance ,e.g. the room size whether is big or small for manage office worker, a high backed, comfortable leather chair is needed for office staffs to sit down to let more comfortable, the door and most of the walls need glass, the office room environment needs have sea-grass rug beneath the desk covering the immediate working area, the office also needs have plants and pictures, mail boxes, telephone and computer facility is needed. When one staff needs to send email or phone call or send letters or deliver documents conveniently. These office elements are essential in order to increase physical well-being and feeling of satisfaction to white-color workers. Hence, geren office and office working space design management is needed in order to influence white color workers' productive efficiency in long term.

●

● Effective workspace design can influence communication to raise productivity

● Office white-color workers often need communication between their managers, supervisors, and themselves. Office communication extends from the way that a user experiences a service. An effective office communication can bring these benefits; Providing positive influence on decision making by presenting a strong point of view and developing mutual understanding, delivering efficient decisions and solutions by providing accurate , timely and relevant information, enabling mutually benefit solutions, building health relationships by encouraging trust and understanding between the high level, middle level and low level staffs.

● Effective office communication needs to clearly communicate its nature and purpose. Good communication ensures that all service staffs are sending out the same messages. Communication is also important for ensuring the service understands what users requires and why he/she talks about understanding users' needs and communication receiver can have effective communication skill to understand what he/she needs the another to do and the another knows he/she ought how to work by his/her task demand. Then, it will shorten much time. If the office has 100 staffs need to often communicate. However, if the office has good space management arrangement to let every staff can communicate easily and walks to anywhere to find the right staff to communicate conveniently. Then, they can spend less time to waste on communication issue. Then, their productive efficiency will be also influence to raise.

●

● Health and safe work environment influences productivity

● Is a health and safe work environment can raise employees' work productive efficiencies indirectly? How and why it can influence employees' productive performance? Some occupations' working environments are easier to occur occupational accidents and diseases risks when the workers are working in the high health and safe risk's working environment. Hence, health and safety issues at these high life risk workplaces can be considered as a key to influence employees' overall performance. The idea that health and safety management program have positive impacts on productivity.

● When one worker needs to work in this high risk of health and safe workplace. He/she will consider whether how his/her work behavior will bring suffer serious injuries for shorter or longer time from work related causes in possible. So, he/she will work carefully in order to avoid injuries occurrence chance. It is possible to influence whose work performance, low productive efficiency in order to avoid any occupational accident occurrences in the dangerous workplace.

● If the employee feels danger when he/she needs to stay in the warehouses stable location to work often. Then his/her absenteeism day number will have increase, due to he/she feels that workplace accidents and occupational illnesses and can lead to permanent occupational disability, when he/she needs to attend the stable dangerous workplace to work in the warehouse. Hence, he/she will choose to apply holiday often in order to avoid injuries chance increasing when he/she needs to stay in the stable workplace location in the warehouse. It explains why companies increase need qualified, motivated and efficient workers who are able willing to contribute activity to technical and organizational innovations. So, healthy workers working in healthy working conditions are thus an important precondition for organization to work smoothly and productively. Hence, a health and safety workplace environment can bring these benefits to organizations as below:

● It can prevent among workers of learning work, due to health problems caused by their working conditions, the protection of workers in their employment from risks resulting from factors adverse to health. The placing and maintenance of the worker in an occupational, environment adapted to his/her physiological and psychological, capabilities, mental , physical and social conditions of workplace and adequacy of health and safety measures are needed to any employees in order to bring positive impact not only on safety and health performance, but also productivity. However, identifying and quantifying these effects will difficult to be measured as well as the quality of a working environment has a strong influence on productive efficiency.

● For one aviation air plane manufacturing factory, where workplace can environment will have high risk to occur occupational related accidents to cause employees' injuries. Hence, employees will be consider themselves safety when they need to work in high accident occurrence workplace. The bad consequence will influence such as absenteeism day number increases, leaving this kind of aviation air plane job of employees number increases, low productive efficiencies, due to there are many proficient experienced employees who choose leave this kind of high accident risk occupation.

● Consequently, any high accident occurrence risk workplace environment , employers need have good safe and health strategy to let their employees have confidence to work in this kind of high risk accident occurrence workplace if they expect low productive efficiencies effect is caused by high accident occurrence risk workplace factor.

●

●

● Employee personal
● empowerment factor influences
● performance

Is empowerment one good method to raise employee himself/herself effort in order to improve productive efficiency in organizations. Empowerment often consists of support groups, e.g. management's effective leading or trainer's training, course educational opportunities. Employee self-management education may impact to improve himself/herself job performance, e.g. increased self-empowerment, self-management skills and job treatment satisfaction.

● Only organization's empowerment strategy can lead every employee to through improvements in the employee individual decision making efficacy, improvement task performance behavior by reviewing whether what are the employee himself/herself errors when he/she encounters any job difficulties, after he/she reviewed his/her task error and his/her manager feels his/her performance can be improved. Then, it can enhance satisfaction with the employee and his/her manage relationship and better access and raising efficient performance in possible . Hence, empowerment can let every employee to discover whether what task related difficulties he/she faces or encounters every day. When his/her manager give ideas to let him/her to know how he/she ought review his/her task error in a supportive education working environment, it aims to let the low performance or low inefficient employees to increase confidence to continue work in the organization. So, the employee turnover number will decrease , if the inefficient employees can feel that they can attempt to solve their task-related difficulties successfully by themselves. So, empowerment can increase social support, leadership and advocacy development , it has resulted in greater employee individual performance psychological empowerment, autonomy and authority to let every employee to feel to achieve to improve themselves efficiencies more effectively in any organizations.

● For hospital organizational efficiency measurement empowerment influence case, how empowerment can influence hospital's efficiency raising? Efficiency is one of the most important indicators of hospital performance evaluation. Why do some hospitals' efficiencies poor? It is possible that mis management of resources, lacking health plan packages, e.g. coverage of basic health insurance, poor quality of care service, more payment demand for out-of pocket payment, quality of primary healthcare, healthcare providers neglect to concern potentially about service efficiency issues.

● In fact, low hospital efficiency is the major problem to influence patients number to choose the hospital's medical service, e.g. when the hospital often needs patients to queue to wait for doctor's care medical service. They need to wait on hour at least or more when the hospital has many patients are waiting for its medical service. Then, it will influence them to choose another hospital to replace it , if the hospital 's medical fee is cheaper and it does not need patients to spend long time to queue to wait its medical service. So, service efficiency is important to influence patients consumers' positive or negative feeling to choose the hospital's medical service. Even, the hospital's doctors are famous or they own many medical working experience, if patients often need long time to queue to wait its medical service . Then, it will cause its patients number to be reduced .

● These are variable factors to influence the hospital's inefficiency. They may include old speed hospital information system and medical record documents based on inefficient input and output variables. Input variables may include the number of hospital admissions, the number of nurses and the number of available beds. The output variable may include average of length of stay and bed turnover interval inefficient paper document record in the patient record administrative department.

● However, to evaluate the hospital efficiency indicators may include technical, scale and managerial efficiency the out-based data development analysis approach and the variable returns to scales assumption was used. Based on the out-input based approach (maximizing the factors of medical service production), to increase efficiency the organization should be increased outputs.

● Hence, when the hospital has good efficient evaluation method to measure every staff's performance , e.g. ward administrative clerk, patient registration clerk etc. Then, it can base on an put-put based approach and assuming a variable return to scale, there is capacity to improve technical efficiency and managerial efficiency in these any hospital different administrative units without an increase in costs and use of same amount of resources in relation to technical efficiency and managerial efficiency and scale efficiency of hospital's administrative labour individual task.

● In conclusion, factors, such as modification of managerial practices, use of modern technologies tailored to the cultural, political and formulation of clinical guidelines to standardize the medical processes in order to reduce medical errors and increase the empowerment of health care buyers (insurance organizations), length of stay, management hospitals by specialist managers, administrative requirement, full time hospital physicians, limiting the authority of decision makers in relation to the recruitment of staff in accordance with the needs of the hospital and optimal allocation of beds, conducting economic evaluations and the type of hospitals ownership had an impact on the hospital efficiency significantly. By increasing the number of beds the hospitals efficiency decreases. Otherwise, optimizing the bed size can increase hospital efficiency.

● However, the important factor to raise hospital overall staffs efficiencies empowerment is needed to let every hospital staff to review whether why and how himself/herself error is caused and he/she needs to review his/her errors to avoid to be caused from any negligence again in order to avoid patients' complaints again or reduce the patients' complaint number aims. So, empowerment of staff himself/herself error review factor is one major raising efficient good method.

●
●
●
●

●
●

CHAPTER SIXTEEN

● Organizational environment factor ● influences the new employees ● production efficiencies

In psychological view ,in any organization's environments, they depend on the types of social and physical environment factors to influence employee personal behavior how to be caused. How and why does the employee select to do whose behavior? If the organization's physical and social environment is better, then it may influence its employees select to work hard. It is possible to bring productive efficient raising consequence.

● In fact, when one new employee enters the new organization to work, he/she needs to learn how to adapt to cooperate with the organization's old employees to work together. So, it explains how and why organization's physical and social environment can influence the new employee individual motivation of behavior to work. In regarding new employee individual behavior by new employer's culture expectations as well as new employees need to adapt of actions that are likely to productive positive outcomes and generally discard those that bring unrewarding or puniishing outcomes by new employer's treatment.

● However, anticipated material and organization environment co-operation outcomes between the new employee and the organization old employees' cooperation, which are not the only kind of incentives that influence the new employee behavior of the new employee actions were performed only on behalf of anticipated external rewards and punishment from the new employer. In actuality, the new employee concerns considerable self-direction in the face of the new employer's organization's old employees competing influences. However, when the new employee has adopted an intension and an action plan. When, he/she works in the new organization for a period, he/she can't simply not back and visit for the appropriate performances to appear.

● The new employee's new job goal will be motivated by enlisting self-evaluative engagement in activities rather than directly. By making self-evaluation conditional on matching personal new job standards, the new employee will give direction to his/her new job pursuits and create self-inventions to sustain his/her efforts for new job goal attainment. The new employee will select to do new task behavior to give him/her self-satisfaction and a sense of pride and self worth for the new job chance.

● Efficacy beliefs also play a key role in shaping the new employees' behavior to do their tasks by influencing the types of new organization's activities and working environments, the new employees choose to set into any factor that influences the employee's choice behavior can affect the direction of employee personal career development in the new organization. This is because the organizational working environment influences operating in the employee how to select working environments continue to work. Thus, by choosing and shaping the new organization's working environments, new employee can have a hand in what they expect.

● In conclusion , when a new employee chooses the new organization to work. He/she must need to adapt the organization's new working environment. If he/she feels difficult to adapt or accept to the organization's new working environment, then he/she will be influenced to work inefficient or poor productive performance , due to he/she feels unhappy to work the new organization's working environment and the new organization's manager will dissatisfy his/her performance and complain or give verbal warning to dismiss him/her. Then, it will bring the poor consequence to let the organization's inefficient productive performance effect. If many new employees feel difficult to adapt to work in the new organization. Then, inefficient productive performance will be influenced to keep a long term. So, it implies that the organization will need to change its organizational culture in order to let many new employees can adapt and accept this new organizational culture to work happily if the organization expects new employees work to raise productive efficiency successfully.
●
●

- Raising efficient and effective
- interview psychological methods
- In human resource department, interviewing and selecting the most right applicants to do different kinds of positions, it is one part of HRM function. If the interviewer need to spend more time to interview to decide whom is the most right applicant to do the position in one day, e.g. 50 at least , even more applicants number as well as he/she can also make the more accurate personal selection decision to choose the most right applicant to do the position after the interview day. Then, the interviewing process needs to be avoided to spend more time to choose the most suitable applicant to do the position within the day. It is difficult to judge whether whom ought be the most right applicant to do the position, if there are more than 50 applicants , they are needed to be interview in the day. The consequence will bring HR department can spend extra time to do the interview task, but it can have enough staffs and time and resource to do other urgent or important task at the interview day. It will bring this question: How to apply psychological method to raise interviewer's efficiency to shorten to spend extra time to do interviewing tasks ? I shall explain some psychological methods to attempt to let interviewers have more confidence to select the most right applicant in short time as below:
- 1. Behavioral interview skill
- The interviewer can apply the actual behavioral interview method to let the interviewee to answer how he/she deals the matters, he/she feels that it is the best decision in order to judge and analyze whether whom applicant is the most suitable to be selected, e.g. describing the situation, he/she needs or the task that he/she needs to accomplish. The situation may be from a previous job, any relevant event, describing the action he/she took and be sure to keep the focus on him/her , e.g. discussing a group project or effort in the team; explaining what results he/she achieved, what happen? How did the event and what dis the applicant accomplishes? What did the applicant learn?
- In the behavioral-based interview. the interviewer can need the applicant to attempt to explain examples clearly in order to judge whose analytical skill whether he/she is the suitable applicant to do the position. The interviewer may ask the applicant to identify some examples from whose post experience where he/she demonstrated top behaviors and skills that employers typically seek. To judge whether his/her examples should be totally positive, such as accomplishments or meeting goals, the other half

should be situations that started at negatively , but either ended positively or he/she made the best of the outcome.

● This behavioral interview test aims to review whether the applicant's every example answer, he/she can provide an appropriate description of how he/she demonstrated the desired behaviors. In the behavioral interview, the interviewer can attempt to judge whether the applicant has good imagine effort to mind any relatively small set of examples to respond to a number of different behavioral questions to satisfy the right example are applied to the right situations in the limited interview time. Hence, behavioral interview can let the interviewer to make more accurate analysis to judge whether whom applicant(s) has (have) good analytical effort to solve any work-related situational problems in the most reasonable way or attitude in order to select whom is the most right applicant to do the position.

●

● 2. E-mail interviewing in qualitative research

● E-mail interviewing is another good interview method to select right applicant to do the managerial level position. E-mail interviewing can be in many cases a viable alternative to face-to-face telephone interviewing. Internet-based qualitative research methods may include online personal interview and virtual focus groups. However, it brings two questions: What opportunities and challenges does online in depth interviewing present for collectively qualitative data? How can in depth e-mail interviews be conducted effectively?

● The applicant targets may be the top-level manager, advertising executive , sales manager, human resource manager etc. management position applicants. They need to answer any complex or difficult interviewing question by email in the limited time, e.g. how to solve one case study problem , how to give recommendation to solve the situation problem. The interview participants may be recruited by tool/method of psychological test questions, the interview questions may be interview guide in a single e-mail and follow yp, length of email data collection period may be up to 10 weeks, the number of e-mail or follow up exchanges may be several number. The electronic formal and require little editing or formation before the applicants are processed for analysis all e-mail interviewing questions. So, they need to answer any managerial case study problem in limited time.

● It is one good managerial interview test method to evaluate whether whom applicant has the best analysis effort in order to the managerial position, because they need to find the best solutions to give recommendations to attempt to solve any situational problems in any un predictive case study problems. For example, when the applicant or a focus group of discussion applicants whom need to spend the maximum half hours to give recommendations to discuss to solve one complex or difficult case study problem either between the interviewer and the another interviewee applicant or between the group of five to ten interviewees (job applicants) themselves. Thus, after the interviewer sent the one case study question to let the applicants to know by every email channel. The interviewer needs to judger whether whom one applicant or one of the focus group applicants their recommendations are the most reasonable to solve the case study managerial situational problem within half hour to one hour. Then, the interviewer can make more accurate judgement to select whether whom has the best analytical effort to do the managerial position.

● 3. The effectiveness of motivational interviewing for young or older adult applicants selection process

● How can apply case management skills to be effective to prepare any interview motivation? How to do the most effective and efficient to meet the objectives of the interview? Some interview techniques used may vary the based on the individuals involved in the interview. For an interview with the young age applicant more require a different approach than an interview with a senior adult applicant. The following are one pointers to assist with preparing for the interview as below:

● Knowing the purpose of the interview and what needs to be accomplished . What is the expected outcome? Gathering all forms that need to be completed or signed having the interview and making list of questions that need to be asked, knowing the key facts and topics to be discussed, during the interview. Gathering factual information that may be helpful. Opening mind is needed in the whole interview process. Making an appointment for the interview and arranging sufficient time to set fully participate in the interview. Taking notes during the interview, let the participants know in general terms the reason notes are being made and how they will be used, opening ended questions invite the applicant to provide more information usually begin with other words who, what, where, how, asking one question at a time and keeping wording simple and specific, defining any terms that may be unfamiliar to the applicant , giving the interviewing participants in the interview an opportunity to ask their one questions or to clarify anything that was discussed, closing the interview with a review of the information discussed and facts gathered, reviewing any follow-up that is to be done by the case manager or others involved in the interview.

● In an efficient and effective interview, the interviewer needs have good body and spoken word communication to the interviewee or the position applicant. Because a good communication can reduce waste time or avoid the extended longer interview time if the interviewer can make good communication to impact good message to let the applicant to understand what is the mean to his/her interview question. What he/she wants to know, the total impact of a message includes ,e.g. 7 % verbal (words), 38% vocal /volume, pitch, rhythm etc. and 55% body movements (mostly facial expression). The interviewer's body and verbal behavior can make more clear message to let the interviewee(job applicant) to understand what answers are he/she wants to know mostly. Hence, an efficient and effective interview can let the interviewer to control and manage the whole interview to evaluate whether whom the applicants' answers or feedbacks are more reasonable to be acceptable to be better to compare other applicants to apply the position more accurately.

●
●
●
●
●
●
●
●
●
●
●
●
●
●
●
●
●
●
●
●

-
-
-
-
- Chapter Three Interview psychology methods
-
- What are common psychology methods of recruitment choice?
-
- Can any psychology methods are used to choose who will be the best recruitment applicant(s) in any recruitment stage more accurate? Can the interviewer observe the applicant's psychological phenomenon to judge whether the applicant can be the best or the most suitable applicant in the recruitment stage more accurate? To answer above these questions. We need to know why a systematic scientific procedure is an essential component to achieve any psychological method(s) to test candidate individual ability to judge whether who is the best or the most suitable applicant to do any position in any organization.
-
- A psychologist can follow a systematic scientific procedure which has theoretical base in order to explain and interpret the psychological phenomenon of the applicant to decide whether who is the best or the most suitable applicant to do the position in the organization.
-
- On the one hand, in order to obtain the applicant's psychological response from individual applicant, there are a number of psychological tools or instruments are used during the interview process. The responses are taken on these tools constitute the basic data which are analyzed to study the applicant experiences, e.g. working experiences, life experiences, mental processes and behaviors. On the other hand, in order to understand every applicant's behavior during the interview process. The different psychological methods can be applied for solving different applicant's individual behavior (individual mental problems) to judge who will be the best or the most suitable applicant to the position in any organization. Because different situations will cause the applicant to choose how to do or perform different behaviors to persuade the interviewer believes who is the best or the most suitable applicant to do the position in the organization. Thus, whose performances will be shaped by many factors both intrinsic and extrinsic to him or her in any interview process.

●

● The common psychological methods of interview process include such as: For observation psychological method example, when shopping in the market , the researcher must have noticed various activities of the consumers . When he/she observes the consumers their activities, the researcher also think about as to why who are doing those activities and probably the researcher reaches a conclusion about the causes of such activities. So, observation is as a psychological method of enquiry is often understand as a systematic registering of events without any deliberate attempt to interface with variables operating in the event which is being studies.

●

● Thus, observation psychological method seems to be applied to judge who is the best or the most suitable applicant to do any position in any organization in any interview process. Such as in any interview process, the interviewer (observer) can use this method to judge or observe every applicant's face and behavioral performance to feel whether who is the best or the most suitable applicant who own ability or confidence or qualification or experience to already to do the job to achieve the recruitment result is more accurate. For example, the interviewer (observer) can attempt to give one simple or difficult task to test whether whom the applicant has the more effort of the induced stress on task performance in the short time observation test in the on part stage of the interview process.

●

● However, observation is also divided into either participant or non-participant both types, depending on the role of observer (interviewer). In the case of interview participant observation, the interviewer mixes up with the job (task) performance event test under study and conducts concerns the interview test, e.g. group discussion interview test, the applicants and the interviewer will discuss one or more than one topic(s) which concern(s) on relating the position requirement issue. So, the interviewer can analyze whom applicant(s) can talk the most reasonable evidences to support whose opinions to argue the topic against the other applicants together among of them in the short time group discussion, e.g. between 15 minutes to 30 minutes. It aims to let the interviewer can have enough time to record whose opinions to analyze whose opinions are the most reasonable argument to support whose main points to win this position among these interview competitors in the short time group discussion.

●

● Thus, the interviewer needs to participate the group discussion to ask every applicant any questions and let them to attempt to solve any challenges in the whole group discussion. After the group discussion, then the interviewer can have more effort or confidence to judge whom applicant (s) is/are the most suitable or the best applicant (s) to do the job for his/her organization more accurate.

●

● Otherwise, as in the case of interview non-participant observation, the interviewer maintains an optimum distance and has little impact on the interview event. Such as the interview group discussion test. The interviewer won't ask any questions to let the applicants to attempt to answer. Otherwise, he/she will let the applicants have chance to ask any questions or answer the questions among of their discussion related to the topic. So the interviewer's role is a listener, who only needs to listen every applicant how who can ask and can answer any questions to decide who can talk the most correct or the right or the most reasonable answers to answer their questions in the short time group discussion. Then, the interviewer can record all applicants' questions and answers to make the judgement to decide who will be the right or the most suitable applicant to do the position in her/him organization more accurate.

●

●

●

● Why does need to test the applicant's psychological behavior in the interview process?

●

● To answer this question, we need to know why any large or middle size organizations which need have human resource department. To challenge of today's HR managers is to create a pool of good employees in the organization. It starts from selection process of the employees. So, interview has been used as an important selection method by HR managers for long time. The cost of rehiring the importance of hiring the right person for right position first. It requires a reliable and valid interview process. Although, any interview won't guarantee 100 percent success in hiring the best employees into any organization, but the proper application is at least, will improve the chances of hiring the best applicant for the job the organization. The importance is given to the selection of right employees for the right positions. Firms are now realizing the value of the good employees because who can make a difference through their job performance. So, various selection methods are now being used to identify the right candidate.

●

● " Interview" has emerged as a very useful tool in this regard. It is a very common selection method and has a high predictive validity for job performance (Robertson, & Smith , 2001). The main purpose of the interview is to select the right candidate for the right job. The importance of conducting an effective interview is also rising. So consensus was found among the HR experts regarding the effective interview techniques. There are a number of existing literatures regarding the techniques of an effective interview, but every few literatures exist regarding a systematic approach of conducting exist regarding a systematic approach of conducting an effective interview.

●

● This is a very few literatures exist regarding a complete interview process that shows a clear path to the employers for selecting right employees. A lot of interview technique are available, but the problem arises regarding the use of these techniques in a concrete manner. A systematic approach of interview will facilitate the tasks of HR managers in selecting the right applicant for the right position.

●

● (Stevens, 1997) author indicated the whole process of the interview has been described in terms of "3D"- Development, discussion and decision. This study is particularly important for three reasons. First , it will help the HR mangers to think about the employee selection interview in a concrete manner. Second, it will help them to use a number of interview techniques in an effective way that will ultimately increase the chance of hiring the right person for the right position. Third, it will enrich the existing literature of selection interview.

●

● (Stevens, 1997) author also explained that the growing importance of good employees will cause a challenge to the HR managers. The selection process of today's HR manager is becoming complex and challenging. Undoubtedly, the overall aim, of the selection process is to identify the candidates who are suitable for the vacancy or wider requirement of the

HR plan. " Interview" has been used as a ' critical selection method ' by HR managers. The interview is the most valid method in determining an applicant's organizational fit, level of motivation and inter-personal selects.

●

● Whetton & Cameron (2002) cited steps of process of conducting an interview, what they named as People-oriented selection interview process. Here is explains the interview process: P=prepare, E=establish rapport, O=obtain information, P=provide information, C= lead top close and E= evaluate.

●

● So, it seems that the candidates' behavior individual performance in the interview process can be predicted whether who is(are) the most suitable or the best to do the position in the organization from the interviewer's observation. So, it also means the candidate's attitude in the interview process can perform to let the interviewer to feel whether who is suitable or the best to do the position in the organization . Thus, observation of the applicant individual performance, it is an interviewer's best interest to find good prospects, hire them and have them stay in the organization.

●

● Therefore, the interviewees are needed to be provided sufficient information about the job and organization to have enough time to prepare before who will go to interview fairly. It aims to let every candidate has enough confidence to prepare to answer any questions in further interview process fairly. So, the development stage is a good preparation for the interview facilitates the effective interview process. To aim to let the candidate have enough preparation to interview , it should begin long before the first question is ever asked fairly.

●

● In conclude, HR department seems an essential department to any middle or large organizations nowadays. It does not attribute only recruitment function to any organization, it also attribute the chance to give one psychological test function to evaluate whom applicant has the more experience and qualification and effort to do any position in any organization. If the interviewer has not prepared any psychological method to test any applicants to judge whether who has the more effort to do the position. Then, I believe the interview result will be more failure and more inaccurate to employ the most suitable applicant , due to who lacks the enough effort and qualification and experience to perform to finish any tasks or duties of the position . So, it is important why any organization needs have good psychological method to test and observe the applicant's psychological behavior in the interview process?

-
-
-
-
- Occupation psychological
- test methods
- How to apply psychological recruitment
- strategies effect/manage in the
- recruitment process?
-
- HR (human resource) managers understand accept that poor recruitment decisions continue to affect organizational performance and limit goal achievement. In this case, many jurisdictions to identify and implement new effective hiring strategies will be serious issue to any HR departments to concern.
-
- Acquiring and retaining high-quality talent is critical to any organization's success. So, recruiters need to be more elective in their choice. Since poor recruiting decisions can produce long term negative effects, among their high training and development costs to minimize the incidence of poor performance and high turnover to impact staff morale, the production of high quality goods and services. Thus, HR managers must seek all possible methods for improve their output and provide the satisfaction to their clients require and deserve. The provision of high quality goods and services begins with the recruitment process.
-
- (Schuler, Randalls, 1989) explained recruitment is as " the set of activities and processes used to legally obtain a sufficient number of qualified applicants at the right place and time. So that the applicants and the organization can select each other in their own best short and long term interests.
-
- Thus, it seems that successful recruitment begins with proper employment planning and forecasting. So any one organization needs analyze what kinds of positions of future needs talent available within and

outside of the organization and the current and anticipated resources that can be expected to attract and retain such talent. Thus, HR manager needs have one successful strategy to be prepared to employ in order to identify and select the best candidates for its developing pool of human resources.

● In common, one successful recruuitment strategy involves these several processes of :

● Step one : Development of a policy on recruitment and giving life to the policy.

● Step two: Needing assessment to determine the current and future human resource requirement of the organization.

● Step three: If the activity is to be effective , the HR requirements for each job category and functional division /unit of the organization must be assessed, identification within and outside the organization of the potential human resources pool.

● Step four: Job analysis and job evaluation to identify the individual aspects of each jobs and calculate its relative worth, assessment of qualifications profiles, job descriptions that identify responsibilities and requirement skills, abilities , knowledge and experience, determination to pay salaries and benefits within a defined period.

● Step five: identification and documentation of the actual process of recruitment and selection to ensure equity and laws.

● Thus, the psychological recruitment strategy for the interviewer includes how to ask interview questions, how to give interview scores and panellists' comments, results of tests (where administered). Because and length of interview time for the interview. There are any interview main contents to any interviewer needs to concern how to arrange interview process.

● For example, nowadays, it is popular internet recruiting. Although, interviewer can reduce time to arrange and spend time to interview any applicants, due to the interviewer can interview any applicants from whose organization website . Specially, there are many similar potential interview competitors to apply to the position at the same time. Otherwise, internet recruiting is not all positive. Such as some applicants skill place great value in face-to-face interactions in the hiring process. Such applicant's are likely to ignore jobs posted, impersonally on time.

●

● I shall indicate these sample recruitment strategy to explain how to influence every applicant's choice to apply the job or not apply the job as below:

●

● The first is online recruiting. This online recruitment strategy has a large percentage of employees are hired by human service agencies for every level jobs are seeking their first career job. The newspaper want ads are not an effective recruitment source for most of today's applicants. Placing vacancy announcements online is more effective and economical than using most traditional forms of advertising. However, online recruitment is designed to close this gap: Not reaching majority of applicants, especially young graduates.

●

● The second is campus recruiting and job fairs. This campus recruiting strategy attracts both professional and paraprofessional applicants, who can be effectively recruited at job fairs sponsored by state workforce development agencies. However, college recruiting can be a very effective method for attracting applicants for professional jobs. The possible psychological advantages to applicants that includes any employers will send team of HR representatives to any colleges to provide an opportunity for job seekers to ask both job specific and hiring process/benefits questions; sending an ambassador to classrooms to quest lecture; schedule experienced employees or supervisors to ask on a hot topic in the human or service field at a local college or university. However, this campus recruiting strategy has a large percentage of employees hired, but need to improve overall applicant.

●

● The third is university partner developing a variety of recruitment strategy. University partnership benefits include to collaborate with university deans and professors to help student interest in the field as well as to develop program partially covering college tuition and other expenses of college students who agree to work for the human service agency for specified periods of time. Its recruitment strategy aims to develop a variety of recruitment strategies with area universities, community colleges and schools of social work to encourage students to pursue careers in the human services. It's weakness lacks enough applicants with specialized social work degrees.

●

● The fourth recruitment strategy is target recruitment. Employers may used a more diverse workforce that better reflects the client population who serve. For example, employers may need to recruit employees with specific language skills or with specialized degrees , e.g. criminal juice. It' weakness lacks of diversity in targeted jobs.

●

● The fifth recruitment strategy is internships. Interns sometimes are paid stipend, but in most instances interns are fulfilling an academic requirement of the college or university. Although supervisors and/or cause work staff must spend time supervising and training interns, the potential payoff is having a known applicant who is familiar with agency operations. Its weakness is needed to improve overall applicant pool.

●

● The sixth recruitment strategy is maintain a pre-screened applicant pool. It has a pool of pre-screened, interviewed applicants always available to be called for a second interview with the hiring supervisor. When, using this approach, it's important to minimize the amount of time between the initial interview and the second interview to prevent top quality applicants from being hired human resources will need to do continuous recruiting and screening , even when there are no current vacancies. It's weaknesses include that some

● human services organizations delay hiring until staff vacancies reach crisis proportions. They than initiate a recruitment process that is designed to bring new employees on board as soon as possible . The unfortunate result is hiring employees who meet the minimum requirements, but nothing more. It also has too many applicants get hired with only the minimum credentials.

●

● The seventh recruitment strategy is realistic job previews. Realistic job previews are designed to prevent applicants from taking jobs that who have life knowledge of or are not suited to perform. It is a recruiting tool is designed to reduce early turnover by communicating both the desirable and the undesirable aspects of a jobs before applicants accept a job offer. It can be in the form of videos, oral presentations, job shadowing opportunities. It's weakness includes unwanted turnover among new workers who did not understand their job when who were hired.

●

● The final recruitment strategy is improved hiring flexibilities in highly centralized systems. It means many public-sector human service agencies are regulated by merit systems that make it different to attract and maintain the interest of top-qualify applicants. Top applicants in today's economy are searching the interest for jobs that are available now. They aren't interested in taking a civil service exam and sitting on eligibility lists for months. In some systems requirements and lengthy inflexible scoring processes wash out well qualified applicants. It's weaknesses include hiring process takes too long, high qualify applicants are looking elsewhere for jobs.

●

●

● How to apply occupational psychological
● test method to test applicant's ability?

●

● Occupational psychological interview method is the application of the science of psychology to test applicant individual work ability. For example, any interviews can apply occupational psychologists' test method to attempt to test applicant individual performance, motivation and wellbeing of the organization in the workplace. If any interviewers can attempt to apply occupational psychologist test method to test any applicant individual working abilities in interview. It brings this question: How can the interviewer develop, apply and evaluate a range of tools and interventions to test the applicant individual working abilities across many different areas of the workplace?

●

● The occupational psychological test method can include these psychological skills to test every applicant individual ability in interview. Such as : Psychological assessment means selecting and assessing the applicant individual ability using interview enquiring method, e.g. in interview, enquiring applicant concerns on how to solve crisis deal issues when challenges cause in any workplace, assessments of what the applicant's main ability centers are. Situational judgement tests, e.g. how to solve challenges in different situations and personality questionnaires and cognitive ability tests. Profiling jobs are matching requirements to the applicant's future performance. Developing and choosing is valid, reliable, fair and suitable selectin procedures.

●

● Thus, the psychological enquiring questions can concern on work motivation, performance, appraisal and management, leadership power influence and negotiation, employee engagement and commitment, citizenship and positive behaviors or counterproductive in workplace, psychology of group teams and teamwork different aspects, which have similar points , such as concern organizational behavior questions. It aims to test the applicant how to deal any immediate crisis in the organization if the interviewer decides to employ him/her.

●

● The key focus of how to achieve one effective psychological test to the applicant in the interview. It focuses on key areas , such as the applicant personal goal attainment, interview performance, the applicant's mind on innovation and creativity aspects, and well being in the workplace how the applicant explains who will perform supposes who did the job in the workplace.

● In the interview, the interviewer needs the applicant to explain to let him/her to understand how the applicant's relation and motivation in the organization. The interviewer also needs to know how the applicant can solve any challenges in workplace in the situation test interview. Because conflict resolution is a challenging environment to work in. However, any downsides are offset by the rewards of being able to help protect both the organization and its employees from the psychological , physiological and economic costs of conflict. Because conflict will occur in possible in any workplaces. Thus, the interviewer ought to ask the question to let him/her to know the applicant will solve if who did this position.

●

● Human factors is a discipline concerned with how the successful interview applicant (future employee) works effectively and safely. It considers a employee's environmental , organizational, job and individual characteristics. These factors will affect the organizational successful interview applicant (future employee) behavior and it is past of the interviewer's job to analyze these and to give recommendations for change to improve human performance to the organization if who selected to employ these applicants in every time interview. Thus it seems occupational psychological test method can give benefits to the interviewer to understand more to the applicants to judge whether who will be the most suitable applicant(s)to do any positions in whose organization more accurate decision in any interviews.

●

●

● Selecting and evaluating

● assessment methods

●

●

● How selection assessment methods are applied to choose the best applicants ?

●

●

● Organizations compete in the war for talent. So, one effective selection assessment method can help any organizations to choose the best applicant(s). Using scientifically proven assessments to make selection decisions, even though such assessments have been shown to result in significant productivity increases, cost savings, decrease other critical organizational outcomes. I shall indicate common misconceptions about selection tests, such as: Screening applicants for conscientiousness will yield better performers , then screening applicants for intelligence, screening applicants for their values will yield better performers , then screening applicants for intelligence, integrity tests are not useful because job candidates misrepresent themselves on these types of tests, unstructured interviews with candidates provide better information than structured assessment processes and using selection tests creates legal problems for organizations rather than helps to solve them.

●

● There are numerous different types of formal assessments that organizations can use to select employees. The first step in developing or selecting an assessment method for a given situation is to understand what the job requires employees to do and what knowledge, skills and abilities individuals must posses in order to perform the job effectively. This is typically accomplished by conducting a job analysis . For job oriented job analysis recruitment example, providing test by stating fact and answer questions, gathering and reviewing information to obtain evidence or develop background information on subjects, integrating diverse information to uncover relationships between individuals, events or evidences.

●

● Other assessment methods focus on how measuring the best applicant who are required to perform job tasks effectively, such as various mental abilities, physical abilities or personality traits, depending on the job's requirements. If one were to assess whether candidates could solve decisive and communicate effectively. Alternatively, if one were selecting an administrative assistant, such as the ability to perform work conscientiously with speed and accuracy would be such more important for identifying capable candidates. Some worker-oriented or job analysis data are used as a basis for developing assessment method, that focus on a job candidate's underlying abilities to perform important work task.

●

● In general, any organization interviews only divide either internal or external both selection. Internal selection refers to situations where organization is hiring or promoting from within, whereas, external selection refers to situations where an organization is hiring from the outside. When some assessment methods are used more commonly for external selection. (e.g. cognitive ability tests, personality tests, integrity tests). There are numerous examples of organizations that have used one or more of the following tools for internal selection, external selection or both. I shall explain what the differences for these interview test methods as follow:

●

● What is cognitive ability tests. These assessment measure a variety of mental abilities, such as verbal and mathematical ability, reasoning ability and reading comprehension. Cognitive ability tests have been shown to be extremely useful predictors of job performance and thus are used frequently in making selection decisions for many different types of jobs (Hunter, J. 1986, Ree, M.J. & Teachout, M.S. 1984, Gottredson, L.S. 1982).

●

● Cognitive ability tests typically consist of multiple choice items that are administered via a paper-and-pencil instructment or computer. Some cognitive ability tests contain test items that need various abilities, e.g. verbal ability, number ability etc. But then sum up the correct answers to all of the items to obtain a single total score. The total score then represents a measure of general mental ability. If a separate score is computed for each of the specific types of abilities, then the resulting scores represent measures of the specific mental abilities.

●

● Job knowledge tests mean these assessments measure critical knowledge areas that are needed to perform a job effectively. Typically, the knowledge arcas measured represent technical knowledge. Job knowledge tests are used in situations m where candidates must clearly possess a body of knowledge prior to job entry. Job knowledge tests are not appropriate to use in situations where candidates will be trained after selection on the on knowledge areas who need to have. Like cognitive ability tests, job knowledge tests typically consist of multiple-choice items administered via a paper-and-pencil instrument or a computer , although essay items are sometimes included in job knowledge tests (Hunter, J. 1986).

●

● Personality tests that assess traits relevant to job performance have been shown to be effective predictors of subsequent job performance. The personality factors that are assessed most frequently in work situations include conscientiousness, extraversion, agreeableness, openness to experience and emotional stability (Barrick, M.R. & Mount, M.K. 1991, Costa, P.T. Jr., & Mccae, r. R. 1982).

●

● Research has shown that conscientiousness is the most useful predictor of performance across many different jobs. Although some of the other personal factors have been shown to be useful predictors of performance in specific types of jobs (Hough, L.M. 1992). It can consist of several multiple choice or true/false items measuring each personality factor. Like cognitive ability and knowledge tests, which are also administered in a paper-and-pencil or computer format.

●

● Biographical data (biodata) inventories, which ask job candidates questions covering their background, personal characteristics or interests have been shown to be effective predictors of job performance (Stokes, G.S. & Owens, W.A. 1994, Shoenfeldt, L.F. 1999). Another form of a biodata inventory is an instrument called an " accomplishment stored". With this types of assessment, candidates prepare a written account of their most meritorious accomplishments in key skill and ability areas that are required for a job , e.g. planning and organizing, customer service, conflict resolution (Hough, L.M. 1984).

●

● Integrity tests measure attitudes and experiences that are related to an individual honesty, trustworthiness and dependability (Sackett, P.R. & Wanek, J.E. 1996). It is typically multiple-choice in format and administered via a paper-and-pencil instrument or a computer.

●

● Physical fitness tests are used in some selection situations. These tests require candidates to perform general physical activities to assess one's overall fitness, strength or other physical capabilities necessary to perform the job.

●

● Situational judgement tests provide job candidates with situations that who would encounter on the job and viable options for handling the presented situations (Mecichmann, D., Schmitt, N. & Harvey, V.S. 2001). depending on how the test is designed , candidates are asked to select the most effective or most and least effective ways of handling the situation from the response options provided. Situational judgement tests are more complicated to develop than many of the other types of assessments. It is because more difficulty in developing scenarios with several likely response options that are all viable, but in fact, some are reliably rated as being more effective than others. Situational judgement tests are typically administered in written or paper-and-pencil test booklet or on a computer.

●

● Assessment centers are a type of work sample test that is typically focused on assessing higher-level managerial and supervisory competencies (Thornton, G.C III 1992). Assessment centers usually last at least a day and up to several days. They typically include role-play exercises in -basket exercises, analytical exercises and group discussion exercises. Trained assessors observe the performance of candidates during the assessment process and evaluate them on standardized rating. Some assessment centers also include other types of assessment methods, such as cognitive ability, job knowledge and personality tests. It should be noted selection purposes that assessment centers aren't only used for comprehensive development feedback to participants.

●

● Physical ability tests are used regularly to select workers for physically demanding jobs, such as police officers and firefighters. These test are similar to work sample tests in that who typically require candidates to perform a series of actual job tasks to determine whether or not who can perform the physical requirements of a jobs. Physical ability tests are often scored in a pass/fail basis. To pass, the complete set of take that comprise the test must be properly completed within a specified timeframe.

●

●

● How to criteria for selecting and evaluating assessment methods in interview?

●

● Properly identifying and implementing formed assessment methods to select employees is one of the more complex areas for HR department to learn about and understand. This is because understanding selection testing requires knowledge of statistics, measurement issues and legal issues relevant to testing.

●

● I recommend any interviewers need to understand important criteria to decide to choose which kind of interview test is the suitable to test applicant individual abilities in every interview such as below:

●

● The first criteria includes validity. Validity means the extent to which the assessment method is useful for predicting subsequent job performance. Adverse impact means the extent to which protected group members , e.g. minorities, females and individuals over 40 score lower on the assessment than majority group members.

●

● The second criteria includes cost. Cost is both to develop and to administer the assessment. Applicant reactions means the extent to which applicants react positively versus negatively to the assessment method. For example, cognitive ability test. on the positive side, this type of assessment is high on validity and low on costs. However, it is also high on adverse impact, moderately favorable. Thus, when cognitive tests are inexpensive and very useful for predicting subsequent job performance, score significantly lower on them than whites. There is no simple, formulaic approach for selecting " one best" assessment method, because all of them have advantages and disadvantages.

●

● However, the most important consideration in evaluating on assessment method is its validity. Validity refers to whether or not the assessment method provides useful information about how effectively an employee will actually perform once who is hired for a job. Validity is the most important factor in considerate whether or not to use an assessment method because identify who will doesn't accurately identify who will perform effectively on a job has no value to the organization.

●

● There are two major forms of validity: criterion-related validity and content validity is a simple example will illustrate how criterion-related validity can be established. Assume that a sales job requires employees to have a high level of customer service orientation and an organization decides to implement a selection test that assesses prospective applicants on their customer service skills. In order to show that the client skills assessment is a valid predictor of performance , it must be shown that individuals who score higher on the assessment perform better. On the job and individuals who score lower on the assessment perform less well on the job. Thus, validity in this case would be defined as a meaningful relationship between how well people performed on the assessment and how well who subsequently performed on the job. Content validity approach to validation involves demonstrating that an assessment provides a direct measure of how well candidates will actually perform to job. This type of validation requires analyzing the job to identify the tasks that are performed.

●

● What are the differences between criterion related versus content validation. Criterion-related validity can be used to evaluate the validity of any assessment where individuals receive scores that reflect how well who perform on the test and these scores are subsequently shown to relate to how well who perform on the job. Content validation can only be used to validate assessments that provide a direct measure of how well candidates perform job tasks or the content of the jobs, such as work sample tests. Otherwise, criterion-related validity evidence or validity . Thus, it is more desirable to obtain if it is possible to conduct a successful unbiased performance measures must be available. Unfortunately, performance appraisal ratings, which are the most commonly used performance measures can be inaccurate and often fail.

●

● Adverse impact is examined by comparing the proportion of majority group who are selected from a job to the protected group members who are selected. When organizations are and should be interested in selecting the higher quality work force possible, many are also concerned about selecting a diverse workforce ought not using measures that will systematically produce adverse impact against protected groups.

●

● In conclusion, either if an assessment method is shown to produce adverse impact and the organization wished to continue the last of that assessment, there are legal requirements to ensure that the method must have demonstrated validity or if an organization uses an assessment that produces adverse impact that produces adverse impact without the validity evidence. The organization will encounter challenges against which it won't be able to prevail. When evidence of validity can be used to justify and defend the use of measures that produce an adverse impact many organizations nonetheless attempt to apply the adverse impact produced be their assessment methods to extent possible in order to minimize potential interview wrong recruitment decisions and lack of diversity concerns issues to recruit any the most suitable applicants to do any positions in any organizations.

●
●
●
●
●
●
●
●
●
●
●
●
●
●
●
●
●
●
●
●
●
●

● Reference
●
● Barrick, M. R. & Mount , M.K. (1991). The big five personality dimensions and job performance: A meta-analysis, personnel psychology, 91, 1-26.
●
● Costa, P.T. & Jr., & McCrae, R.R. (1992). Four ways five factors are basic. Personality and individual differences, 13, 653-665.
●
● Gottredson, L.S. (Ed). (1982). The g factor in employment, Journal of vacational behavior, 29(3).
●
● Hough, L.. (1992) The big five personality variables construct confusion: Description versus prediction human performance, 5, 135-155.
●
● Hough, L.M. (1984). Development and evaluation of the " accomplishment record" methods of selecting and promoting professonals. Journal of applied psychology, 69, 135-146.
●
● Hunter, J. (1986). Cognitive ability, cognitive aptitudes, job knowledge and job performance, Journal of vacational behavior, 29, 340-362.
●
● Meichmann, D., Schmitt, N., & Harvey, V.S. (20010. Incremental validity of situatinal judgement tests , Journal of applied psychology, 86, 410-417.
●
● Ree, M.J. Earles, J.A., & Teachout, M.S. (1994), Predicting job performance: Hot much more than g. Journal of applied psychology, 79, 518-524.
●
● Robserton, I. T., & Smith, M. (2001). Personnel Selection. Journal Of Occupational And Organizational Psychological Psychology, 74(4), 441-472.
●
● Sackett, P.R. & Wanek, J.E. (1996). New developments in the use of measures of honesty, integrity, conscientiousness, dependability, trustworthiness and reliability for personnel selection, personnel psychology, 49, 787-829.
●

● Schuler, Randalls, S: Personnel and human resources management. Third edition, 1987.

●

● Shoenfeldt, L.F. (1999). From dustbowl empiricism to rational constructs in biodata. Human resource management review, 9, 147-167.

●

● Steven, Kay Cynthia (1997). Effects of pre-interview beliefs on applicant's reactions to campus interviews. Academy of management journal, 40(4), 947-966.

●

● Stokes, G.S. Mumford, M.D. & owen, W.A. (Eds.) (1994). Biodata handbook paloacto, CA: CPP Books.

●

● Thornton, G.C. III (1992). Assessment centers in human resources management Addison-Wesley,

●

● Whetton, D.A. & Cameron, K.S. (2002). Developing Management , Skill 5th edition, reading, MA: Addison Wesley Longman.

●

●

●

●

Employee efficiency psychological research

CHAPTER SEVENTEEN

Employee satisfaction measurement ●

● How to measure employee satisfaction ?

● It has close relationship between employee satisfaction and work motivation. The right staff can work in the right position which can affect the effective productivity of the company. Also, if employees feel satisfactory , then the company can have more chance to raise (increase) productivity, responsiveness, quality and good customer service performance. However, if any company want employees to work efficiently, then which needs to know that one of the biggest internal strength of the organization is the relationship and communication between employees and the managers. Besides, the biggest improvement is also needed in the field of the financial rewards, because most of the employees are not showing high satisfaction to them.

● Whether how to measure what the level of employee satisfaction is accepted to achieve the stable productivities? The main subjects will be leadership and motivation to answer this question. For example, supermarket organization, whether which factors could be improved in the target work in supermarket organization every day? I shall assume it has perhaps to cause job dissatisfaction if the supermarket has only the power of money as motivator in supermarket organization. Any organization has its culture. As supermarket organization has also itself culture. However, I believe that cultural traits that can affect the employee satisfaction in any supermarket organizations. Although, any supermarket organization has usually different departments to cooperate work together. Hence, if it has good organizational culture to make different departments, e.g. store, food, wine, stationery, clerical, counter etc. departments staff who can have good communication to work in comfortable cultural supermarket environment together, then its staff can have more ability to achieve the best work performance. How to solve this department cultural difference of challenge, I suggest any supermarket needs have good HRM plan to control its department's employee behaviors.

●

● Human resource means the staff who work in a organization and the contribution who make with whose skill, knowledge and competence. The most important successful factor of knowledge based economy in which intelligent organizations are the key aspects of economic growth in the global economy. Why does organization need to satisfy employee needs? Because any staff trend to change working places often, any staff can change their workplaces to gain more respect and to feel more valued in their jobs. So, it can avoid staff turnover (leaving) whose organization very easy if the employer can satisfy whose staff needs. Thus, human resource plan is needed to achieve policies, recruiting and selecting work force, training and development, workplace planning, ensuring fair treatment of employees, ensuring equal opportunities, assessing the performance of employees, managing employee welfare, providing a counseling service for employees, managing the payment and rewards systems, supervising health and safety procedures, disciplining individuals, dealing with dismissal or promotion, negotiation, ensuring the legality of organizations etc. concerning about managing employees' positive psychological issues, in order to build positive emotion to them.

●

●

●

● How can leaders satisfy employee needs?
● Any organization needs have good leaders because leaders act to provide satisfaction or more likely to offer means of satisfaction to whose team members. Leaders don't necessarily motivate. A successful leader understands the needs of the others and persuades them to act in a certain way. A good leaders can make whose workers see that following the views of the leader's workers will get the most satisfaction out of their work. However, a person can be motivated without leadership. But leadership, however, can't succeed without the motivation of the follower's side. If a

staff has the feeling that who can perform a higher level job, himself/herself who have the motivation to attend courses or train in another way to be able to perform at the required higher levels.

●

● Douglas Mc Gregor's famous classification of theory x versus theory y is applicable for leadership approaches. In general, any staff has two kinds of psychological characteristics of either theory x person or theory y person. Theory x assumes that in general most staff find working distasteful and usually avoid doing it if it is possible . That is why most staff must be controlled and directed, even threatened to perform the way the organizational goals will be reached. Theory x also assumes that staff want to be controlled and directed rather than take responsibility and that staff lack ambition. Otherwise, theory y on the other hand, is more likely to have roots in the recent knowledge of human behavior. It assumes that physical and mental effort in work is as natural as play or rest. So, leaders need to judge whether whole managing staffs (team members) who belong to theory x or theory y kind of staff. Then, who will have more accurate method to lead whose team members easily.

●

● What level of satisfaction to the organization's staff can achieve the best performance. I feel that when the organization can reach the willingness level to be told the extent to which any one of staff has motivation and commitment or self-confidence to accomplish a certain task. So, the willing level is the most satisfactory maturity level to achieve the best performance psychological factor to any organization. Because of the maturity satisfactory level of employees is high, the employees are both willing and able to do the tasks given more efficient. Otherwise, if the maturity satisfactory level is moderate, leaders can concentrate on the relationship and participate in the decision making and willing processes as workers are able but may be unwilling to complete their tasks. Only a little bit of encouraging is needed. Otherwise, if the mature satisfactory level is low, workers are willing but may be unable to complete the tasks, so leaders must push to sell the tasks and let the workers do the rest or leaders must tell workers what to do.

●

● In this supermarket organization case, if supermarket's grocery department and logistic department and clerical or cashier departments and fishing/meet etc. department whose employees' maturity satisfactory level is low, then it is possible that who are unable and unwilling to complete whose individual department daily tasks efficiently and these different department managers need to concentrate on both relationship and task aspects to raise whose maturity satisfactory level to be moderate level, even the high level in order to achieve the best performance.

●

● Leaders also need to concern staff job satisfaction issue. Job satisfaction is the reflection of a good treatment. It also can be considered as an indicator of emotion well being or psychological health, even job satisfaction can lead to behavior by an employee that affects organizational functioning. Furthermore, job satisfaction can be a reflection of organizational functioning. Why can job satisfaction influence any organizational performance? The reason is some people like to work and who find working is an important part of their lives. Some people on the other hand find work unpleasant and work only because who have to do support their lives. However, job satisfaction tells how much people like their job. Job satisfaction is the most studied field of organizational behavior. It is important to know the level of satisfaction at work for many reasons and the results of the job satisfaction studies. In the workers' point of view, it is obvious that feel respected and satisfied at work, it could be a reflection of a good treatment. In the organization's point of view good job satisfaction can lead to better performance of the workers which affects how the result of the organization to achieve its productivities for long term.

● So, any employer or leader can not neglect whose staff what job satisfaction level to whose staff in any time. In general, if whose staff can not feel job satisfaction, who will choose to leave whose current employer more easily.

●

●

●

●

● How does one company raise employee
● efficiency
●

● What makes one company more successful than another? It is possible to concern better products, services, strategies, technologies or perhaps a better cost structure. However, the final source is the best staff performance of good productive factor, because it can cause these result, also employees who are engaged significantly outperform work group and who are tangible asset to raise the company's competitive advantage where employees are the differentiator, engaged employees are the ultimate goal. What factors can affect job satisfaction. I find that agency theory might be helpful to explain how organizations need to think of their human resource responsible in producing the output needed by organizations to meet shareholders value. Agency theory is concerned with issues related to the ownership of the firm when that ownership is separated from the day-to-day running of the organization. It assumes that in all but owner managed organizations, the owner or owners (known is agency theory as the "principle" of an organization must best authority to an agent -corporate management to act on their behalf) Shenkel, R. Gardner, C. (2004, pp. 57-59).

●

● The principle recognizes the risk, here and act on the assumption that any agent will look to serve its own as well as the principle interests as it fulfills it contract with that principal. However, this is not the situation in real life situation. As all agents are perceived to be opportunistic. Agency theory is therefore used to analysis this conflict in interest between the principal (shareholders of organizations) and their agents (leaders of these organizations). The agents in keeping with the interest of the shareholders and organizational goals turn to use financial motivational aspects like bonuses, higher payrolls, pensions, sick allowances, risk payments to reward and retained their staff and enhance their performance. However, given this perception, the principal in an organization will feel unable to predict an agent's behavior in any given situation and so brings into play various measures to do with incentives in other to tie employee's needs to those of their organization. However, the fundamental problem, dealt with is that drives or induces people to exploit their potential resources in the way they do in organization. The issue of motivation and performance are who positively related. By focusing on the financial aspect of motivation problem like bonus system, allowances perks, salaries etc. I believe financial motivation and trying to Mallow's Basic needs non financial aspect why comes in when financial motivation has failed. So, employers need to evaluate the methods of performance motivation in whose organization in organizing some motivational factors like satisfies and dissatisfies will be used to evaluate how employees motivation is enhanced other, than financial aspects of motivation. I believe that with the changing nature of the work force, recent trends in development, information and technology, the issue of financial motivation becomes consent on one of the most important assets in an organization. The potential role of money is as conditioned reinforce and an incentive which is capable of satisfying needs and an anxiety reducer and serves to erase feelings of dissatisfaction.

● In general, any organization can use performance or efficiency to measure its productivities. Such as, performance means the act of performing; of doing something successfully; using knowledge as distinguished from merely possessing it; a performance comprises an event in which generally one group of staff (the performer or performers) behave in a particular way for another group its staff.

● Efficiency means the ratio of the output to the input of any system. Economic efficiency is a general term for the value assigned to a situation by some measure designed to capture the amount of waste or friction or other under desirable and undesirable economic feature present. It can also be looked as a short run criterion of effectiveness that refers to the ability of the organization to produce outputs with minimum use of inputs.

● Why does employer need to know how to motivate whose staff? What is meaning of motivation? Motivation means as the psychological process that give behavior purpose and direction to behave in a purposive manner to achieve specific unmet needs, an unsatisfied need, and they will to achieve respectively. So, salary, job satisfaction, job goal , reward will be task -related motivation since goals direct staffs' thoughts and action. So, motivation to staff needs have these factors expected. For example, phychological needs are the bottom of the staff, such as foods, air, water and shelter. Any staff needs a salary that enable then to afford adequate living conditions. Then, staffs need safety, psychological needs. They need to work for a secure working environment free from any threats or harms and organizations can provide these need by providing employees, with safety working equipment e.g. hardhars, health insurance plans, fire protection etc. Next, staffs need social needs and the needed to be loved and accepted by other people. Esteem includes the need for self-respect and approval of others. Finally, self actualisation is the top psychological need, it is capable of being to develop the staff himself/herself full potential. The rationale holds to the point that self actualised employees respect valuable assets to the organization human resource.

●

● Why do employers need to concern flexible working arrangement? Employers need to concern flexible working arrangement if who hope employees can raise productivities and efficiencies to achieve the best work performance. Flexible working describes any types of working arrangement that gives some degree of flexibility on how long, where and when employees work. Because employees need time to learn a familiar phase with workplaces, flexible working arrangements have been an option in many employment sectors for a long time, helping employment meets the changing needs of their customers and staff. The reasons include customers expect to have products and services available outside of the traditional 9 to 5 working hours; employees want to achieve a better balance of between work and home life and organizations want to meet their customers and employees needs in a way that enables them to be as productive as possible. Organizations need to produce any products and services of the right quality and at the right price, under constant pressure. To meet customers' demands, sometimes new ways of working have to be found to make the best use of staff and resources. Flexible patterns of work can help to solve those pressures by maximising the available labor and improving customer service.

●

● At employers, organizations also have a duty of care to protect whose staff from risks to their health and safety, e.g. stress caused by working long hours or feeling pressure to need to balance work and home life. However, flexible working can help to improve the health and wellbeing of employees and by extension, reduce absenteeism, increase productivity, and enhance employee engagement and loyalty. Flexible working time includes per time works often used in hotels, restaurants, warehouses etc. flex time. Mostly used in office based environments for staff below managerial level in public and private sector service organizations; annualized hours often used in manufacturing and agriculture where there can be big variations in demand throughout the year.

●

● Thus, I feel the flexible working and work life balance benefits can include a more efficient and productive organization, a more motivated workforce, better retention of valuable employees, a wider pool of applicants can be attracted for vacancies, reduced levels of absence and increased customer loyalty and working hours that the best suit the organization, its employees and its customers applications of knowledge about how people as indicators and groups, act within the total organization, analyzing the external environment's effect on the organization and its human resources, missions, objectives and strategies. So, it concerns how to predict staff psychological feeling to learn how to motivate who to work efficiently.

●

● Why does manager need to concern employee's individual diversity need? Also, manager needs to know each person is substantially different from all others in terms of their personalities, needs, demographic factors and past experiences and/or because who are placed in different physical settings, time periods or social surroundings. This diversity needs to be recognized and viewed as a valuable asset to organizations. Selective perceptions may lead be mis- interprectation of single event work or create a barrier in the search for new experience. Managers need to recognize the perceptual differences aiming the employees and manage them accordingly. These whole person effects between the work life and life outside work and management focus should be in developing not only a better employee but also better person in terms of growth If the whole person can be developed, then benefits will beyond the firm into the larger society in which each employee lives. Because individual's behavior are guided by their needs and the consequences that results from their acts. In case of needs, people are motivated not by what others think who ought to have but by what who themselves went. However, motivation of employee is essential to the operation of organizations and the biggest challenge faced by managers. Organizations ought give more opportunities to let employees who can contribute their talents and ideas because many employees actively seek opportunities at work to become relevant decisions the stay or leave the organization, also managers ought concern any employee's individual skills and abilities and to be provided with opportunities to develop themselves.

●
●
●
●
●
●
●

-
-
-
-
-
-
-
-
-
-
-
-
- Chapter Two Organizational behavior theory
-
- What is system approach?
- What is system approach? All parts of an organization interact in a complex relationship. Systems approach takes an across, the board view of people in organizations and analyses issues in terms of total situations and as many factor as possible that may effect people's behavior. Three theoretical frameworks, the cognitive behavioristic and social learning frameworks, the basis of any organizational behavior model. The cognitive approach is based on the staff and organization expectancy, demand and incentive concepts. Because staff behavior on the basis of the connection between stimulus and response in any organization. The social learning approach incorporates the concepts and principle of both the cognitive and behavioristic frameworks. In this approach, staff behavior is explained as a continuous interaction between cognitive is explained as a continuous environmental determinants. In the organizational behavioral model, there are some dependent variables like productivity, absenteeism turnover, job satisfaction, deviance absenteeism, turnover, organizational citizenship behavior etc. The reason of which staff try to understand. The cause of these outcomes like with some variables of individual, groups and individual level, these variables are called independent variables.
-
- It seems different organizational workplace environments will influence staff's different variable causes to decide how to do whole daily behaviors, how to fit to work in the organization. So, any manager needs to know what every staff is individual characteristics to judge how to manager himself/

herself. For example, if the staff is theory x person, who will dislikes work and will avoid it if possible, who lacks responsibility, has little ambition and seeks security above all who must be controlled, threatened with punishment to get who to work. So, the manager's attitude is needed to control whom. Otherwise, if the staff is theory y person, who will feel work is as natural as play as rest. People are not inherently lazy, who have become the way is as a result committed, the staff has potential, under proper condition who learn to accept and seek responsibility, who has imagination creativity that can be applied to work, so manager who is to develop the potential to the staff and help who release that potential toward common objectives.

●

● Any organization depends on the external environment for two kinds of into outputs, which it transforms into outputs and then releases in the hope that external environment will accept them. First, human input, employees and natural resources. Second, non human inputs, e.g. equipment, information, raw materials. However, organization needs to adjust to environmental demands, e.g. customer complaints, market research, financial reports, in order to keep to improve performance easily.

●

● How to raise organizational efficiency? As systems theory indicates organizational effectiveness and time is considered as one element of a larger system of number of elements. The organization takes resources (inputs) from the external environment, processes these resources and returns them in changed form (output). According to system theory, effectiveness criteria must reflect the entire input process, output cycle, not simply output and must also reflect the interrelationships between the organization and its outside environment. In relation to environmental circumstances organization passes through different phases of lifecycle like forming, developing , maturing and declining and the appropriate criteria of effectiveness must reflect the stage of the organization's life cycle.

●

● The criteria of effectiveness are also time based short run (results of actions concluded in a year or less), intermediate run (when effectiveness of individual, group or organization is considered for a longer period, perhaps five years and long run for this the time frame is indefinite future. The four short run effectiveness criteria are quality, productivity, efficiency and satisfaction. Three intermediate criteria are quality, adaptiveness, efficiency and satisfaction. The two long run criteria are quality and survival. So, any organization needs have effectiveness criteria because effectiveness criteria can reflect the stage is of the organization's life-cycle (which includes stages of growth, maturation and decline) and short, intermediate and long term perspectives. Quality means the total quality control rank among the most used programs to meet customers' changing demand. Hence, employee's individual satisfaction will influence productivity. Because productivity reflects the relationship between the organization's inputs and outputs and measures of productivity include profit, sales, market share. For example, patients released, clients served concerns the relationship between employees' satisfaction and clients' overall satisfaction. When the employee feel more satisfactory, then who will work more efficient or who will serve the clients more pleasant. Then, the customers will have more chance to feel more satisfactory from the staff's individual service.

●

● Efficiency is the ratio of outputs to inputs. It focuses on the entire input process output cycle, emphasis in out and progress. Measures of efficiency include rate of return on capital, or assets, unit cost, waste, downtime, occupancy rates and cost per patient/student etc. customers. Satisfaction meets employee needs. It recognizes the organization is as social system that benefit its participants. Measures of satisfaction include turnover, absenteeism and employee attitudes. Adoptive means the degree to which the organization can and does respond to internal and external changes. It relates to management's ability to sense environmental changes and changes within the organization. There are no specific measure of adaptiveness, but certain progress, e.g. employee training and career counseling increase its capacity to deal with it. Finally, development means the ability of the organization to increase its capacity to deal with environmental demand. So, if the organization hope to be survival in the long term, then it needs to achieve training programs and organizational development to be represent the organization's investment in survival.

●

●

● How can satisfy to employees' needs ?

● How can satisfy to employees? Because a high rate of employee is directly related to a lower turnover rate. Thus, keeping employees' satisfied with their careers should be a major priority for every employers. Reasons why employees can become discourages with jobs and design, including high stress, lack of communication within the organization, lack of recognition, or limited opportunity for growth. So, management need actively seek to improve these factors to avoid if who hope to lower turnover rate. However, some employee will often be feel bored with the work because there is no intrinsic motivation to succeed. Finding the daily same job duties can reduce the individual's motivation to succeed to raise desire to show up to work and to do the job well. In this case, the employee may continue to come to work, but whose efforts will be minimal.

-
-
- Stress is another factor to cause low performance. Branham (2005) indicates that " it seems clear that one quarter to one half of all workers are feeling some level of dysfunction, sue to stress, which is undoubtedly have a negative improve on their productivity and the probability that they will stay with their employers."
- However, stress can be caused by these factors, e.g. in the situation, when a company can't or won't supply the tools necessary to produce or work efficiently on the job. This produced higher stress levels because these workers are expected to perform at certain rates, yet who are unable to do so. This results in lower productivity and higher turnover because quotes can't be met by the employees. On staff knowing that management is able to provide the tools essential for the position is important to employee trusting the intentions of their employer.

-
-
- Dissatisfaction with the job many come from sources other than stress or poor fit between employee and the job. Employers that are deemed unethical by workers because who appear to care about company revenues, rather than the employees that are working for them. In the result, the employer may lead to job dissatisfaction, and raise the company's turnover rate.
-
- Lack of communication in the workforce is another major contributor to dissatisfaction. Bad communication leaves employees feeling disconnected from the organizations. This is detrimental to wellbeing of the company because when an employee feels neglected, who will trend to perform at a lower level because who feels unsure of whose position within the

company and wonders what whose purpose is within the workplace. Also, employees may be unaware of how whose performance measures up to that of their co-workers and have no sense of who can improve. So, without communication, it becomes difficult for employees to make any progress in their efficiency. The employee may feel uncomfortable in the workplace, of who feel rarely be praises for the quality of whose performance. Finally, those factors cause the failure to provide employees with opportunities to grow within the company results in employee frustration to cause whose poor performance and low productivity.

●

● Whether can bonuses increase raise employee satisfaction and team performance? In some occupations, I feel bonuses can raise staff performance, such as bonuses lead to happier and it can be used in the form of donations to charity organization or bonuses in the form of expenditures to pharmaceutical sales teams and sport teams organizations. However, employees are becoming more and more unhappy, more and more of time at work, hardly a formula for a healthy and productive workplace. In this increasingly negative environment, how can employers incentivize their employees to increase their happiness, job satisfaction, and job performance? Certainly, designing effective incentive schemes is a central challenge for a wide range of organizations form multi-national corporations to academic departments. Identifying the most effective strategies, a variety of incentive schemes and are suggested such as bonuses from fixed salaries to pay-performance from commission to end-of-year bonuses. It is based to assume that the best way to motivate employees is to reward them with money that who then spend on themselves. In general, existing methods of increasing workplace performance, including individual-based and team based bonuses schemes, which trend to reveal both benefits and unexpected cost. Whether the benefits of improving social life in the work phase can increase employee citizenship behaviors to satisfy the organization actual needs from these bonuses compensation schemes.

●

● What is the effect of money on employee's job satisfaction and performance? On one hand, monetary bonuses have been found to have positive effects, increased productivity effort, performance and job satisfaction. Individual bonuses increase job satisfaction in part. On the other hand, individual incentives, such as large bonuses are often surprising ineffective increasingly employee morale and productivity. In an effort to prevent such negative competitive dynamic that can result from individual based-bonuses, organizations often change to incentivize employees for their collective performance, encouraging cooperation and teamwork rather than competition. Otherwise, in some cases, team based compensation schemes have been shown to raise this sense of cooperation between team members, inducing them to exert additional effort toward helping another worker to work together linked to employee morale and performance.

●

● Whether bonuses can have a causal impact on employee. In fact, individual incentives, such as large bonuses are often surprisingly ineffective in increasingly employee morale and productivity. Also, rewarding individual employees can produce negative outcomes, as employees become reluctant to share information with others even at the expense of reduced output. In an effort to prevent such negative competitive dynamics that can result from individual based bonuses. Importantly, such increased cooperation due to interdependent rewards has been shown to improve team performance, suggesting that team based bonuses may be an effective means of improving employee social life. As with individual based bonuses, however team based bonuses offer important advantages, but also potential drawbacks. I suggest that prosocial bonuses can have a causal impact on employee satisfaction and performance, such that providing employees with money to spend on themselves.

●

● How effective organizational communication can affect employee attitude, happiness and job satisfaction. Communication has been studied with regard to performance and job satisfaction, but the relationship with employee attitude and happiness has not been done in a higher education setting. The value of communication in an employee's choice to be happy is explained as it affects the individual, team and overall organizational culture. Attitude and happiness have been recognized by communication examination of organizational culture and emotion in the workplace. For example, for frontline employees are needed have cheerful and positive in the face or any situation. So, it requires the owners, managers and supervisors communicate to whose team efficiently.

●

● Communication with telecommuting or remote workers is a consideration that organizations must take seriously more than 24 million people were working remotely in 2008 year (World at work, 2009) and that number is steadily rising. Teleworkers report feelings of isolation, uncertainty, a lack of trust and lower organizational commitment with lower job satisfaction. Managers may not communicate the save way with remote workers as who do with employees who are in the workplace each day. Improve communication is important to hold employee engagement initiatives together, particularly in government public sector organizations must communicate throughout the entire cycle of planning, conducting and acting on engagement. So, I suggest some effective communication method to raise productivity and improve performance. Such as ensuring that employees understand their work expectation between their jobs and the organization's mission, meeting regularly with staff members, providing feedback as performance , as well as opportunities to grow and developing , even fail as a way to learn and holding employees accountable for performance, including with poor performance.

●

● How to make a difference at work be more meaningful and purposeful workplaces. The workplace provides a wealth of opportunities and possibilities through which anyone can make a difference every day. Whether it's one person, one team or one organization, everyone has the capacity to create positive and meaningful change in their workplace in both small and large ways. How to foster the work motivation of individuals and team? Nowadays, some evidence supports claims that motivational programs can increase the quality and quantity of performance from 20 to 40 percent. Moreover, motivation can solve three types of performance challenges: first, staff are refusing to change often, second, allowing themselves to be distracted and not persist at a key task and/or third, treating a task as familiar, making mistakes but not investing mental effort and taking responsibility because of overconfidence.

●

● Imagine that more than 50% of staff in your organization decided that from this point, who would work one extra day a work without an extra day of rest. What impact would their decision have on your organization's bottom line? What is the value of a 50% increase in performance by 100% of the workforce? Assuming that you may know some of the 50% , who do the minimum and a few of the 80% who could work much harder, do you think that there is anything that would convince people to work harder than who are now? Is it possible that half of your staff who admit that who could work much harder might actually decide to increase whose performance by 20% or more if they were adequately motivated? The best evidence suggests that highly significant performance increases are possible when motivational strategies are implemented (Clark & Estes, 2002).

●

● How to achieve work motivation strategy ?

● Work motivation is the process that initiates and maintains goal-directed performance. Without motivation , even the most capable person will refuse to work hard. Thus, motivational performance gaps exist whenever staff avoid starting something new, resist doing something familiar, stop doing something important or attention to a less valued task, or refuse to work smart on a new challenges, instead use old familiar, but inadequate solutions to solve a new problem (Clark, 1998).

●

● How can we make sense of such variety and get benefits as performance technologies? Is any given situation where we want to increase work motivation, we must determine what will convince staff to start doing something new or different increase their persistence at an important task and investment mental effort. The staff must believe that the motivator driving their enhanced performance will directly or indirectly contribute significantly to what who need to feel successful and effective. The motivator's work has to cost less than the value of the increased performance and it must meet both ethical and legal requirement. When it might appear that solutions have to be tailored to the different demands of individuals in a team. In the absence of a clear vision leading to work defined business and performance goals, people substitute their own goals and whose goals may not support the organization. So, it is important to ask about evidence for the benefit of all work rules and what might be cost of the rules more eliminated. What is gained by rules that staff can't take or eat in certain areas? Why can't they decorate their work space in ways that suit them? How much of staff's behavior must you control to achieve business goals? One way to motivate and staff and simplify organizational work processes is to eliminate all unnecessary rules, policies and procedures.

●

● To learn how to motivate staff, we need to learn how to predict staff's individual psychological behavior. Organizational behavior is a scientific discipline in which large number of research studies and conceptual developments are constantly adding to its knowledge base. It is also an applied science, in that information about effective practices in one organization is being extended to many others. Organizational behavior is the systematic study of human behavior, attitudes and performance within an organizational setting, drawing on theory methods and principles from such disciplines as psychology, sociology and cultural anthropology to learn about individual perceptions, values, learning, capacities and actions when workings in groups .

●

● Nowadays, why employees hope employers can give them to enjoy well life balance. The reasons may include care commitments to children or elderly relatives, education commitment that limit availability at times of the week/month/year, duties and/or interests outside of work, needing to be available for people making a greater sense of well being and reduced stress levels. How to arrange flexible working in organization? For example, an employer may be thinking about introducing annual hours in order to increase production levels to meet infrequent rises in demand because who can work well where, there are peaks in works, the workforce is required to be available with little notice. The employer could decide to meet these increases in demand by introducing overtime because it provides flexibility to meet fluctuations and it could be a smaller change to the organization than annual hour. However, there are many different forms of flexible working. Flexible working can cover the way working hours are organised during the day, week or year. It can also describe the place of work, such as homeworking or the kind of contract, such as a temporary contract. Anyway, flex time can operate in different ways depending on business need. On the one hand, there may be a system to allow employee to build up additional hours, which can be used to leave early, come in late, or take longer periods off with early, come in late, to take longer periods off, with approval from line management. An example of this might be an assembly line or call center where staffing must be scheduled to meet customer demand. For example, an employer needs to extend the hours that whose business is open to 8 AM to 8 PM, but can't afford the extra overtime. how to manage flex time approach could help provide the additional hours, reduce staff numbers at quiet times and minimize the need for overtime. Employer may benefit from the opportunity to travel outside of peak hours and/or accommodate personal responsibilities, such as the school runs part time work is the must common types of flexible working. It's potential benefits include customer demands on be met and machinery can be caused more efficiently if part time workers cover lunch breaks/evening shifts and weekends, the working day can be arranges around caring responsibilities and/or other commitments, employees can continue to work increasing whose own leisure time. But part time work also have potential challenges, such as increase in training, increase in administrative and recruitment costs, e.g. recruiting two part timers could longer than one full times and providing a continuous level of service may be difficult.

● Overtime is normally hours that are worked over the usual full time hours. It can be compulsory or voluntary . A recognized system of paid overtime is more common with hourly paid staff than salaried staff. Potential benefits include that employer can provide flexibility to meet fluctuations in demand, short term labor shortage without having to recruit extra staff overtime. Even with premium payments, is often less costly than recruiting and training extra staff or buying extra equipment. However, overtime work has also potential challenges, include when working excessive overtime can affect an employee is performance health and home life. It can result in higher absence levels and unsafe working practices.

●

● Job sharing is a form of part time working where two or more people share the responsibility for a full time job. They share the pay and benefits in proportion to the hours each works. They share the pay and benefits in proportion to the hours each works. Job shares may work split days, split weeks or alternate weeks. it's potential benefits include that if one job sharer is absent, due to illness or holiday, the other can carry on with at least half the work, who can help meet people demand , e.g. both shares being present when workloads are heavy, a wider range of available, who can help people with caring responsibilities and/or other commitments to continue working. It is potential challenges also include extra induction, training and administration cost, replacement may be difficult if one job sharer leaves, added responsibility on supervisors/managers, who must allocate well fairly and ensure that the job shares communicate effectiveness. If the shared role involves managing on supervising staff can find it is difficult working for two managers.

●

● Shift work is a pattern of work in which one employee replace another doing the same job within a 24 hour periods. Shift workers normally work in crews, which are groups of workers who make up a separate shift team. it's potential benefits include it can reduce costs by using equipment more intensively and taking advantage of cheaper off peak. It's potential challenges include it can increase wage and labor costs, it can disrupt employees' social and domestic lives, it can upset employees' body and affect an employee's performance and health.

●

● Employers ought concern employee engagement issue. Different professions have their own specific, which need to be addressed during the engagement building process. For example, for hospital workers, safety issue is of a high importance as who deal with different kinds of sicknesses, whereas for teachers or the issue of stress and emotional exhaustion many be of more importance.

●

● To learn how to satisfy employees, content with their work experience, was a good formula for success, as a satisfied employees, who wanted to stay with a company, contributed to the workforce stability and productivity. However, satisfied employees may just meet the work demands, but this won't lead to higher performance. In order to compete effectively, employers need to go beyond satisfaction. Therefore, modern organizations expect their employees to be full of enthusiasm to work. Other researchers state that employee engagements is the best fool in the company's efforts to gain on competitive advantages and stay competition. Though, the notion of engagement is relatively new, and it is already a hot managerial topic and it is rare to find an HR or managerial related that doesn't mention employee engagement. These researchers agree that engagement creates the prospect for employees to attach closely with their managers, co-workers and organization in general and engaging environment is the environment when employees have positive attitude toward their job and are willing to do high quality job.

●

● It seems that how to develop good engagement workplace environment can influence employees' satisfaction, then it can influence whose performance or productivity. So, they have close relationship. however, it is even harder to build engagement within the specific group of employees in the situation, when the knowledge about the specifics of their work-life is missing. Different occupations need have different engagement workplace environments and engagement methods to let employees to feel satisfaction. For example, engagement of administrative workers in the educational organizations is rarely studied and poorly understanding, even though these employees have a significant influence in the institution and the quality of their performance contributes to the quality of relationships with faculty students and the public. So, understanding the administrative personnel work life perception is important to educational organizations. How schools can implement engagement to achieve target to improve administration employees (administrative workers) whose performance, students, faculty public satisfaction and other organizational outcomes. Because whose performance is not save to factory workers to cause how many product quantities manufacturing per hour to calculate, whose need to use service quality to measure performance.

●

● I feel it is better in the situation when organizations have a better understanding of the administrative personnel work-life perceptions, it is easier for them to create appropriate engagement building tools. Such as, administration employees working at small sized education organizations are more engaged, and this might be due to the reason that they have better relationships with colleagues and experience a greater sense of belonging than their collages from larger education organizations. Futhermore, Johnsrud and Rosser (1999) also suggest that the smaller the institution, the more positive administrative workers moral and consequentially the higher chances for their engagement. Therefore, result of this study can be applied only to the educational institutions of the similar size. Furthermore, results of this study can't be used for similar organization in order contributions.

●

● What factors can influence the engagement of administration staff. I feel that significant variables factors include: working conditions, job fit, role fit, time spent interacting with students and length of employment on campus. As some researchers working conditions were found to be a significant and positive factor influencing engagement, this means that better working conditions increase the chance that the employee will shoe in higher level of engagement person job fit was defined by Edwards (1991, as referenced in Kristof, 1996, p.8) as " the fit between the abilities of a person and the demands of a job , i.e. demands-abilities or the desires of a person and the attributes of a job needs supplies". Job fit also focuses more on the formal aspects of the work, when role-fit includes both established and new tasks, which core out in teams, as team members' roles include formal tasks as well as informal socially defined tasks. The only factor , which was found to have a negative influence on the engagement of administrative workers was employment history, meaning that the higher level of employees were working within an educational organization, the lower level of engagement who showing.

●

● I shall recommend to measure the engagement level of employees and to find out the specific engagement that need to be improved, the quantitative research with questionnaires as the main source collecting data was needed to choose to any educational organizations. Because questionnaires can produce number data, which is a quantitative approach. The educational administrative workers can be compared with each other within the category of engagement and can point out the factors driving engagement, which need to be improved. These numbers are the basis for further analysis and recommendations. The factors, which can be chosen for the investigation, include meaningful job autonomy at work, performance feedback, institution development opportunities, organizational support, procedural justice, social support from colleagues, supervisory support, social climate etc. The reasons to choose these factors to investigate because the meaningful job can increase psychological meaningfulness for the employee and therefore increases engagement. The above factor meaningful job has been included in the list. Besides, job characteristics can increase meaningfulness for the employee and are positively rarely to job engagement. However, educational administrative workers' moral has an influence on their perception an attitude to the job. The same study pointed out that the moral of administrative workers in educational organization is influenced by number of factors, such as working atmosphere, relations with colleagues and supervisors. For example, social support from colleagues and supervisory support is concerned to moral issue. Social climate factor is concerned to reward and recognition issue.

●

● Why employers need to concern employee moral issue. For example, any clinic organization has complex interpersonal relationships within the clinical domain and the critical issues are faced by nurses on a daily basis, indicate that morale, job satisfaction and motivation are essential components in improving workplace efficiency, output and communication amongst staff. Drawing on educational , organizational and psychological research, that the ability to inspire morale, staff morale which is a fundamental indicator of sound leadership and managerial characteristics. These includes role preparation for managers, understanding internal and external motivation, how internal motivation to nursing staff and the importance of attitude when investing in relationships. Because this factors can influence nurse performance. As the field of nursing, amongst money others, the concepts of developing emotional self-awareness in staffs, self-control, adaptability in initiating in management, and organization teamwork in social networks have been poorly applied. Despite this, it has been suggested that nurse and physical collaboration is one of three strongest predictors of psychological empowerment of nurses (Larrabee et. 2003).

●

● Relationships on the ward can influence to nurse satisfaction and personal professionals are closely linked to self-esteem or person's own morale. So, morale of nurse occupation can influence performance to serve patients. In health care industries, how to create healthy working clinical environments and encourage nursing staff for leadership and management roles, the issues of morale and motivation need to become primary concerns in the ward setting. Because any nurse service will fill with dread, fear and anxiety to whose patients if who neglects to concern care morale. So, nurses need to concern motivating behavior and discourages pessimistic feelings and performance. The reality is that some people naturally posses a high level of this internal motivation, these who focus on the internal feelings of satisfaction who will attain despite any difficulties who face along the way. Executives are coached, athletes are coached, why not health care professionals? The nature of helping others through clinical care provision may preclude staff from asking for help themselves.

●

● Has it relationship between boosting morale and improving performance in the nursing occupation? For example, healthy working environment and system may be assisted through the regularity of coaching key staff, e.g. nurses in hospitals need to create any clinic ward organizations. Clinical will environments with good retention, work satisfaction and high quality measures. Nurses can also learn how to self-coach be more self aware and develop themselves. In the nursing occupation, linking nurses' daily work to long term ambitions will impose their motivation, boost their self-confidence and assist them to function at a higher performance level.

Coaching will also help staff recognize their own management styles, and identify their leadership strengths and areas for improvement. Because nursing work is frequently rewarded by patients' gratitude. Nurses within clinical settings often comment on the patients' capacity to say thank you and their appreciation of how nurses contribute to their well being. So, the success of their health care service. In fact, performance appraisal is ideally about recognising the direction an individual nurse wishes to pursue concern how health care moral behavior to nurses to achieve to satisfy patient's individual need to reduce complaint occurrences to build healthy clinic environment to let nurses to work enjoyable.

●

● Why absenteeism will influence performance? Unscheduled absenteeism is a popular problem for U.S. employers, conservatively costing $3,600 per hourly employee per year and $2,650 per salaries employee per year, the majority of employers have limited ability to accurately and regularly track how much absenteeism is reducing their bottom line earning, effective absence management systems can track absenteeism, manage absence policies and work schedules, and control overtime, allowing management to reduce lost earnings, also reducing absenteeism will also help employers better meet production and service demands without requiring an increase in headcount. Commonly, the un schedules absenteeism rate in the U.S. hourly workforce is approximately 9% almost one in ten workers is absent when who would be at work. There are considerable direct and indirect costs are increasing. Not only should managers be motivated to reduce absenteeism because of the excess costs, but without absence tracking tools, employers can't adequately estimate their accurate liabilities. However, absenteeism causing is probable due to poor health to the individual employee. So, who will perform poorly to influence whose productivity to be worse. Why is there such little focus on absenteeism, compared to other costs, health care or low productivity or poor service performance costs for example? So absenteeism can raise much different workforce related costs. The excess costs arise cause disruption to the business, make it difficult to deloy the workforce, and have a profound effect productivity, profit margins and poor employee morale.

●

● However, improving employee health can at most, only reduce absenteeism by one-third, as two-thirds of absenteeism is caused with non-sickness (personal reasons, feeling of entitlement, family issues). In the result, the direct impact is reduced or poor delayed production or customers are not being served. How to solve absenteeism challenges? Generally, the employer was using a five day schedule, but demand was such that employees were asked to come in on the weekend on a regular basis. The employees disliked working, so many consecutive days with no time off, which led to very high absence rates. The shortages of employees results in demand not being met and customers were dissatisfied. The organization has to replace missing workers with other employees or contractors and pay overtime or higher rates. Overtime levels are 28% higher in facilities with low absenteeism. Excess staffing plan, such as headcount is higher than necessary in order to cover unplanned absences. For example, the employer routinely increased headcount by 13% on weekends to cope with extra absenteeism on a Saturday and Sunday. It is less usual for a salaried employee to be replaced when absent. Instead, the demands of customers (internal or external) are not met and depending on the employee's position in the company, the ability to create revenue may be affected. Excess absenteeism can also lead to increased health care cost, greater safety issues and accidents, high turnover, and poor morale or performance. To achieve significant reductions in the excess costs with absence, the manager must reduce the rate of absenteeism and the subsequent effect that absenteeism has no the business. The first step is accurately and efficiently tracking absenteeism rates and patterns on a regular basis. The majority of organizations don't have an automated means to track every instance of absence in one system and therefore lack the visibility necessary to address this business problem. Once the root causes of the problem are known. The manager can consider what steps need to be taken. There may include using rules engines and process automation to consistently enforce absence policies, compliance with union, state and rules, improving absence management technology and increasing employee satisfaction with the workplace, reducing overtime costs by selecting employee to cover for absence based on their competence, training and hours worked during the week, accurate reports of absenteeism , patterns over time and root causes.

●

● In order to take full advantage of opportunities for business expansion and growth. Human assets investment strategy is very important to any organizations. For example, airport organization, it needs good employees serve to provide excellent customer services to satisfy the increase flight slots at airports. So good human assets investment strategy can drive focus on safety, innovation and globalization and create programs for motivating employees to enable them to fully demonstrate their abilities. Such as airport training is needed to be given by lecturers, include rank based and elective training to airport service industry. Methods are such as on site courses, supporting the career development to any airport different rank of staffs to promote on environment where individual employees can display their capabilities to the maximum possible extent in their respective roles. In special, giving women career training establishing a mentor system under which senior employees provide ongoing direction and support for junior and new employees and introducing role models through an intranet, supporting for working includes holding seminars for woman who are pregnant or on maternity leave and introducing a system or part employment. As a result, the number of employee and nearly all of tem return to the workforce. Because airport service industry needs have a large female workforce, including cabin attendants and airport passenger service staff. Besides, airport service industry also needs to hire women for career track administrative and maintenance positions and flight crews and working to increase the percentage of women in management positions.

●

● Better work life balance is also needed to satisfy airport service industry staff. Besides, airport service industry also needs to hire women for career track administrative and maintenance positions and flight crews and working to increase the percentage of women in management positions. Because airport job duty is common needed to be shift duty. Hence, the working time is flexible time to work when new employees decide to attribute to airport service career. However, due to many passengers need, so airport service workers need to work overtime hours. But, commonly, who do not hope to work overtime often. So, airport management needs to create an comfortable and enjoyable working environment in which each new or old employee can rethink whose own working style to contribute will help vitalize society, companies and individuals.

●

● How to leverage technology to improve employee engagement? Nowadays, employee engagement has evolved from a relatively unknown trend to a term in common usage, which leads itself to a variety of forms and levels of understanding. Employee engagement is about the ability of leaders to inspire their people around the way forward at the desired pace, involving a planned communication effort that is integrated with all the other leadership and change activities. Employee engagement is the emotional commitment the employee has to the organization and its goals. However, technology can play an important role in making engagement a practical part of everyday work. As companies move towards a digital workplace, understanding the impact of technology on employee engagement is critical.

●

● What is the digital workplace? The digital workplace is the digital environment in which staff work, and a place to find corporate knowledge. It includes a collection of election tools that enable productive, effective, work from anywhere. In the future, according to the workplace of the future survey by Teknion corporation predicted 88% of companies offer their workforce personal devices, such as smartphones and tablets. Nearly 90% of companies plan to increase their investment in productivity enabling technologies, such as voice activation and video conferencing by 20 15 year. Organizations are seeking the workplace as which search for ways to be more efficient, more collaborative and reduce their physical workplace to realizing higher levels of productivity with their workforce. So, it seems digital workplace can assist to raise performance. Two important reasons why new technology tools will be represent great return on investment for internal use with employees.

●

● The first reason is technology helps us comment with and engage remote or disconnected employees, those with little or no computer or internet access during their work time . The second reason is peer-to-peer engagement and using technology can drive the generation of more ideas, which drives innovation and improvement to produce in any workplace. So, creating an actionable roadmap that fully technology in any organization's staff engagement initiatives can improve bottom line performance. So, technology can assist organization to measure employee engagement, connect disconnected workers, encourage collaboration and social interaction.

●

● I assure engagement lies in sound decision making and action, then driving good decision making and action should be a communicator's core strategy. Many communicators are already doing good work to drive action. Then, good decision making is driven, in part, by the availability f good information. Even employees who are less digital connected at work can contribute great ideas that improve that work situation and organizational productivity. Examples, of ways technology helps to that such as: one employee posts about a project who is working on, another employee in an office on the other side of the world sees the post and realizes who is working on a similar project. If the two teams combine their effort, who can solve the problem and the company gets a global solution. So, corporate internet is a new digital workplace tools. To effectively solve challenge as making the right information available to the right people at the right time. Organizations must begin by clearly identifying the core types of information that must be shared to engage employee and bring about maximum organizational benefit.

●

● What critical organizational information should all employees access? What types of knowledge are suitable for collaboration? What informational exist today and how are these pockets of information affecting business performance? When analyzing your environment for knowledge sharing, take the time to understand knowledge sharing objectives and how to get employees on information that empowers them to be more successful and therefore more engaged. Remember, anyone can serve in this knowledge management role as long as who are contributing relevant and engaging information.

●

● When looking at any new technology to improve organization knowledge transfer and employee engagement for your employees you should consider the following questions: How does the proposed technology create for information sharing? Are they create for information sharing? Are they easy to use for people of all levels of the organization? How does the technology solution you are examine help employees get work accomplished? This is especially important when examining enterprise social technologies. How can the technology provide more information about company vision, people, business processes. How effectively does the technology support key organizational scenarios, such as identifying the best talent for a particular department or initiative? For example, hospital environment can give conversation about the patient benefits of a new in-room online information display at a hospital.

●

●

● How can influence organizational positive behaviors ?

● Nowadays, there are key forces are affecting daily organizational behaviors and continuing challenges, such as staff structure (work relationship), technology (resources inputs)are needs to transform to with people work and affects the tasks that who perform, environment (internal and external) factors influence the attitudes of staff, affect working conditions and provide competition for resources and power. So, based on these four forces, managers need to face the different challenges, such as managing chances in a global environment, managing ethical issues at work.
●

● How to raise staff performance to satisfy clients' needs? Customer service and satisfaction is not limited to the private sector, public sector also needs , e.g. education reform, private, managed case. So, staff need have excellent performance to raise quality of service to satisfy students, patients etc. needs. Why organizations focus on customer satisfaction. Business monitor customer satisfaction in order to determine how to increase customer base, customer loyalty, revenue, profit, market share and survival. Besides, government needs to monitor customer satisfaction to achieve citizen needs. What is customer satisfaction? Customer satisfaction can be experienced in a variety of situations and connected to both products and services. It is a highly personal assessment that is greatly affected by customer expectations, satisfaction also is based on the customer's experience of both contact with the organization , the moment of truth and personal outcomes. Private sector means it is as one who receives significant added value as well as public sector means it is to whose bottom line. However, customer satisfaction differs depending on the situation and the product or service. A client may be satisfied with a product or service on experience, a purchase decision, a salesperson, store, service provider or an attitude. So, staff performance can influence or client's decision to choose to buy the product or consume the service indirectly. For example, in hospital organization , patient surveys often ask customers to rate their providers and experiences in response to detailed questions, such as " How well did your physicians keep you informed?" These surveys provide "actions" data that reveal obvious steps for improvement.
●

● Client satisfaction is highly personal assessment that is greatly influenced by individual expectation. In the public sector, the definition of client satisfaction is often linked to both the personal interaction with the service provider and the outcomes experiences by service users. For example, satisfaction with client worker interaction whether in person, by phone, or by mail or by email communication, satisfaction with the support payment , e.g. its accuracy and timeliness and satisfaction with the effect of child support enforcement on the child. For hospital organization, staff performance need have these service quality factors to raise or improve whose service satisfaction experience to whose patients (clients), e.g. timeliness and convenience, personal attention, reliability and dependability, employee competence and professionalism, empathy, responsiveness, assurance, availability and tangible, such as physical facilities and equipment and the appearance of the personnel.

●

● Satisfaction and engagement are two important distinct measurements that provide valuable and actionable insights into the workforce. The problem is that how many organizations still view them as one and the same thing. As a result, they may be missing critical opportunities to foster the kind of workforce engagement that drives innovation, boosts performance and increases competitive success. However, some organizations think which don't have to worry about engagement because turnover is how and employees seem satisfied when employee satisfaction is important to maintaining a positive work environment. Is it enough to help you retain top performers and drive bottom line impact? Probably not, by focusing more employee engagement, organizations are more likely to maintain a strong, motivated workforce that is willing to expand extra effort, drive business goals and deliver a return on HR's talent management investment. How to achieve actionable strategies for maximizing workforce engagement and subsequently, driving higher performance across the organization. It addresses critical questions, such as: Do you want satisfied employees or engaged employees? Which has a greater impact on the organization's bottom line? What are some proven techniques for addressing both satisfaction and engagement? Employee satisfaction can typically measured through surveys to gather opinions about HR related issues like bonus programs, benefits and work/life balance. Some employee satisfaction can refer to how employees feel, that happiness about their job and conditions, such as compensation, benefits, work environment, career development opportunities. On the other hand, engagement refers to employees commitment and connection to work as measured by the amount of discretinary effort, who are willing to expand discretionary effort, who are willing to expand on behalf of their employer. High engaged employees go above and beyond the core responsibilities outlines in their job descriptions, innovating and thinking outside the box to move their organizations forward, much like volunteers are willing to give their fine and energy to support a cause about which they are truly passionate.

●

● Can an organization have a satisfied employee who isn't engaged? Chances is an engaged employee is also a satisfied employee. However, it is certainly possible to have a satisfied employee a with a low engagement level. That's why focusing on satisfaction without addressing engagement is unlikely to foster the kind of expect workforce performance that drives business results. Why do organizations need to care about their workforce engagement level? The primary goal of a business is to make money, even non profit organizations exist to fund their specific causes. Many studies have linked organizations need to get employees at all levels focused on driving revenue. Also which indicates to link employee engagement to workforce preference, customer satisfaction, productivity absenteeism, turnover. Employee engagement is a concept that is rooted in science and at the most fundamental level reflects the human condition itself.

●

● It makes sense that this human motivation process would apply in the workplace just as in other areas of life. By motivating employees beyond basic satisfaction to achieve higher levels of engagement. HR professionals have more significantly impact business outcomes and drive bottom line results. Top-performing organizations understand that measuring employees' contentment levels and emotional commitment to the organization on a regular basis can put them at a competitive advantage. Since satisfaction measures on employee happiness with current job and security opportunities to use skills and abilities, the organization's financial stability, relationship with immediate supervisor, compensation and benefits. In general, these factors can contribute to job satisfaction, such as job security, opportunities to use skills and abilities, organization's financial stability, relationship with immediate supervisor compensation and benefit, communication between employees and senior management, the work itself, autonomy and independence, management's recognition of employee performance. However, fact engagement condition can have these difference with job satisfaction, such as relationship with co-workers, opportunities to use skills and abilities relationship with immediate supervisor, contribution of work to organization's business goal, meaningfulness of job, variety of work, overall corporate cultures. In general, staff tend to receive more pleasure and satisfaction from what who do if who are in jobs or roles that match both their interests and skills if staff feel who are making meaningful contributions to whose jobs, their organizations do society as a whole, they tend to be more engages. Staff want to be recognized and rewarded for their contributions. Rewards and recognition come in many forms, including competitive compensation packages, a healthy work/life balance, or sales trips etc. benefits. So, lack of motivation will affect productivity. In addition, a number of point to low morale: declining productivity, higher incidence of absenteeism and friend, increasing defective products higher number of accidents or a higher level of waste materials and scrapes. How much money (salary) will you give to your employee to satisfy whose needs? However, staff's needs differ some can be motivated by opportunity for growth and development, job security, good working condition more than high salary.

●

● In conclusion, as a manager, if you want to develop and encourage good employee performance, and good performance comes from strong employee motivation. But managers can't motivate employee. Motivation is an internal state, like emotions and attitudes, that only the individual can control. Managers can however, create a workplace environment to attempt to motivate staff. Nowadays, workplace is affected by a number of factors, including a decreasing emphasis on money, an increasing amount of work, an increasing need to work together in teams. Hence, employers concern to consider these above different psychological factors which can influence employee's individual behavior to perform efficiently in any organization.

●
●
●
●
●
●
●
●
●
●
●
●

-
-
-
-
-

- Reference
- Branham, L. (2005). The 7 Hidden Reasons Employees Leave: How To Recognize The Subtle Signs And Act Before Its Too Late. New York, NY: Amacom.
- Clark, R.E. (1998). Motivating Performance, Performance Improvement, 37 (8), 39-47.
- Clark, R.E. & Estes, F. (2002). Turning Research Into
- Results: A Guide To Selecting The Right Performance Solutions. Atlanta, G.A: CEP Press.
- Johnsrud, L.K. and Rosser, V.J., 1999. College and
- University Midlevel Administrators:
- Explaining and improving their morale. The
- review of higher education, 22(2), pp. 121-141.
- Kristof, A.C. 1996. Person-organization fit: An
- Integrative Review of its conceptualizations, measurement and implications. Personnel psychology, 49(1), pp.1-49.
- Larrabee J.H. Janney M.A., Ostrow C.L., Withrow M.L.,
- Hobbs G.R. And Burant C. (2003) Predicting
- registered nurse job satisfaction and intent
- to leave., Journal of nursing administration,
- 33 (5), 271-283.
- Shenkel, R. & Gardner, C. (2004), " Five ways to retain good staff", Family Management, Now-Dec. , pp.57-59.
- World at work (2009). Telework trend lines. Retrieved from http://www.workingfromanywhere.org/
- News/Trend lines_2009.pdf

-
-
-

● How to learn qualificative research ● interviewing in order to raise ● efficiency and effectiveness

●

● I assume that if the interviewer can learn whose what errors are in order to let him/her to review from past every time interview experience, then he/she can know how to improve future every time interview, e.g. controlling or managing time arrangment to every new interview process, asking what knids of questions to let the interviewer to attempt to answer for any kinds of position applocation suitation, how to make judge whose feedbacks or answers to any kinds of interviewing questions to be more reasonable in order to select the most right applicants to improve the interviewer's interviewing efficiency and make the more effective interviewing consequences, e.g. when the interview has 100 applicants or more on that day , and it has only one to three interviewer(s) number. Hence, time controlling and managing and how to ask interview quetions will be one value considerable questions to the interviewer(s), if the interviewer does not want to waste time to make wrong judgement to select the applicant(s) who is(are) not the most right applicant(s) to do the position(s). Hence, how to learn the qualitative research interviewing, it will be one value question to any interviews for whose organizational economic benefits, because their interviewing behavior will influence their organizations time and resource and human resource lose or waste to do other important or urgent tasks every day, when they use the limited working time to concentrate on the interviewing and selection task only , but on more time to do other efficient and effective interviewing tasks. So, it brings this question: How can the interviewer learn past interviewing experience in order to improve next every time qualitative research interviewing consequence?

●

● Steinar, K & Svend, B. (2009, p.2) explains thatdifferent forms of interviews serve different purposes: Journalistic position application interviews are means of recording and reporting important events in society, theapeutic position application. Interviews seek to improve debilitating suitations in people's times, and research interviews have the purpose of producing knowledge. Hence, the interviewer needs know whether what kinds of position, the applicant is applying, e.g. above different kinds of professional jobs. They need the applicant owns the kind of professional knowledge and technique and educational level to do the kind of professional job, in order to do the kind of position more proficient. So, above of all these kinds of professional job interviews, they have need have these basic application requirement to let the interviewer to select, but how to ask different kinds of interviewing questions to every applicant, he/she can follow whom educational background and owning related working related experience to choose the interviewer ought ask him/her, the application what kinds of interviewing questions in order to let him/her to answer or give feedbacks in order to make more accurate selective decision to every applicant in fact.

●

● The research interview is based on the conversations of daily life and is a professional conversation to any interviewer's daily interviewing task. It is an interview, where knowledge is constructed in the inter action between the interviewer and the interviewee. Any one interviewer needs to know an interview is a conservation that has a structure and a purpose and it becomes a careful questioning and listening approach with the purpose of training thoroughly tested knowledge.

●

● The research interview is not a conversation between equal partners because the inteviewing researcher needs to define and control the situation for interview. The positive application interview researcher needs to introduce the topic of the job interview and also critically , follows up on the subject's answer to hir /her interviewing questions. So, it is one time spending tasks to any interviewers, when any interview needs to be carried on. I shall indicate the main interview learning points as below:

●

● The first interview learning point is any job interviewing is an active process where interviewer and interviewee through their relationship produce social knowledge. Interview knowledge is product in a conservational relation. The conception interview knowledge presented to contrast with a methodogical positivison conception of knowledge as given facts to be quantified, e.g. in one journalist position application interview, the interviewer asks the same question to ten applicants. The question: How do you have more confidence to apply your past journal writing working experience and knowledge to do this journalist job? When these ten applicants listened this question. They will have different feeling to answer this question. Hence, the interviewer can follow their different answers or feedbacks to compare these 10 applicants' consumers to judge whether whose answers can have more reasonable to be accepted as well as the interviewer also needs to record how much time , that they need to answer this question. Hence, a conception of conception of research interviewing is as a rule governed method, it will lead to different job application interview practices than an inderstanding of research interviewing as a tool, where the quality of the kind of job interview knowledge is more important to comapre the skills and the personal judgement of the interviewer.

●

● The another interview learning point is the interviewer needs to understand whose interview tasks is a semi-structured life and he/she needs to attempt to understand the applicant's lived eveyday world from his/her subjects' own perspectives, when the interviewee attempts to answer the interviewer's any interviewing questions by whose owning methods. This kind of interview seeks to obtain descriptions of the interviewees' lived world wit respect to interpretation of the meaning of the described phenomena. It comes close to an everyday conservation, such as the interiewer's everyday asking interviewing questions and listening the interviewer's every job applicant's answers or feedbacks, but when the interviewer assumes whose interview tasks, it needs to involve a specific approach and technique, it is semi-structured and it is neither an open everyday conscrvation nor a closed questionnaire between the job interviewer himself/herself and whose any job applicants. It is conducted according to an intervew guide that focuses on certain themes and that may include suggested questions. The job application interview is usually transcribed, and the written text and sound recording together constitute the materials for the subsequence analysis of meaning after every time interview. It aims to let the interviewer himself/herself can make more accurate judgement to select whom is the most right applicant to the job.

●

● Steinar, K. & Svend, B. (2009, p.28) indicates one qualitative research interview has any one of these twelve aspects characteristics. They incude as below :

●

● The topic of qualitative interview is the every day lived world of the interviewee and the interviewer his/her relation to it; the interview seeks to interpret the meaning of central themes in the life world of the subject; the interviewer needs to register and interpret the meaning of what is said as well as how it is said between the interviewer himself/herself and the interviewee(s) in every time interview; the interview seeks qualitative knowledge expressed in normal language, it does not aim at quantification, the interview attempts to obtain open descriptions of different aspects of the subjects life worlds, descriptions of specific situations and general opinions , the interviewer needs to exhibit openness to new and unexpected phenomena, the interview is focused on particular themes, it is neither strictly stim-structured with standardized questions, interviewee statements can sometimes be reflected, contradictions is the world the subject live in, the process of being interviewed may produce new insights and awareness, and the subject may in the course of the interview, come to change the interviewer's descriptions and meanings about a theme, different interviewers can produce different statements can produce different statements on the same themes , depending on their sensitivity to and knowledge of the interview topic, the knowledge obtained is produced through the interpersonal interaction in the interview, a well carried out research interview can be a rare and enriching experience for the interviewee, who may obtain new insights into his/her life situation.

●

● The final interview learning point is that the interviewer also needs to have ethical issues in research interviewing, to control or manage himself/ herself interview behavior. Ethics is basic to an interview inquiry. It situations of conflict, the applicant's selective decision about which rules to follow with to a large extent depend upon the interview researcher's experience and personal judgement experienced interviewers. The interviewing skills, the knowledge, and the interviewer personal judgements necessary for conducting a qualitative interview of a high quality require extensive job interview training. The flexible , content and content-related skills of interviewing are acquired by doing interviews. Whereas, the interview of questiond can be communicated verbally, other aspects of interview skills, such as the kinds of interview questions, sensitive listening and the establishing of good environment in the interview situation all these ethic factors are very important to influence one efficient and effective interview achievement.

● In conclusion, to achieve one qualitative interview learning method in success. The interviewer needs to learn, such as one good interview practice consists of more than carrying out practical act , it also involves a situated judgement of what knowledge and techniques to apply when acting in a given interview situation, and when every interview is needed to carry on with different goals and values that interview demand careful choice. Hence, a research interviewing is learned by practicing interviewing, preferably within a personal interview experiene of whether the interviewee needed to use how much time to answer this interview question(s) in order to make more effective and qualitative accurate and fair researching selective decision to employ whom is the most right applicant to do as above this journalist position example among these journlist applicants.

●
●
●
●
●

● Reference

● Steinar, K & Svend, B. (2009) interviews learning the craft of qualitative research interviewing, US: SAGE publications, Inc. pp. 2, pp.28.

●
●
●
●
●
●
●

-
-
-
-
- Chapter Four
- How to apply psychological methods to predict employee individual productive efficiency and service performance
-
- It has one interesting question concerns whether organization's in-house training management and/or human resource training course program has close relationship to influence the reducing or raising employee individual productive efficiency and better or worse service performance consequence. I shall recommend that any organizations can apply psychological methods to judge whether they need to implement their facility management department to change their working environment to be better in order to let their employees feel comfortable to work to raise productive efficiency or implement training course program to let employees to learn in order to raise productive efficiency.
- How to apply psychological methods to evaluate whether the organization has need to implement in-house facility management service and/or any employee train courses program? I shall explain as below:
-
- Some essential concepts in psychological research concerns employees' raising productive efficiency and improving service performance may include as below:
- Cause means something which results in an effect, e.g. The organization's employees overall service performance is worse (effect) and/or overall productive efficiencies are worse (effect), it is due to the poor working environment factor and/or lacking effective training courses program provision (cause).
-
- Action or condition means that the organization's employees often perform worse (action), it is due to they feel worse working environment (condition) to influence their emotions are negative.
-
- Data means that the information from which are drawn and conclusions reached. For example, the organization gather much data concerns workplace environment variable facilities factors, e.g. enough air

conditioners, clean canteen facilities, large warehouse space allocation available etc. variable data as well as training course contents data. Then it will analyze all these both kinds of data to make the accurate conclusion reached to make the more accurate conclusion reached to judge whether its employees overall worse productive efficiencies and/or worse service performance effect is due to either worse workplace working environment and/or lacking enough training work-related course programs provision to let them to learn.

●

● In any large organization's improving employee performance and/or raising productive efficient research. A lot of data are collected in numerical form , e.g. how many employees feel their workplace environment is satisfactory or comfortable? The workplace environment comfortable and satisfactory feeling rank:

●

● 1 means the most comfortable,

● 2 means more comfortable,

● 3 means worse comfortable,

● 4 means the worst comfortable,

●

● But it is equally viable to use data in the form of text for an analysis and randomized experiment means a type of research in which participants in research are allocated at random by chance to an experimental or control condition. For example, when one organization needs 20 employees to do one performance improving experiment in one day 9 working hours. The 10 employees are arranged to manufacture watch product in one large warehouse space available and more cool temperature feeling working environment factory. The other 10 employees are arranged to manufacture the same kind of watch product in one small warehouse space available and less cool temperature feeling working environment factory. Hence, their watch manufacturing skills must be same proficient level, due to they manufacture the same kind of watch and the two factories' equipment supplies are same number and their qualities are the new purchase, and these two factories' worker number is same , the two variable factors are different , it is only that one factory's space is large size and the another factory's space is small size as well as one factory's temperature is much cooler, but the another factory's temperature is less cooler. This organization's one day working hours experiment aims to research whether these two factories' warehouses' space size variable factor and temperature variable factor whether they can influence these two groups of 20 workers overall productive efficiencies to bring the much difference of watch manufacturing number of the day. For example, if the large space available and much cooler warehouse's 10 employees can manufacture more than 500 watch number in the day. Otherwise, the small space available and less cooler warehouse's 10 employees can only manufacture less than 300 watch number in the day. Then, the organization can judge the conclusion concerns whether the better or worse workplace environment will influence its employee individual emotion to manufacture its watch number.

●

● All above these elements are each employee performance psychological research needs. Any employee psychological researches are needed to evaluate the evidence. Employee individual performance psychology is not simply about learning what conclusions have been reached on a particular topic. It is perhaps more important to find out and carefully evaluate the evidence which has led to these conclusion. For example, in the newspapers and on television, one comes findings from advertising influence consumers (audiences) media research. IS it simply to accept what the newspaper or television report claims or world it be better media choice to be advertised to check the original research in order to evaluate what the best advertisement media choice to attract customers (audiences') attention actually meant?

●

● The evaluation of employee performance improving evidence involves examining the general findings that the employee psychological research is making about an issue and the information or data that are relevant to this finding, e.g. The organization has not implement any training courses to let employee to learn, (it is the issue), the organization discovers many employee individual productive efficiency is worse, it is the information, this organization will gather different variable data, e.g. the equipment number whether is enough to supply to them to apply to work, the equipment quality whether is good or bad, new or old, the worker individual proficient skill level is high or low or their working related skillful experience is long or short years. Then, it can make more accurate analysis to find whether the lacking enough training courses program to be supplied to let them to learn any work-related skills, whether this variable factor is the major variable factor to influence their performance to be worse. For example, if this organization had enough equipment number supply and all are new and these workers' overall proficient skillful level is high and they own many years working experience about this kind of tasks. Then, it can judge the lacking training course program implementation is not the major factor to influence their performance to be worse, due to their performance ought not need to be improved. SO, it ought have other variable factors to influence their performance to be worse suddenly.

●

● Then, the organization needs to check whether the evidence or data support the finding or whether the finding goes beyond what could be confidently concluded. However, in any employee performance psychological research, there is nothing wrong with speculation as such since hypotheses.

●

● What is causal explanation in employee performance psychological research view point? Dennis , H & Duncan, C. (2005, pp.9-10), they stated one prisoner suicide risk case example of causal explanation, a psychologist who wishes to predict suicide risk in prisoners does not have to know why the causes of suicide among prisoners. So, if research shows that being in prison for the first time is the strongest predictor of suicide, then this is a possible predictor. It is irrelevant whether the predictor is in itself the direct cause of suicide. Hence, the two authors assume that in general, the prisoners choose to suicide in prisons. Usually, they are the first time to enter the prison. Because the two authors assume the psychologist does not know what the reasons cause prisoners choose to do suicide behavior in prison, because it is possible that these first time prisoners who feel difficult to adapt to live in prisons' strange environment, they afraid to be fright or hurt by another/other prisoners' hurt in prison, they also feel alone , when they can not live with their families together forever. SO, the reasons of not adaptable living in prison, which is possible to cause the first time prisoners to choose to suicide in prisons. Hence, the first time prisoners suicide in prisons, it is one assumption , when the psychologist does not know what reasons cause prisoners suicide in prisons in general. Such as employee performance research, organizations usually do not know what reasons cause their employees' overall performance to be worse suddenly, it is possible that their families relationship is worse, or they feel wage/salary level is too low to compare the industry's average salary/wage level, or they feel their company's promotion chance is less, or they hope to change another new job. However, the organization needs to assume that poor workplace environment and/or lacking effective training course program , these both factors will cause its employees' performance to be worse suddenly. Thus, causal explanation view point, it will need to be considered to any organizations when they need to do any employee performance psychological research.

●

●

●

●

● Aims and hypotheses in employee performance psychological research

●

● The possible aims of employee psychological research is to examine research objectives as three research aspects, such as below:

●

● 1. Descriptive or exploratory studies, it concerns case studies are reports that describe a particular case in detail, for example, the case study research aim can be conceived as investigating the factors that how they can be created, to find what factors cause the consequences which can be the psychological research aim. Such as employee performance psychological research case, when the organization needs to investigate whether in general, some employee individual productive efficiency is worse, the causes are due to themselves family relationship or lacking money spending or changing new job desire etc. non –related its organizational weaknesses factors or it's organizational weaknesses factors, such as poor working environment , lacking enough facilities supply, or poor manger individual attitude, or lacking enough training to improve their efficiency. So, when the organization discover its employees perform worse suddenly. It needs to gather data to investigate whether what are the major factors to cause its employees perform worse suddenly.

●

● 2. Evaluation or outcome studies, it aims to test the effectiveness of a particular feature. This kind of research often seeks to develop theory to explain why the outcome occurrence. It simply concentrates on the consequences of certain activities without attempting to test theoretical or ideas to explain how any why the consequences are caused. For employee performance research case example, when the organization knows its employees' overall performance is worse, e.g. this month car manufacturing number is less than 50 % to compare last month . The less than 50% car manufacturing number to this month, it is the effectiveness feature. The organization expects to find the reasons why this month's car manufacturing number reduces less than 50% to compare last month suddenly. It is possible due to the machines qualities are worse and old obsolete when they are used to manufacture cars long term, needed new technologies , e.g. artificial intelligent manufacturing robots, employees feel tried to work, when they often need to overtime to work or the employees number is not enough. SO, its poor productive efficient consequence must not be caused by poor manufacturing workplace environment or lacking enough training to workers both factors. It is due to the organization itself resource shortage problem. Then, the organization needs to gather different category of data to evaluate whether why its overall employee's performance is worse to compare last month suddenly.

●

● 3. This kind of research is meta-analysis studies. It aims to summarize and analyze the results of the range of studies which have investigated a particular topic . It is in a systematic and structured way using statistical techniques. These trends may be used to calculate what is known as an effect size. This is the size of the trend in the data adjusted for the variability in the data. For employee performance psychological research example, when the organization expects to find whether the other similar competitors between owning training department and lacking training department , what are the advantages will be possible to bring or/and what are the disadvantages will be possible to bring as well as whether it has need to implement one training department to bring the possible advantages to itself. Then , it needs a systematic and structured way using statistical techniques. These trends may be used to calculate what is known as an effect size. This is the size of the trend in the data adjusted for the variability in the data for its reference sources. It aims to analyze whether the training department is needed to bring what the good or bad influences to its similar competitors in order to help itself to make the judgement whether it ought need to set up one training department or not.

●

● What the employee performance research aim?

●

● The employee performance researcher needs to have an understanding of what purposes the research will serve and how likely it is to serve these purposes. The employee performance researcher needs to be able to present the aims of their studies with enough clarity to justify just why the research was done in the way in which it was done. More importantly, the aims of the research need to be clearly justified by providing their rational.

●

● In conclusion, justifying the aims research can involve: Explaining the relevance of the research to what is already known about the topic as well as reference to the wider social situation, e.g. competitors' productive efficiency and organizational development growth situation for research, employee performance psychology research is often a response to the concerns of whole society by government, social institutions, such as the legal and educational system, business organization.

●

● What are employee psychological research hypotheses?

●

● The use of hypotheses is more common in employee psychological performance research than in concerning , such as sociology, economics and other related subjects. A hypothesis does not have to be true since the point of research is to examine the support or its aim is for the hypothesis, e.g. One car manufacturing organization assumes that all first time new car manufacturing employees , they lack enough skills to manufacture its different kinds of cars , so it assumes that they all need to be trained to raise their car manufacturing skills to be proficient, if it expects that they can raise productive efficiency in short time, e.g. one month. It implies that it needs have one training department to provide effective car manufacturing training courses to let them to learn satisfactorily if their car manufacturing technique can be improved in short time. SO, it has both assumptions, the first is all car manufacturing workers' skills are not enough as well as the second is that an effective training courses program can improve their car manufacturing skills in short time in order to raise productive efficiency after one month.

●

● A hypothesis does not have to be true, such as car manufacturing firm case, since the point of research is to examine the support of it's aim is for the hypothesis. So, hypotheses are assumptions to link to the aims of the study. Such as the car manufacturing firm aims to raise its car manufacturing worker's skills to be proficient after one month, so it assumes that its all new workers' skills are not proficient and it is one an effective training courses program can improve their skills to manufacture the increasing car number after one month in possible. So, it does not concern other variable factors will influence their car manufacturing performance.

●

● However, hypotheses can contain three variables: Attitude importance, attitude similarity, interpersonal attraction variables. These assumptions concern to research the firm's employee personal individual working attitude can be either similar, e.g. many employees' working attitude is positive or liking to work or many employees' working attitude is negative or disliking to work, or interpersonal attraction , e.g. many employees can be influenced to reduce productive efficiencies , due to the poor performance of employees' personal influence, or attitude importance in a group of student's learning behavior, such as business organization case, the team employees' overall working performance behavior can influence the other team members' working behavior obviously.

●

So, this psychological research can assume the Classroom students' learning attitude can be either similar to hard to learn, or these students can influence interpersonal attraction to influence themselves learning attitude together in classroom or all these students' feeling which is their whole classroom's all student their learning attitudes are very important factor to influence themselves whole learning behaviors in classroom. So, such as any organizations' employees , organizations can also assume that many employee individual performance can be influenced to perform better or worse when they need to cooperate to work in different teams working environment together.

●
●
●
●
●

● What are variables, concepts and measures meaning to any employee performance psychological research

●

● The variable means a key concept in psychological research. A variable is anything which varies and can be measured , e.g. the organization's overall employees performance or productive efficiencies can be raised or decreased the product number in any time, it is tangible, such as manufacturing number's increasing or decreasing number. These is a distinction between a concept and how it is measured. Otherwise, hypothetical is not variable, but theoretical or conceptual inventions, which explains what we can observe in our psychological research. It is feeling and intangible.

●

● Variables are what we create when we try to measure concepts. So, we will use the term variable without discussing the idea in any great details. Variables are the things what we measure. They are not exactly the same thing as the concepts that we use when trying to develop theories about something. For example, if one social psychological student wished to measure social influence how to influence people's behaviors in the country, the social psychological student might so, so in a number of different ways, such as number of people who disagree with a participant in s study.

●

● The use of concepts of independent variable and dependent variables was being encouraged by experimental psychologists to replace the response. The term variable tool prominence between psychologists concludes psychological phenomena in terms of the variables familiar from statistics. In this way, psychological phenomena in terms of the variables familiar from statistics.

●

● Dennis, H & Duncan, C. (2005, pp.39-40) indicated variables in psychology can include these sample different types: causal variable, it is only psychological domain. It is not possible to establish cause and effect sequences , simply on the basic of statistics, e.g. the organization can not find what factors cause its employees overall performance to be worse. It can only find data gathering of all similar competitors' overall worse performance analysis; hypothetical construct , it is only psychological domain, it is not really a form of variable , but an unobservable psychological structure or process , which explains observable findings, e.g. the organization assumes all new employees' overall productive efficiencies will be worse to compare the old employees and it assumes that an effective training program can improve the new employees' performance in short time; independent variable includes psychological or statistical variable in the dependent variables. As a psychological independent variable has a causal effect on the dependent variable. This is not the case when considered as a statistical concept. Ratio variable is only statistical domain, it measured on an numerical scale which has a proper new point. This allows the researcher to make ratio statements, such as person it is twice as tall as person is, such as organization's performance research, e.g. this month, this organization's manufacturing number can raise to manufacture more than three times to compare last month.

●

● However, it is given close relationships between psychology and statistics, many variables do not readily talk into just one

● of these categories. This is sometimes because psychologists have taken statistical terminology and observed it into their professional vocabulary to refer to slightly different things.

● It brings one interesting question concerns variable: How

● can a variable be the independent variable of the causal direction of the relationship between two variables is not know? E.g. When one organization believes that there is possible to cause worse performance, due to either lacking effective training or worse workplace environment, how

● it can prove that these two variables both can influence

● their employees' worse performance in the same time.

●

● For example, variables which can be calculated number

● and which are characteristic of the participant , subject variables , variables can be example: How old the person is, how intelligent, they are, how anxious , they are etc. when

● the organization employ any one of its employees. All these variables may be described aas the independent variable by some researchers. Such as this psychological research what characteristics the participant, it can not be explained how the causal direction of the relationship between the participant's age and whether his age has relationship to cause his intelligent level, e.g. when he is younger, then he is more intelligent, so when he is older, he will be less intelligent, however, these two variables are not known by the psychological researcher. Such as the organization's employee individual age variable, which will influence their intelligent level in order to learn training courses more easily to bring effect of the raising productive efficiency in short time or the employee is younger and he is health, so the worse workplace can not influence his productive efficiency to be worse.

Hence, in the organization case, it will need to try to predict what the value is of the criterion variable to the participant's psychological research from the values of the predictor variable or variables in order to decide whether what are /is the main factor(s) to influence its organizational performance.

●

● What is quantitative variables mean?

When we measure a quantitative variable, the numbers or values we assign to each person or case represent increasing levels of the variable. These numbers are known as scores since they represent amounts of something. For example, in one quiz game to research whether whom game player is

more clever, the independent variable might be age and the dependent variable may be scores on a quiz game or some other measure of general knowledge, older people do better

on the general knowledge quiz game. So, age itself, is not responsible for higher scores on the quit game. Otherwise, these may be more than one variable, e.g. educational experiences to raise the quit game player's skill to earn higher scores to win any quiz game competition. So, it seems that younger age quit game player must not earn higher scores to compare the older age quiz game player.

Age factor is not the main factor . Otherwise, education all experience will prove any quiz game players' skill to raise quiz playing skill to learn how to win the quiz competition more easily. So, age and clever is not the main factor to assist quiz game player to win easily. Learning experience will be one main psychological factor to assist the quiz game player to win any quiz competition.

It concludes there is an individual effect of age to influence the quiz game players' on the scores on the quiz. Otherwise, these may be more than mediator variable , e.g. educational experiences to raise the game competition. So, it seems that younger age quiz game player must not earn higher scores to compare the older age quiz game player. Age factor is not the main factor. Such as employee psychological performance research, organizations ought assume many different factors, include the non-related organizational as well as related organizational factors in order to find whether its organization ought need to implement effective training or/ and implement facility management strategy to improve workplace environment to achieve the raising productive efficiency or improving performance aim. Because each factors will be possible dependent or independent.

Reference

Dennis, H & Duncan, C. (2005), Introduction to research methods in psychology , 2 edition: New York, US Person Prentice Hall, pp. 9-10., pp. 39-40.

CHAPTER NINETEEN

Human resource department and organizational performance relationship

In any large organizations, whether human resource department can assist organizations to raise employees' effective and productive performance, instead of its basic main functions, such as selection, interviewing , performance management, reward management, training functions. I shall follow these several aspects to analysize whether human resource can assist to any organizations to raise efficiency and productive performance in possible. They may include these several aspects to analyze: The impact of training factor influences performance, the impact of recruitment and selection factor influences performance, the impact of facility management environment factor influences performance , the impact of reward and performance management factor influences performance.

Firstly, I shall explain how and why training provision factor may influence performance. In organization, training is one kind of method to assist employees to learn. The organization's technique and culture. Any organizations expect to survival, they will need employees to work or grow in one organizational learning and creation of learning environment in order to raise their skills, techniques and knowledge of level to work efficiently.

Hence , one learning organization needs employees to change mindset knowledge and values as well as improved organizational performance. Organizational learning may be any one of these processes occurring and organizational levels. Individual learning means to change in individual's knowledge, beliefs and ideas. Learning means to share understanding and interaction among employees.

Hence, in any organizations, they belong to this kind of learning team , employees need learn together in their deparments as well as organizational learning , it requires something more than shared understanding among employees, different departments' employees need to share understanding with other departments' employees. At this level of learning organizational factors need to be linked together and to individual and group learning to facilities organizational learning.

It brings this question: Can organizational learning bring the organizational overall performance improvement consequence? In fact, in any training, when employees attempt to apply the different training methods to solve their tasks difficulties. They will be possible to encounter fundamental barriers should be identified and removed. It seems that in their process of encountering barriers and finding solving methods to remove. This is one learning process to let them to attempt to accept problems and threats, and train them to learn to analyze which is the best method to solve the problem from training learning knowledge.

It is possible to raise employee individual efficiency from the training and learning error review process. The reason is that performance is the process of determining the efficiency of past activities. Organizational performance is in general concept means to how organizational operations are performed. Organizational performance measurement determines whether the organization has been successful as well as it is much discussed , but little understood.

However, there are other factors that influence organizational performance either directly or indirectly. For example, learning culture is one the important internal factors affecting organizatonal performance. A creative company needs to employ high levels of organizational learning and could use the information more efficient employees to work more than one non-creative company. So, it seems that effective training may create high creative learning culture to increase the high creative level of employees number to attribute a positive high levels of learning and financial and knowledge performance to the organization.

Hence, management tcnds to follow approaches that may guarantee organizational success. Since, any one organizational learning training chance provision is considered as an important factor in the efficiency of dynamic organizations. Learning and training is a process that brings about changes in performace through acqusition of knowledge and experience as well as training. Learning at the individual level includes changing in skills, attitudes , knowledge and values of individual employees. For example, a sport professional needs to be trained to learn the kind of sport knowledge from his/her sport trainer every day. So, sport practice and sport learning techniqie will assist the sport professional to raise whose individual sport skill in order to win the award achievement. For another example, one teacher can be trained and practice his/her teaching skill from his/her university's education course. So, university organization can provide skill to raise teacher teaching effort in order to improve whose teaching performance and adapt whose teaching career more easily. Hence, some occupations , such as teacher, sport professional etc. they ought need to be trained by teachers in order to help their organizations to improve overall performance more easily than without training provision.

Why can training learning provision internal variable factor impact organization's overall performance? Human resource is the main capital in any organizations. Efficiency and productivity of any organization is depended on the behavior and performance of its staffs and employees. Any training learning provision can being innovation benefit to the organization. The concept of innovation means a important enabling tool to create value and competitive advantage within organizations in a changing environment with increasing complexities. In fact, the starting point for innovation strongly relies on knowledge, expertise and commitment of human resources as key inputs to the process of value creation to an effective training is a good way to bring successful innovation to the organization. Because after a big improvement in managerial processes, the organizations would need motivation and ability, driven from human capital in order to create innovative ideas, develop innovative methods and build new business opportunities.

For example, IBM 's old kind of desktop computer product needs to be innovated to invent new kind of laptop computer product, its advantage is that the user can easy to bring the laptop computer to go to anywhere because it is not too heavy. Even, nowadays, it invents the iphone computer,it is one phone, but it has also computer functions. It can download any photos , documents, typing words, sending email. Hence, IBM's innovation is successful and it will continue to attempt to invent any kind of undiscovered new kinds of computer products to satisfy computer users' needs. If it has no one effective training department to train excellent computer professionals to help it to research and invent any kinds of unique computer products. IBM will be possible to be one failure business organization, if the other computer competitors, such as Apple computer can invent any new kinds of computer products in the future. So, one effective training departmen can provide new techniques to let trainees to attempt to mind any new ideas , innovates the old products' knowledge to change the new product's concept. Such as the computer product case, it is from the desktop computer stage, then to change the laptop computer stage, till to nowadays to change the iphone computer stage.

In computer industry case, all of these innovations, such as the computer organization needs have strategic human resource practices to affect the selection, capacities and behaviors of employees, e.g. programmer, computer handware and software engineers etc. computer professionals to achieve the computer organization's goals and to change them. So, each one of these computer professionals is playing a major role in necessary conditions, classify and conduct individuals towards innovative activities. So, it seems that an effective training department, internal variable factors can help the computer organization's computer professionals to improve their software and hardware program design techniques in order to innovate the computer's old computer design to change to new computer design product. Hence, when the computer organization owns one effective training department , then it can provide good creative ideas to let its computer professionals to bring new mind creative ideas. if their any new mind creative ideas are success to assist the computer organization to innovate new kinds of computer products to attract future new computer users' attention in order to attract their purchase choices. Then, the computer organization's overall sale performance will be raised. It is due to the proficient and excellent computer professional's computer invention skillful level are raised from their trainers' training provisions. Thus, it seems that an effective training department can improve some organizations' overall sale performance in possible.

Secondly, I shall discuss how and why the recruitment and selection factor may influence performance. Can an effective human resource management activity , such as job analysis, recruitment, selection and development which can influence organization's overall performance? I shall assume that if the organization has no effective job analysis then it will lead to poor selection to recruit the not best employees to serve its organization. It is vital for the managers to ensure all the workers are fairly paid and they work in the desired working environment. So, when the organization has poor job analysis, it will influence some employees feel workload and work difficulties, if the employees has low knowledge level and skillful to do the job, but her/his salary / wage is higher to compare another high or other high knowledge and skillful level staff/staffs. Then, the high knowledge and skillful staff /staffs will feel unfair, due to whose salary is / salaries are lower to compare her/him. Then, he/she will perform low efficiency or inefficiency or low productive behavior in order to complain whose manager's unfair treatment in whose department. So, it seems that poor job analysis will influence poor selection and unfair recruitment internal variable factor as well as it will influence the high knowledg and skillful employees to attempt to perform low productive behavior to achieve the inefficient performance aim. This situation is popular in manufacturing industry, when one factory whose one product manufacturing worker feel whose knowledg and skillful level is better than another worker, he/she can manufacture many good quality of products number to compare another worker's number every day. But, he/she knows the another worker's wage is higher than him/her, it is possible that due to he/she works long time in this factory or he/she and his/her manager relationship is good. Hence, he/she may feel unfair and it can cause he/she choose to produce products number in order to perform his/her complaint to whose manager or factory employee.

However, in fact, he/she has absolute effort to produce many product number to compare the another worker's number. However, when the factory manager discovers the excellent performance worker's productive efficiency is poor. He/she plans to make the decision on selling the given employee, it means that finding another new employee to replace him/her (unemploying him/her). So, the manger will do wrong decision, he/she only believes the employee's knowledge and technique level is poor to compare the others. The manager does not know the employee perform low productive behavior, he/she aims to complain to the manager himself/herself for unfair treatment. So, if the manager finds the another new worker to replace the high performance worker. But the new worker's productive number can be improved to achieved the old high productive worker's performance. It will influence the factory's overall productive performance in long term.

Thus, it implies that the internal changing factors between the new and old workers or the variables on the factory workers' productivities should be analyzed as well as the number of the factory's workers in the affected manufacturing department in the factory. This phenomenon can as well as take place from within the factory when the factory's workers show a competent ability and therefore, needs promotion. Thus, it explains why that effection in job analysis internal variable factor will influence the more accurate selection and recruitment to the most right employee in order to avoid the high knowledge and high technical employees choose to perform low productive and inefficient behaviors to achieve aim to complain their dissatisfactory treatment from whose employer. Then, it will influence the organization's overall productive performance to be poor , due to the high knowledge and high technique of employees' low productive behavioral performance. Every one of their low productive behaviors can influence the organization's overall productive performance to be poor in long term. Thus, one ineffective job analysis, selection and recruitment , human resource strategic internal variable factor will influence the organization's overall productive performance to be poor in possible long term.

Thirdly, I shall discuss why and how the facility management environment internal variable factor can influence the organization's overall performance in possible. The main idea indicates that the HRM performance presumption is that HR practices affect the employees' attitudes and behaviors, which further affects the operational performance, such as productivity , quality and innovation . It can bring a positive or negative effect on the financial and market performance to the organization. However, in any small, medium and large size organizations, they must need workplace and facilities to let their staffs to work in the stable locations. If the organization's location is not comfortable to let many staffs to feel in long term, e.g. factory, office, working environment. It is possible to influence its staffs' emotion to be bad, due to they need often to work in the poor working environment. It affects the employees' emotions negatively, this includes increased work intensity, stress, burn out and ripple effects from work into private life. It has relationship to influence the organization's employee individual productivity or service performance between the organization's internal variable facility management environment and employee individual emotion. It seems that if the employee has good emotion, it will influence his/her efficiency to be raised, otherwise, if the employss has bad emotion, it will influence his/her efficiency to be reduced. However, I assume that any organization's facility management workplace environment will influence employee individual emotion to be good or bad, then it will bring consequence , such as how the employee perform to do his/her task to be better or worse. For example, in one school classroom, its size is small, it only allows to the 30 students maximum number . If there are students need to sit in the classroom every class. Then, it will be possible to cause some students feel uncomfortable to sit in the classroom.. Then, it will be possible to influence these feeling uncomfortable students' learning emotions to be negative or they can not concentrate on learning when they still need sit in this small size classroom. Even, if these are 50 students ,even more students , they will sit in this small size classroom. Thus, it will bring the consequence in possible, such as the increase poor negative emotion student number as well as the poor learning performance. Thus, it seems that school organization's classroom size and learning material supply facilities, e.g. tables, chairs, computers, library books number, etc. these any one of the school's internal variable facilities number supplying and learning classroom size, attending lecture hall size , library size etc. facilities management factors will influence the student's learning emotion. Even the school's teachers' teaching emotions will be also influenced, due to they also need to go to classrooms or lecture halls (learning workplaces) to teach their students in the school. If the school has good teaching facilities management environment to let teachers to feel. Then it will be possible to influence their teaching performance to be better. Otherwise, if the school has worse teaching facility management environment. Then, it will possible to influence their teaching performance to be worse . Hence, it implies that any organization's facilities management environment will be possible to influence its employees' emotions to be negative or positive as well as it can also influence their services or productive performances to be good or bad indirectly. For example, in one poor factory environment, the workers need to work in one without air conditioners working place to work. Although, their working environment has fans, but they still feel hot in summer to work. Then, this poor workplace will influence the high knowledge and technical level workers whose performances to be poor in summer to work , due to their good working emotions will be influenced to be bad, due to they need to often to work in this high temperature factory's stable workplace or this high temperature warehouse's stable workplace in summer.

Thus, whether the working place environment can let employees to feel comfortable or not comfortable to work. This internal variable facility management factor will influence employee individual emotion to be good or bad in order to cause efficiency or performance to be improved. Thus, the organization's internal workplace facility management factor will influence efficiency and performance indirectly.

The final factor is that whether the reward and performance management factor can influence performance. Can the organization provide effective reward and performance management strategy influence limiting productive efficiency and profitablity. An effective reward can follow the individual performance, it depends on whether his/her performance is poor average, high or excellent level in order to give the reasonable reward to the employee fairly.

It seems that when there is one employee feel the organization can provide reasonable and fair reward to him/her. Then, the limiting factor (the stable fixed or unchanging staff number) will be possible influenced to raise productive efficiency, due to many of them feel their organization can provide fair and reasonable reward to encourage them to raise efficiency in order to earn more extra tangible reward, e.g. increasing salary/wage amount, increasing extra welfare , or intangible reward, increasing promotion chance, appreciation, job satisfaction. There are many employees feel their organization can not provide reasonable or fair reward. Then, it won't be encouraged them to work hardly. They will produce inefficiently. Thus, it explains why two organizations have same number of high knowledge and skillful level employees. The one orgnization's overall efficiency can be raised absolutely. Otherwise, the another organization's overall efficiency can not be raised absolutely, even its overall efficiency will be poor in possible. It is possible due to that the organization has many employees feel it can provide reasonable and fair reward when the employee performs better, he/she can earn more reward. Otherwise, the employee can not perform better, he/she can not earn more reward. Anyway, the another organization has many employees, they feel it can not provide fair and reasonable reward to them. When they work hardly, they can not earn more reward. Then, they will be possible to reduce their productivity and inefficiency. So, unfair and unreasonable reward can not encourage them to work hardly. Even, they will perform poorly, they aim to achieve the same productive level to the low productive employees to satisfy the same reward level feeling. Thus, it explains why effective reward and performance management factor has relationship to encourage many efficient employees to raise productivity as well as improve organizational overall productive performance in possible.

In conclusion, above these psychological factors will influence how human resource performance to be either improved better or inefficient productivity. It depends on the organization's internal variable factors to influence any one staff individual performance effectively. So, any organizations ought consider how to achieve its human resource strategic plan in order to keep their staffs overall performance can not be influenced to be worse from any one of these internal variable factors.

Factors influence organizational overall performance effectiveness

What is efficient achievement of technological inputs factor in construction industry

What is organizational efficient raising actual mean? I shall indicate construction industry case to explain technological factor is the major factor to assist construction organization to raise efficiency. For construction industry example, improved productivity could be attributed to advances in and increased usage of information technologies, increased competition, due to globalization and changes in workplace and organizational structures.

For construction efficiency, the construction process can reduce waste in coordinating labor and in managing, moving and installing materials, loss avoidance. It can achieve efficient aim. The construction productive efficient concept can be defined efficiency improvements as ways to cut waste and labor. So, one construction organizational efficient achievement means that it implemented through the capital facilities sector, these activities would significantly advance construction efficiency and improve the quality, timeliness, cost effectiveness of projects in construction processes.

On construction industry technological factor influence hand, it can influence that construction productivity how well, how quality, and at what cost buildings and infrastructure can be constructed, directly affects prices for homes and consumer products and the robustness of the national economy. Construction productivity will also affect the outcomes of national efforts to renew existing infrastructure systems; to build new infrastructure for power from renewable to renew existing infrastructure systems; to build new infrastructure for power from renewable resources to develop high-performance " green building" and to remain competitive in the global market. If the construction organization expected to achieve effficient aim. It ought consider how to change in building design, construction and renovation and in building materials and materials recycling, will be essential to the success of national efforts to minimize environmental impacts, reduce overall energy use, and reduce greenhouse gas emissions.

However, construction industry analysts differ on whether construction industry productivity is improved by efficiency outcome. They indicate construction efficiency needs to reduce 25-50 percent waste in coordinating labour and in managing, moving and installing materials. This is the most minimum standard efficient achievement level to any construction organizations.

What are the factors influence efficiency to any construction organizations? An efficient construction task process is made possible by a range of information technological tools and applications, including computer-aided design and drafting, three and four dimensional visualization and modeling programs, laser scanning, cost-estimating and scheduling tools and materials tracking. So, high technological tool will assist to raise efficient construction process to any construction organizations. It can help them to shorten time and avoid materials waste and control cost effective estimation for any construction projects.

Effective use of interoperate technologies requires effective team cooperative processes and effective planning up front and this it can help overcome obstacles to efficiency created by process fragmentation. Interoperable technologies can also help to improve the quality and speed of any construction project related decision making, integrate processes, managing supply chains, sequence work flows, improve data accuracy and reduce the time spent on data entry, reduce design and engineering conflicts and the subsequent need for rework, improve the life-cycle management of buildings and infrastructure.

All of these factors will influence whether the construction organization can implement efficiency in success. For example, interoperable techcholgies include legal issues, data-storage capacities and the need for " intelligent " search applications to sort quickly through thousands of data elements and make real-time information available for on-site decision making. How to improve job-site efficiency through more effective interfacing of people, processes, materials ,equipment, and information. The job site for a large construction project is a dynamic place, involving numerous contractors, subcontractors, trades people and labors, all of whom must require equipment, materials and supplies to complete their tasks. So, they need to know how to manage activities and demands to achieve the maximum efficiency from the limited available resources. Time, money, and resources will have possible to be wasted when projects are poorly managed, causing workers to have to wait around for tools and work crews are not on-site at appropriate time or when supplies and equipment are stored in complexity or difficulty, requiring that they can be moved multiple time (time waste).

How to improve job site safety and improve the quality of projects, significantly cut waste? The use of automated equipment, e.g. for excavation and earthmoving operations, pip installation, concrete placement, and information technologies, e.g. radio-frequency identification tags for tracking materials personal digital assistants for capturing field data. These high technological tool can help any construction projects to raise efficiency to process improvements and the provision for real -time information for improved management at the job site.

Moreover, on mannal research and development tools hand, instead of data technological tools hand, any construction organizations also need to consider how to take a variety of forms: How to test field on a job site? How to arrange lecture shows in efficient way, seminrs, training and conference, and scientific laboratories time, human resource available arrangement, spending expenditure budget to finish. Moreover, effective performance mearements are enablers of innovation and of corrective actions throughout a construction project's life cycle. They can help any construction companies or organizations understand how processes led to success or failure, improvements or inefficiencies and how to use that knowledge to improve construction products , processes and outcomes of active projects.

The nature of construction projects, the industry itself, any construction organizations ought consider the construction working environment how to influence construction workers' emotions. For example, when the construction site is high levels, of noise, dust and airborne particles, adverse weather conditions,and other factors that can cause injuries and thereby reduce efficiency and productivity. New types of equipment can make an active physically easier to perform, easier to control, move precise , and safer for construction workers. Similarly, changes in materials can reduce the weight of construction components, make them easier to handle, move and install. Manufacturing building components off-site providers need more control conditions and allow for improved quality and precision in the fabrication of the component, One study that examined the relationship between changes in material technology and construction productivity based on 100 construction a related tasks, the study found that labor productivity for the same activity increased by 30 % at least when higher materials were used and labour productivity also improved when construction activites were performed using materials that were easier to install or were pre-fabricated. So, it seems material heavy can influence construction worker individual productive efficiency in site, if the material is higher , then the construction worker's productivity will be influenced to improve (Goodrum et al. 2009).

Thus, the factors influence construction organization's efficiency. It focuses on whether the construction firm applies how advanced construction technologies to assist its construction workers to work as well as whether its construction environment can let workers to feel safe to avoid life danger or accident occurrence. When the workers do not worry about whose life safety as well as they can apply advanced construction technology to assist them to work. Then, their productive efficiencies ought need to be improved easily. Thus, facility management and advanced technology will be the main factor to raise construction workers' efficiencies.

CHAPTER TWENTY-ONE

Can effective departmental communication factor influence successful organizational effective change

In any organizations, their staffs must need communication either between the supervisor and low level staff(s) or between the same level staff(s) himself/herself/themselves. Has it relationship between communication and organizational efficient change? Can effective communication bring advantages to improve effort of employees to raise productive efficiency and execute change strategies more effective? Does organizational efficient change depend on effective communication in overall organization from low to top level, or top to low level? Why does effective overall organizational communication raise efficiency?

It is possible to consider that poorly managed change communication results in rumors and resistance to let every employee to know whether he/she ought know how to do it in order to finish whose task efficiently and effective result aim. Otherwise, an effective communication can let the employee to understand whether he/she needs how to do it clearly. Then, he/she will be possible to finish his/her task efficiently. So, it seems that employee individual job satisfaction will bring positive (effective) organizational outputs or negative (incffective) organizational outputs, when he/she can be often communicated either efficiently or inefficiently.

In one big organization, if every employee feels difficult to communicate daily. Then, it is possible to influence his/her low productive , or inefficient performance. So, managers, supervisors and low level staffs ought have effective communication between them. Communication can include writing communication,e.g. memos are needed to delivered between internal different departments or between external departments daily immedicately by the delivered staff. Because it will influence the department delivers what message to another department to know to be delayed if the memo can not delivered to the department on the day. Then, it may influence inefficiency. Communication can include oral or verbal. The supervisor or manager ought take hir/her low level staff how to do the task to be improved immediately if he/she feels that the staff her error. If he/she can't tell the staff to let him/her to know whether he/she ought need how to do to be better. Then, it will cause the employee does not know whether what his/her error is and he/she ought need how to review to change his/her error to be right or reasonable acceptance in order to satisfy her/his supervisor/manager's task need. So, it seems that effective communication can influence how the staff's performance indirectly. Due to his/her misunderstanding how to do whose task to be improved or better. Then, it will bring inefficiency outcome in possible.

Any organizations need to depend on achievement of efficiency and effectiveness of themselves staffs communication behaviors every day. During the staffs' communication , they will face problems of different understanding of communication related issues. Communication is either thus, such as negative communication phenomena that must be prevented or avoided; examples of difficult communication channel unavoidable problematic phenomena within the organization; they result from person/ personality communication problems of participants or as positive (creative) phenomena that enable the organization's development. For example: the both different departments or single department communicator(s) can present in possibility to active more effective communication participation and they can encourage creation of new and opportunities, as well as they can contribute significantly to introduction of changes; when they enable additional forms of either verbal/oral or writing form of memo or report communication. For example, when one marketing team needs to write a report to recommend new idea concerns hoe to promote the new product to the global market. If the marketing team member can cooperate to discuss easily. Then, they can communicate how to gather data to cooperate how to communicate to sale team members in order to achieve sale target easily. Hence, when the marketing team members can communicate to sale team members to give ideas to let them to know what their new marketing plan will be implemented in order to follow their marketing plan to prepare how to sell their firm's new products strategically. When the organization is large size, e.f. IBM computer organization , the marketing team members will need effective communication to sale team members if they expect to implement any new product market plan to promote to sell to global computer users more easily/ If the IBM large computer organization sale department members need to spend much time to contact marketing department members in person. Then, due to difficult communication problem causes their plan to implement the marketing promotion plan in long time. It seems that marketing and sale departments' staffs inefficient performance, it is due to ineffective communication between departments in possible.

Moreover, ineffective or different communication environment also causes individual conflicts impact organization in different ways(e.g. indirectly , directly) are of different importance to influence the organization's overall different department cooperation relationship to be poor (e.g. highly urgent communication matter, less important communication matter). They organization's different departments may not know whether what is the highly urgent matter needs to be dealt immediately and what is the less important matter does not need to be delat immediately of the organization's department staffs feel difficult to communicate, due to time management is poor causes the department staffs do not know whether the department staffs ought spend time to do the communication tasks with another department staffs in prior in order to let the another department staffs know how they ought to follow their demand to finish their task in short time cooperation efficiently. Thus, effective communication can help the organization to effectiveness present the level at which the organization achieves its goals , when its different department staffs can communicate to cooperate to work team work to finish effectively any tasks effectively and efficiently in short time. So, effective departmental communication can bring the limited staffs number the benefit, such as invested less efforts and less time input to help the organization to achieve the most maximum outcome output of its aims and goals of the organization. The effective communication concerns the staff's communication behavioral factor, e.g. (message content) inputs, (writing or verbal communication method) operations, and (how long time to finish the mission) outputs relation between the factors (internal, external departments).

In conclusion, when one organization has many different departments as well as many staffs who need to often cooperate to communicate how to do evey task together. Time management is one important successful factor to every department individual staff, he/she needs to know whether what is the highly urgent important messages are needed to be communicated to let the another department staffs to know, that is the less important messages are needed to be communicated to the another department staffs to know. Hence, effective communication is concerned how the employee arranges time to work daily. If the employee is one poor time management person, then his/her communication will ineffective, the consequence will bring the organization's different departments' cooperation inefficiency ,even it can cause the organization's overall productive performance to be poor, due to long term inefficient departmental difficult communication between departments factor.

CHAPTER TWENTY-TWO

Can human resource development training factor influence organizational productive performance

Can HRD has relationship efficiency of HRD training and development in organization growth? HRM is the function within an organization that focused on recruitment of management of and provision of direction to people who work in the organization, performance measurement and rewarding management of effective HRM enables employees to contribute effectively and productivity to the overall company direction and the achievement of the organization's goals and objectives in possible.

How any why effective HRD can influence organizational efficiency? HRD is administrative activities with HR planning , recruitment , selection, training , appraisal , motivation, reward strategic focuses on employees. So employees are any organization's assets. It assumes that when the organization's employees (assets) can be trained effectively. Then, the assets (employees) efficiencies will raise in long term. HRM designs the effective activities to be arranged to provide to every employee individual task and coordinates , all human element within the organizations. When, every employee individual effort can be attributed to the most maximum . Then, it assumes the organizational overall efficiency will be raised. So, effective training is one suggestive method aims to raise employee individual effort level to the maximum. Then, thc organization's overall efficiency will be raised in possible. However, HRD of training needs to be spent much money to invest in large size organizatons. Although, large size organizations, e.g. IBM computer firs, its training provides to spend much expenditure to train computer programming staffs to teach them how to create different new softwares in order to raise its competitive effort, it is long time investment value to its computer programming staffs because it is possible that it can upgrade its computer programming staffs' creative programming skills to be invented any new kinds of software products or designing new kinds of computers to sell. Hence, IBM 's HRD in training function has difficult evaluation its future human element of programming staffs' worth in long term. When, its programming staffs' skills can be upgraded to create special software products. Then, its overall staffs' efficient performance will also be raised because their software creative skills have been improved, due to effective training provision.

Effective training can solve the challenges of lack of skilled labour, heavy competition among firms, technological problems, low productivity and poor product implementation when placing a serious limitation on product expansion and increase in productivity. So, effective training needs have these characteristics: The trainer needs have good teaching skills or methods to raise employss individual creative effort, the training's content must need useful to satisfy the trainees' task need. So, the HRD's factors, such as organizational culture, job satisfactin, training and development and stress will have close relationship to influence the organization's overall employee productive performance or efficiency to be raised. For IBM computer example, it's organizational culture is that encouraging different department computer professionals create themselve software designing effort, providing effective training courses to raise their software designing creative effort in order to raise efficiency to achieve how to create new softwares in short time efficiently. Then, their job satisfaction may be increased, due to they feel that their software creative efforts and writing programming skillsa re raised or improved. Their stress will be also reduced, due to they do not need to worry about when they can create any new kinds of softwares or computer engineering systems to be invented to sell. So, if the IBM's HRD 's training function is one effective training course, it can assist IBM's programmers to raise their software and hardware creative effort to achieve raising IBM organization's overall productive performance and every software and hardware employee individual efficiency is also raised in possible.

Hence, any organization's training (HRD) will be one successful factor to influence the firm's productive performance and efficiency in possible.

An organization's HRD of training and development function concerns with organizational activity aimed at improvement of organizational performance, including employee development, human resource learning and development. Training has traditionally been defined as the process by individuals change their skills, knowledge, attitudes, and/or behavior. Similarly, training involves designing and supporting learning activities that result in a desired level of performance. In constrast, HRD refers to long-term growth and learning, directing attention more on what an individual may need to know or do at some future time. In fact, training focuse more on current job duties or responsibilities, development points to future jon responsibilities. It emphasizes either the product of training and development or how individuals perform as a result of what they have learned.

However, an effective training is real an educational process, trainees can learn new information, re-learn and re-improve existing knowlege and skills , and more importantly have time to think and consider what new options can help them improve their effectiveness and performance at work in possible. Effective trainings are taught useful information that inform employees and develop skills and behaviors that can be transferred back to the workplace. The goals of training is to create an impact to cause the consequence , such as inefficiency can be changed to efficiently as well as ineffectiveness can be changed to effectiveness of the training itself's final goal. An effective training, the focus is on creating specific action steps and commitments that focus trainee's attention on incorporating their new skills and ideas back at work. However, training can be offered as skill development for individuals and groups. In general, trainings involve presentation and learning of content as a means for enhancing skill development and improving workplace behaviors.

These are both processes, training and development are often closely connected. Training can be used as a method for developing or improving or creating or upgrading skills and expertise to prevent problems from arising and can be an effective tool to reduce the performance gaps among staff . Training learning development can be used to create solutions to workplace issues, before or after the trainee had encountered any problems when they are working. Hence, an effective human rcsource training development can help the organization's overall employees on a team, in a department and as part of an institution identify effective strategies for improving performance. Also, it means that when the organization's employees overall performances are improved or efficiencies are raised, it may be concerned to an effective training is provided to teach them before in possible. It implies that how to measure whether the training is effective, it is decided by whether the organization's overall efficiency is raised or not. If the organization's employees overall productive performance whom are improved. Its efficiency is raised, then it is possible that it had implemented an effective trainess to provide them to learn useful knowledge to raise their creative effort to solve their job-related problems in possible.

Thus, it seems that it has relationship between training and efficiency to any organizations. HRD process aims to find ideas and solutions that can effectively return the group to a state of high performance. Training and HRD describes the formal, ongoing efforts that are made within organizations to improve the performance and the employer self-fulfillment of himself/herself through a variety of educational methods and programmes. Hence, in the modern workplace, training development process indicates that the trainer needs to teach from short term specific job skills to long term professional development.

All of above issues, they are based on these assumptions , such as these relationships: There is a relationship between organizational culture and employee performance, there is a relationship between job satisfaction and employee performance, there is a relationship between stress and employee performance as well as there is a relationship between training and development and employee performance. However, training and development is the main factor to improve employee performance. When the organization has effective training and development to provide to its employees (trainees) to learn , then their stress will be influenced to reduce, job satisfaction can b raised and they can accept to adapt their organizational culture more easily. Then, their efficiencies will raise more when they can perform better or improve performance between to compare their prior work performance in their organizations. Hence, training and development element will be the most influential element to compare the other organizational culture, job satisfaction and stress elements in a human resource management factor, which can influence whole firm performance (every employee individual performance) obviously. Because I assume when the organization can have an effective training and development deparrment to provide any kinds of effective training courses to let its employees (trainees) to learn. Then, it is possible that it can help all employees (trainees) to increase themselves confidence to work more easily. Due to an effective training development can influence they can accept more easier adaption to their organizational culture, bring more job satisfaction, when they feel more easier to do their tasks and their stress will also be reduced, when their any job-related difficulties will be solved every day. The final consequence will being that the organization's every employee (trainee) whom efficiency will be raised in possible as well as it will bring the firm's overall employees performances to be raised or improved or the firm itself overall performance to be raised or improved.

In conclusion, it seems that an effective training and development can assist the organization's employee(trainee) individual efficiency to be raised or improved, then it can assist the firm itself overall employees(trainees) whose performace to be raised or improved, due to the effective training can influence the trainees overall efficiency to be raised or improved, then it can influence the firm itself overall performance to be raised or improved in possible.

CHAPTER TWENTY-THREE

Factors influence employee motivation to achieve organizational effective performance

In fact, one organization can influence employee motivation, instead of external fairly management workplace environment, effective training provision better reward attractive strategies, fair performance measurement policy, accurate selection and recruitment interview method factors. The intrinsic factors that are also importance to influence employee motivation. For example, employee achievement and recognition work itself satisfaction, role and responsibility itself, salary structure, the level to which the employee feels appreciated and the building good or bad relationship between the employee and his/her supervisor or manager. There are influential psychological factor to impact on the employee performance in the organization.

Motivatin is the personal intrinsic emotion factor how to influence the employee to develop a certain mind set regarding his/her job. In fact, the exterinsic factors in the organization's human resource management practices particularly to ensure that the employees are influenced well motivated to perform their tasks. In addition, the organization may need extrinsic factors, such as encouraging employee involvement in the decision making participation and innovation in the decision making participation and innovation and increases the promotion appreciation or effective or useful training opportunities for the personal growth: It can positively influence the intrinsic factors of employee motivation.

Similarly, when one employee feels he/she acknowledges his/her role in important to influence on organizationa; effectiveness in order to assist the organization to overcome challenges, it can create a strong and positive job cooperation relationship with its employees as well as improving task fulfillment and ensure they have job satisfaction. In special, any large size organizations, they have low, middle and top level staffs. If they only feel the middle and high level management staffs too feel their roles are important , but they neglect to let the low level staffs, e.g. workers, clerks , salespeople, teacher etc. low level staffs. These staffs themseleves can also feel their roles are important in their organizations. Then, these large size organizations' effectiveness or efficiency or performance will be poor, due to these large size organizations feel they are not important staffs and they can be replaced from other new employees any time easily. Then, these low level staffs will have plan to find another organization (new employee) to replace their current employers any time. In the consequence, the organizations will be possible to lose any one of these important low level high efficient or good performance staffs (workers) or main HR asset. It will lead to failure of these organizations when these high efficient staffs (workers) high staff turnover number is increasing. The reason is because they feel that they hace hgh efficiency, so they can another new job very easily. So they have poor job satisfaction, due to their orgaizations can not motivate their low level staffs take more reward and good salary to attract them to work efficiently. These emplers do not understand the benefits of motivation in the workplace, then the investment in these low level employee related policies ca be easily justified. They only consider to satisfy the middles and top level managemet staffs' tasks need and reward need. If these low level employees are motivated to fulfill their tasks and achieve their goals, e.g. the organization's salespeople don't attmept to help their organization to sell their products hardly, the school's teachers do not attempt to find good teaching behavioral method to attract their students to raise interest to learn or let they feel fun to learn from their teaching in classrooms. Then, their poor sale or teaching performance will bring the students or product buyer number to be reduced. For this reason, it is essential for a manager/supervisor to understand what really motivates the low level employees without making on improvemen performance or inefficiency or low productive assumption.

Motivation means an individual's intensity, mind set, direction and spending effort toward attaining a goal. It can be either individual goal motivation to achieve any matter or visiion from personal benefit or the organization goal motivation to persuade its employees to help it to achieve its improvement performance, raising profit, raising sale , raising productive growth, raising efficiency , vison or aim . In this chapter, I shall discuss how the organization's motivation to employees can impact organization's overall performance or efficiency or productivity to be either good or bad. So, motivation to employees can include extrinsic motivation, e.g. increasing salary level, increasing welfares, as well as intrinsic motivation , e.g. job satisfaction, appreciation, promotion chance/opportunity, feeling important role. I shall assume that if the employee lacks motivation emotion to work, then he/she will only spend less effort, nervous , time to attribute to work more hardly in the organization. Because they do not feel enjoyable to work , they won't raise efficient work performance, as well as their intrinsic motivation can not energize personal enjoyment, interest, or pleasure to let them they feel, they play one important role to earn unfair external reward to compare other same level or not same level staffs, e.g. the top level manager feels he/she earns unfair reward to compare another top level manager or the low level worker feels that he/she earn unfair reward to compare another low level worker, or the low level staff feels his/her organization gives excellent reward to the middle level or top level manager/supervisor only. So, it implies that the poor motivateion will occur to the overall organizational low middle and/or top level staffs , it is not only occur to the low level staffs. For example, if the organization's CEO feels his/her reward treatment is poor or unfair to compare to other companies' CEP reward. It means that it is possible that the organization's poor motivation or effort can be caused by the top, middle or low level staff, he /she needs to compare to othe companies; same level staff reward in general job market reward structure. Hence, any one organization needs to consider whether its reward is poor to compare other organizations' rewards. They can not only consider whether its reward is fair treatment to the low to to[level staffs issue only, but it neglects to consider whether wha tis the current market reward structure to its same competitors' rewards. It seems that one organization's employees will be possible compare whether their rewards are fair between themselves in their organizations as well as they will be possible compare whether their rewards are fair to the similar sale or service organizations or competitors. Hence, fair and reasoable reward can motivate or encourage every staff to accept to spend more effort, time, nervous to attribute to serve his/her organization.

Consequently, when the staff has good motivation, it may bring better efficiency, improving performance, raising productivity in possible. Otherwise, when the staff has bad emotivation, it may bring poor efficiency, or inefficiency, worse performance, reducing productivity in possible. So , it seems that it has indirect relationship between motivation and the organization's overall performance.

CHAPTER TWENTY-FOUR

Performance measurement influences effectiveness

Performance means understanding as achievement of the organization in relation with its set goals. It may include outcomes achieved, or accomplished through contribution of individuals or teams to the organization's strategic goals. It brings this question whether effective performance measurement can raise the organization's effectiveness. Performance has a linkage with the individual potential and how best it is realized by the individual organization needs performance measurement because it needs to measure every employee individual job behavior in order to evaluate whether his/her performance is acceptable to either raise salary/ wage or keep the same level salary/wage or appreciate to promote higher or senior position or unemploy (fire) the employee, when his/her performance is poor or unacceptable task level to earn this position level's reward with regard to manage. The employee's potential becomes the input to the productive process and performance is the out. It seems that when the one organization has many good performance employees number, then its effectiveness can not be improved to be better to compare the another similar industry organization has less good performance employees number , then its effectiveness can not improve to be better. The actua reason many include any company is one cooperative organization, it needs different teams or departments' members , workers, staffs to participate to work in low, middle, top level organizational structure. Hence, one organizational behavior can not be influenced only by one employee individual behavior or performance. The organization's overall performance or effectiveness ought be influenced by group (team) and organizational purpose, group (team) or organization capacities and resources, human climate in the group or team or the organization, the (team) group every member personal performance quality, efficient level , productive level. So, organization needs to consider how to make reasonable or fair feedback on group (team) overall performance. It does not only consider how to make reasonable or fair feedback on the top or middle level management employee individual performance only and it neglects to consider the low level employee individual performance measurement.

There are three abilities in an individual are said to be essential for performance achievement to evaluate whether the employee individual performance to excellent , good, common, poor level. They include the employee individual desire or motivation himself/herself ability, knowledge or know-how quality or action to actualize ability. Hence, one excellent performance employee whom ought have these above personal quality or ability characteristics, then he/she can perform the esscellent job performance. If the team or group or department owns the employees whom own above these abilities , then group, team, department's effectiveness will be improved, or efficiency can be raised, or productive growth can be raised more easily. However, effective performance measurement model was based mainly on financial measures and considered as one component of the planning and control cycle view, it is based on multipl non financial measures where performance measurement acts as an independent process includes in a set of activities.

How to design an effective performance measurement ? I shall assume that it has relationship between organizational effectiveness and performance measurement, also it means that whether organization is either effective or ineffective, it depends on whether its performance measurement is effective or ineffective. In essence, an organizational effectiveness represents the outcome of organizational activities when performance measurement consists of an assessment tool to measure effectiveness. In fact, the team " performance" and " effectiveness" are used interchangably because any organizational problems are related to their definition, measurement and explanation when their different groups, teams or departments' staffs are encountering the similar or same general problems when they are feeling in their departments. It seems that any organizations need to find whether what kinds of task problems to influence its different teams feel difficult to work , different department's staffs whom are feeling in general. Then, when the organization cna ensure whether what kinds of taxk problems that its staffs are facing. It can let its staffs to know how any why it needs its any ony one of its staffs to suggest useful ideas or opinions to help it to solve its organizational tasks problems in themselves department. If any one staff can know that whether he/she ought need how to do to solve whom task difficulty and the organization can attempt to use whose opinion to confirm his/her opinion is effective or useful to help it to solve his/her department general problems to its this department 's staffs' facing. Then, the organization can make more accurate judgement or evaluation to ensure the staff can be one excellent performance employee because he/she can attempt to find the effective or useful method(s) to help him/her deparment or team or group to solve his/her department overall member whom are facing or encountering general task difficulties or problems that they feel needs to solve immediately. It seems that one excellent performance employee needs own have one unique difficult solvable ability that the other members can not find the effective or useful solution method(s) to help the department to solve. Its overall daily task difficulties that its department members can not solve easily. Similarly, it means that effective or fair performance measurement is based on whether the employee can find the best solution(s0 to help whom department to solve any task problems(difficulties) when it's overall members feel whom are encountering the same problems daily. When the department has one staff whom can suggest the best opinion(s) to help the department's staffs to raise efficiency or improve productivity to achieve whose department overall performance effectiveness to be improved better. Then the department staff ought be the excellent performance staff and his/her reward must be the best to compare other same level staffs in the department. Hence, the fair or reasonable performance measurement is based on the employee individual ability, it is not based on the department overall ability. It means that one department, however, its department structure level is the low, middle or top level, even the low level department ought have one or some staff(s) whom own personal ability is above to compare the same job responsibility level staffs in the department. The owninf above-average ability staff(s) ought earn more appreciation or promotion opportunity increasing to compare the owning low-average ability staffs in the department. When the department's low-average or general ability staffs who had been working in the department long time acknowledge why the staff(s) can be appreciated to promote to do the senior position or increase salary immediately to compare themselves. Then they will be influenced by the owning above-average ability of employee(s) to work hardly or attempt to find any solution(s) or method(s) to help themselves to solve any unpredictive task difficulties in order to achieve appreciation or increasing salary or senior position promotion personal aim or desire. Then, they can influence the department's overall effectiveness to be improved in long term possible. Hence, it seems to explain one effective or good performance measurement can influence the organization's effectiveness to be improved successfully.

An effective performance measurement model needs have an effective is measured in the terms of accomplishment of the outcomes to every department, it do not neglect the importance to review its error to help its different departments to solve themselves difficulties when their any one employee individual opinion is failure or unsuccessful to help it solve whom department's prior problems, also every employee ought have chance to let himself/herself to express opinions to let it to know whether what task difficulties when he/she is possible to encounter, and it ought let every department staff has opportunity to carry on group meeting discussion how to solve himself/herself department's overall facing general problems as well as it also needs to adopt the different solutions to attempt to find which one solution is the best in order to evaluate whether whom ability is above to any one in the department. It aims to make the more accurrate performance measurement decision to give the fair and reasonable reward or welfare to any one in any department.

In conclusion, an effective performance measurement has these requirements: It needs to find whom the employee(s) has/have good decision making ability to help himself/herself department ot the other employees to solve general task difficulties in order to improve of decision process though (setting performance and strategies goals and ensuring an adequate level and mix of resources) and coordination to parts of a business to achieve objective; it needs have effective control to feedback to ensure the input-process-out system. Input means that different reward structure to be designed to the low , middle and top level employees' performance measurementevaluation and reward evaluation need, process means that an effective employee performance measurement evaluation startegic system and ouput means that an fair and reasonable reward structure implementation to every low, middle and top level employee. It is properly and to motivate and evaluate employees, managers need and it also needs to consider the overall organization how is related to its values, preferences and where themsleves department employees should be focusing their attention and energy how to attempt to solve solve themselves task difficulties in order to find whom is/are the above -average ability employee(s) in themselves department and to be recommend to appreciate to earn the more fair and reasonable reward immediately. So, an effective performance measurement organization is not only composed of individuals, but also interdependent groups with different immediate goals, (desired from specializations), different ways of working , different formal training and even different personality types. For example, staffs who work in accounting department , often have every different personality, goals , training and styles of work and socialization than staffs who work in advertising or marketing departments. So , the organization ought need to follow whether the staffs are working in which departments in order to arrange the most reasonable job task responsibilities to let him/her to work. It means that one accounting deparment will need to employ different accounting skillful staffs to do these different accounting task functions, such as financial and finance function, salary and performance measurement calcuation function, cost accounting and management budget function. So, if one employee whom is proficient on financial accounting, but he/she is arranged to do the management and cost budget function task duties. Then, it will influence whom performance to be poor, due to he/she is not proficient do do management and cost budget analysis task duties. Although, he/she has accounting knowledge and working experiences, but it does not mean that he/she has ability to do management and cost budget task duties better in the accounting department. So, any manager needs to select the right employee to arrange the right task function to let the employee do the right task responsibility duties in his /her department. If the manager selected the wrong employee to be arranged him/her to do the wrong job task reponsibility position in whose department. It is possible to influence its department's overall efficiency or productive performance to be poor.

Hence, it has close indirect relationship between performance measurement and the organization's overall effectiveness. Because effectiveness oriented companies are concerned with output, sales, quality, creation of value added, innovation, cost reduction. It measures the degree to which a business achieve its goals or the way outputs interest with the economics and social environment. When the organization has an effective or fair and reasonable performance measurement strategy. Then, its employees will feel more satisfactory to improve productive performance or efficiency in order to earn more reasonable awards easily. When the organization has many employees can improve their productive efficiency. Then, its overall productive number will be increased or service performance will be improved . Consequently, its effective performance can be also improved, thus it explains why and how when one organization has one effective performance measurement strategy , it can improve its organizational overall performance to be more effective because every department will have more employees whom like to attribute more nervous, effort, time to do themselves job duties in order to achieve appreciation, promotion, increasing salary opportunity when they acknowledge their organization has fair and reasonable performance mangement policy to evaluate themselves performance fairly.

Similarly, in one fair and reasonable performance measurement organizaional workplace environment, it will influence every department employee individual emotion to be positive, he/she can feel whom need to spend more effort, tiem and nervous to work in order to assist his/ her department to raise efficiency or productivity or improve service performance aim. Then, if the organization has many department's efficiency and productive growth can be raised. It means that the organization's overall performance can be more effective also. So, it has indirect relationship between performance measurement and organizational overall performance.

CHAPTER TWENTY-FIVE

Facility management brings economic benefits to organizations

May one organization implement facility management " FM" straegy bring long term economic benefits to itself organization in possible? I shall indicate both school educational organizations and theater performance leisure organizatons to explain whether if they can attempt to implement " FM" strategy which may help tmem to bring themselves organizations long term economic benefits.

Firstly, I shall explain one school educational organization how it can apply ' FM" strategy to help itself to gain long term economic benefits. One school educational organization, it's customers must be students. However, if its pupils must need to go to classrooms or halls to listen teachers' teaching every day. If the school can have good air conditions or warm heaters system to let students can feel cool when they need to spend long time to sit down clasroms when weather is summer or they can feel warm when they need to spend long time to sit down classrooms when weather is winter. Then, the school's air conditions or warm heaters' temperature facilities can let all its students feel comfortable to sit down in classrooms or halls to listen their teachers' teaching speaking often .

So, the school's " FM" on temperature system aspect, which can influence all pupilas feel comfortable and enjoy to enter its any classrooms or school hall indoor environment, to learn . It is one important " F" on temperature psychological factor to influence all this school's pupils to like to enter this school's classrooms or halls to learn often.

Otherwise, if this school's " FM" on temperature system can not satisfy their learning comfortable environment needs, e.g. they often feel too hot to sit down in any classrooms or halls to listen their teachers' teaching in summer or they often feel too cold to sit down in any classrooms or halls to listen their teachers' feeling in winter. Consequently, this school's ' FM" on temperature system every influence their learning desire to be poor due to this school's "FM" on temperature control system to its all classrooms and halls indoor environment is very ppor.

Hence, it is one good example to explain any school's " FM" on classrooms and halls temperature control aspect, it may influence its pupil individual learning attitude, when they can often feel comfortable and learn classrooms and halls indoor learning environment in this school, it's learning facility environment can bring indirect influence to their learning behavior and learning attitude to be improved more easily, instead of this school's every teacher individual teaching method factor. Hence, one school can provide excellent " FM" learning environment, it may bring long term students number increasing and tuition fee increasing benefits in possible.

The another " FM" example to organization's economic benefit, I shall indicat theater leisure performance organization. Any theater performance organization, any theater ought need have excellent " FM" strategy on theater its inside performance hall, because every audience must need to buy ticket to choose the theater's hall to listen music or see actors; art performance. When they sit down in every chair in the theater's performance hall. They must need to spend at least one hour to see any art performance or listen music. If the theater's hall environment is one noise environment, it's "FM" sound control system is poor, every audience can not feel quiet and they can not listen the art performance's soft music clearly. They can not feel enjoy the musician's music performance as well as they can not satisfy the music performance, due to the theater's inside hall's " FM" sound management system is poor, it can not be controlled to let all audiences feel enjoy to listen the music performer's msic performance, e.g. they may feel the theater's hall has poor sound control system to let they feel noise. Then, they can not concentrate on listening every music performance more easily in this theater's performance hall.

So, any theater's perfomance hall , its "FM" on sound control system must be often repaired and check in order to avoid noise influence to every listening music audience when he/she sits down in this theater's hall. If this theater's hall's ' FM" sound control equipment system is por and old, then it can influence every music performer can not feel easy to concentrate on their nervous to play any music tools in order to satisfy every music audience individual listening music enjoyable and pleasure feeling and needs.Hence, instead of music performer individual music performance skill aspect, any theater must need to consider its " FM" hall sound control equipment system aspect, in order to let every music audience can enjoy to listen every music performance in the quiet and comfortable hall.

Consequently, the theter's music audience number may be influenced to increase, it can have good sound " FM: control system in its hall. So, if the theater can have excellent sound " FM" control system may help the theater to increase music audience number indirectly. It implies that this excellent sound " FM" control system also may help this theater to bring long term economic benefits, during every music audience can feel this theater's music hall environment is comfortable and its sound "FM" equipment control system can let every music audience feels comfortable as well as they can feel to listen every music performer's sound easily in the most quiet theater hall inside environment.

On conclusion, "FM" strategy can be influenced to any organizations. It depends on whether whom are the organization's customer target. For example, one school organization's customer target is pupils. Hence, its classroom's size, tables and chairs whether they can let students to feel comfortable to use to write and sit down, temperature control " FM" control may let its pupils whether they can feel comfortable or not to listen their teachers' teaching . So, any schools' "FM" on classrooms and teaching halls must need have good " FM" strategy . Also, one music performance theater organization's customer target is audience. Hence, its music hall's sound control " FM: system, chair number and comfortable feeling, hall size, temperature control etc. different facilities in the music hall, which may influence any one music audience feels pleasure to listen the music performance and comfortable when they need to spend at least one hour to sit down chairs to listen the music performance in the music hall. Hence, the music theater's sound " FM" contrl system facilities may influence every music audience's listening music feeling to be more comfortable or worse.

Hence, it seems that any organizations ought need to judge whether whch aspect " FM" can influence its customer individual feeling to be satisfactory or which aspect " FM" is the major influential factor to influence their satisfaction in order to implement their "FM" strategy to bring long term economic benefits.

Ingram Content Group UK Ltd.
Milton Keynes UK
UKHW021643290323
419359UK00013B/1565